DIAMOND PEOPLE

DIAMOND PEOPLE

Text

A. J. WANNENBURGH

Photography

PETER JOHNSON

Design

JOHAN HOEKSTRA

NORFOLK HOUSE

British Library Cataloguing
in Publication Data
Wannenburgh, A. J. (Alfred John) *1936* –
DIAMOND PEOPLE.
1. Diamonds industries & trade
I. Title
338.2782

ISBN 1-872093-00-0

First edition, first impression 1990.
Published by Norfolk House Publishers,
5th Floor, St. Andrew's House,
40 Broadway, London SW1H OBT,
England.

CONTENTS

CELEBRATED BY THE ANCIENTS in myth and legend, for centuries the preserve of monarchs and potentates, diamonds, as the symbol of love and enduring relationships, today occupy a special place in a popular culture that transcends disparities of wealth and status and extends across national and regional boundaries to the ends of the earth.

World-wide some three hundred million women own at least one piece of diamond jewellery, and each year husbands, lovers and women themselves spend almost forty billion dollars on about sixty million pieces containing some fifteen million carats of diamonds.

Behind these figures is an industry that is not only international, but in which all the component enterprises, wherever they may be, are interdependent. It is an extraordinary mix of the competitive entrepreneurial spirit and co-operation in matters of common interest, involving the Third World just as much as the industrialized countries.

Diamonds are mined in some twenty countries on four continents and give employment to over two hundred thousand people in the formal mining sector and countless independent diggers, legal and illicit. Diamond cutting and polishing in thirty-odd countries occupies eight hundred thousand people. Just as many are engaged in manufacturing, wholesaling and retailing diamond jewellery. All told, about two million families are directly dependent on diamonds for their livelihood.

What distinguishes diamonds from other luxury products is that every stone is unique, a separate creation of nature, cut and polished to individual perfection. And just as every diamond is different, so too is every gift of diamonds unlike any other. For the individual who gives or wears a diamond, it is a deeply personal, enduring expression of the occasion it honours and the loving relationship it seals.

The entire industry is founded on the traditional perceptions that men and women have of diamonds and the value they place on love. Owing to the nature of the product, and because the industry is relatively small, it is built up of personal relationships at all levels, and is an intimate association that combines the specialist knowledge and skills of a great many highly individual people. From the prospector and the miner, through the sorting and distribution network of the Central Selling Organization, to the diamond cutter, jewellery manufacturer and retail jeweller, the people are the industry. It is for them that this introduction to the world of diamonds is titled.

The chapters that follow have been fashioned from personal observation and interviews with hundreds of Diamond People in many parts of the world. The contribution made by those who are not named in the text is at least as great as that made by those who are. This is the fascinating story that collectively they have to tell.

CHAPTER 1 MAGIC AND MYSTIQUE

A crown for the King of Kings, set with diamonds and other precious stones donated during the last century by parishioners of St Andries church in Antwerp.

Jewelled crowns have for centuries been the symbol of monarchy, worn by sovereigns temporal and spiritual. In other settings too, from the tiara of a duchess to the solitaire ring displayed by a young woman to indicate that she is engaged to be married, diamonds have long been an emblem of status.

Their mystique lies not only in their beauty, but also in the talismanic properties that have been attributed to them since ancient times. Because of their clarity and brilliance, diamonds have been regarded as both a test and a guarantee of chastity, while their durability made them an assurance of permanence – of eternal love.

At the entrance to Border Cave (right) Peter Beaumont, of the McGregor Museum in Kimberley, briefs a party of international specialists in dating techniques on work done at the site. In the picture with him are (from left) Dr Reiner Gruen, of Cambridge, Ebby Visser, of the South African Council for Scientific and Industrial Research, and Israeli Joel Kronfeld.

At Border Cave (above), high in the Zululand Lebombo Mountains, archaeologist Peter Beaumont, assisted by the Anglo American and De Beers Chairman's Fund, found evidence that over a hundred thousand years ago the earliest representatives of Modern Man used specularite they mined in the area to decorate their bodies. His discovery raises new questions concerning the origins of Modern Man and gives greater antiquity to the art of body adornment, which has its highest expression today in the wearing of diamond jewellery.

Allah hu akbar – God is great – the call of the muezzin greets the dawn as the rising sun lights the sky behind the ruins of Golconda Fort, ancient citadel of maharajahs, sultans and nizams, and once the greatest diamond trading centre in Asia, if not the world, to which merchants from Turkestan, Persia and Arabia came to buy diamonds mined on the tributaries of the Krishna.

Following a daily pattern that has probably remained unchanged for centuries, sari-clad women from the village pass through a vaulted arcade (left) in the Rani Mahal, once a magnificent palace at the foot of Golconda Fort, to draw water from a well. Inviolate in death, as Muslims, the Qutb Shahi sultans, under whose rule the diamond trade flourished at Golconda during the sixteenth and seventeenth centuries, are present still in the domed tombs (above) they had built for them in a flint garden outside the wall.

Amid the bustle of village commerce, children play and old men mutter in the street outside their homes, formerly the booths where the diamond merchants of Golconda plied their trade.

FIRST LIGHT SUFFUSES THE COUNTRYSIDE south-west of Hyderabad, imparting faint grey definition to the granite hills about Golconda Fort, tinting pink and gold the domed tombs of the Qutb Shahi sultans, who ruled there in the sixteenth and seventeenth centuries. Doves fill the vaults above the sarcophagi with the sound of their awakening, like a murmuring assembly of departed souls. Viewed from the bastioned perimeter wall of Golconda, a kilometre from the flint garden of the tombs, daybreak raises a fiery banner behind the sharp silhouette of ruined palaces and crenellated fortifications on the hill within. Cocks crow among houses clustered below, and the voice of a muezzin calls the azan from afar, summoning the faithful to prayer. A villager's transistor radio adds the exultation of sitar and tabla to the medley of sounds, as women drive small herds of water-buffalo out to graze on the slopes between the inner and outer defences, silently, timelessly.

Behind the Balahisar gate of the citadel, which is studded with metal spikes to resist the elephants of invading armies, the crumbling walls of palace and harem, mosque and Hindu shrine speak of ages when Golconda was the stronghold successively of maharajahs, sultans and nizams. They tell of times when it was a thriving commercial city, the leading diamond trading centre in Asia, if not the world, to which merchants came from Turkestan, Persia and Arabia, to buy there and sell again in the West. Today the massive granite walls of the royal apartments have been stripped of their plaster by weather and avarice; gaping holes reveal where, according to local tradition, the conquering Moguls used gunpowder to expose the hoards of diamonds that they believed the former rulers had cached within them. The merchants' booths in the old diamond market are now small family homes, facing a narrow street, busy with bullock carts, bicycles and motorized rickshaws.

The celebrated diamonds of Golconda are dispersed in collections around the world, the mines that produced them have been idle for some two hundred years and the ruins (left) are a reminder of past glories. Holes in the crumbling masonry of the Rani Mahal (right) are said to have been blasted by the conquering Moguls searching for the hidden treasures of their predecessors.

It is engaging to imagine the scene as it was in the mid-seventeenth century, when, during the reign of Sultan Abdullah, the French jeweller Jean Baptiste Tavernier visited the Golconda mines on tributaries of the Krishna River, some days' journey to the west and the east of the fort. In the record of his travels he related that even ten-year-old children were active in the diamond trade. His account enables us to picture them, with their diamond weights and stuffed purses, gathering early each morning under a shady tree in a square, to buy diamonds from the miners, and then sort and resell them to the great merchants. We can imagine too the great merchants themselves, lying abed in their houses until ten in the morning, and then washing and eating at leisure before receiving the mine owners, who waited outside with the parcels they wished to sell. Re-creating the past from the ruins, we may visualize the sultan living in refinement and comfort in his palace on the hill, levying a percentage on all the merchants' transactions and receiving from the mine owners royalties based on the number of diggers they employed, which could have amounted to an appreciable sum, for one of the twenty-odd mines alone employed some sixty thousand diggers.

Until the second quarter of the eighteenth century, when diamonds from Brazil began reaching Europe, it was from these and other Indian mines that all the world's diamonds came. Among them were the legendary Great Mogul and Great Table, portions of which, after the sack of Delhi by the Persian Nadir Shah in 1739, became dispersed among the crown jewels of Europe and the Middle East. Among them too were many of the largest and most celebrated polished diamonds we know of today: the 189.6-carat Orlov, set in the Russian Imperial Sceptre by Catherine the Great; the 140.5-carat Regent, which once graced the hilt of Napoleon Bonaparte's sword; the reputedly "unlucky" 69-carat dark-blue Hope diamond, once worn by the Sun King, Louis XIV of France, now in the collection of the Smithsonian Institution; the 108.93-carat Koh-i-noor, formerly worn by the Lion of the Punjab, Ranjit Singh, and set since 1937 in the crown made for Queen Elizabeth the Queen Mother.

India had been the source of diamonds many centuries before Tavernier visited Golconda. The great Indian epic, the *Mahabharata,* refers to diamonds that adorned its heroes four thousand years ago. There were so many diamonds in the country during the twelfth century that, in the course of founding Muslim dominion in India, Mohammed Ghori was able to amass by plunder some two hundred kilograms weight of them. But the mines they came from have long ceased to produce; today only a few hundred carats a year are still recovered in the country, chiefly from alluvial deposits in Madhya Pradesh.

Much of what is recorded about diamonds in ancient times belongs more to romance and legend than to fact. The fabled "valley of diamonds", wherein a large bird deposited Sinbad the Sailor in the *Arabian Nights,* is mentioned too by Aristotle, who noted that his pupil, Alexander the Great, had visited the fabled valley while campaigning in India in 327 BC. According to an Arab handbook written centuries later, he had found the valley guarded by snakes, and so had resorted to tossing down to the valley floor lumps of meat, to which the diamonds stuck, and from which they were retrieved after the eagles carried the meat to their nests. There are differences of detail, but the story remains essentially the same. Perhaps it was, after all, a tale that Indian diamond merchants told to discourage outsiders from seeking the source of their goods. If so, their ruse succeeded for some hundreds of years, because the Roman, Pliny the Elder, writing in the first century AD, gave a "valley of diamonds" as the principal source of these stones. We find it mentioned again several centuries later in Liang Dynasty China, recorded in accounts of Chinese merchants who had traded in India. Fanciful though such tales may be, they reflect the mystique that the diamond has had through millennia for people of diverse cultures, in both the East and the West.

Thai teenagers, Nattakarn Paosila and Nissra Siddhichai, receive from their grandmother, Piroah Paosila, their inheritance of Thai jewellery containing the nine gems of different colours that traditionally constitute a blessing.

By the fourth century BC the Arab and Persian trade in Indian diamonds was well established. But it is difficult to say when diamonds from India first reached the lands bordering the Mediterranean. Linguistic evidence suggests that Old Testament references to diamonds, which go back to the twelfth century BC, are probably mistranslations from the Hebrew. Similarly, the Greek word *adamas,* from which the word for diamond in several European languages is derived, was applied also to hard substances other than diamonds, although it is tempting to speculate that the traditional association of diamonds and romantic love began with the mythical diamond-tipped arrows of Eros. An anonymous Greek text named the Indian ports known for their diamond trade in the first century BC, when the main trade route followed the coast from the Gulf of Oman to the head of the Persian Gulf. For perhaps a thousand years Arabs and Persians dominated the trade between India and Europe. In the twelfth century an Arab, Teifaschius, issued the first diamond price list. By the thirteenth century Venetian merchants had secured a monopoly in supplying Indian diamonds to Europe. They enjoyed exclusive rights to their purchase where the trade route ended at Aleppo, in present-day Syria, and also sent them on from Venice, by way of the Rhine valley, to the diamond cutters of Nuremberg and Bruges.

In India, diamonds were sometimes set in the eyes of statues of the Hindu deities, and potentates vied with one another for the possession of renowned gems, using them as instruments of diplomacy, wearing them as symbols of status, sewn into their clothing, or of power, encrusting the scabbards and set in the hilts of their scimitars. Indeed, the esteem for precious stones extended throughout South-East Asia, where they were and are to this day valued for their talismanic as well as their aesthetic qualities.

The Chinese scholar Wang Chen, wrote in AD 270 about a hard stone, looking something like a pearl, found in the southern provinces, and remarked that strangers set

these stones in rings to protect themselves from poisoning and other dangers. In Thailand, nine gems of different colours – diamond, ruby, emerald, topaz, garnet, blue sapphire or spinel, pearl or moonstone, zircon and cat's eye – traditionally constitute a blessing. Wrapped in a piece of cloth, they may be buried beneath the central pillar of a house to bring blessings upon it. They protect from harm, bring good fortune and success in ventures, counteract the effects of unpropitious astrological events, and invest the wearer with charm and the ability to attract others. The larger these gemstones are, the more effective they are held to be. An ancient body chain of Nine Gems is worn by the King as a decoration of rank, and from it hangs his sword of office, sheathed in a gold scabbard set with many diamonds. The conical Great Crown of Victory, worn by successive Thai kings, has a large diamond, the Maha Vichai Mani, symbolically set at its pinnacle. So too do the three crowns belonging to the bejewelled seasonal costumes in which, thrice yearly, the King ritually dresses the Emerald Buddha, which is enshrined in the royal Wat Phra Kaeo temple in Bangkok as the object of the highest Thai Buddhist veneration, symbol of an ancient tradition, a faith and a civilization.

A practising alchemist in the suburbs of Adelaide, "Professor" Manfred Junius knows of several diamond preparations for treating cancer, which he says are accepted by schools of Indian alchemy and have been used for generations by traditional Indian physicians.

Europeans initially valued diamonds most of all for their practical uses – however impractical these might in fact have been – as talisman, panacea and poison. In the first and second centuries AD Romans wore rough diamond crystals set in gold rings, less for ornament than for protection against illness, misadventure, evil spirits and a host of other natural and supernatural hazards. But they prized diamonds for their hardness as well as their magical powers, fashioning them into tools for carving jade and drilling pearls, and exporting these to China, where they were regarded as gifts fit for kings.

The talismanic virtues of diamonds, which had doubtless long been recognized in folklore, were formally listed at this time by Pliny the Elder, who, in an age when speculative philosophy was more honoured than empirical verification, at the same time gave currency to several misconceptions concerning diamonds that have persisted to this day. There are still those who believe with Pliny that a diamond placed on an anvil will not shatter when struck with a hammer. Few would agree with him, however, that the best way to cleave a diamond is to place it in the fresh, warm blood of a goat.

Diamonds such as this large twinned crystal in the De Beers collection of unusual diamonds must have given rise to the notion, unchallenged for centuries, that diamonds are capable of gestation and giving birth.

Other notions, of even greater antiquity, but too preposterous to retain a following today, nevertheless remained largely unchallenged for two thousand years. In the fourth century BC, Plato averred that precious stones were living beings, the embodiment of celestial spirits, and that the diamond was the transparent distillate of the noblest part of gold. Aristotle's pupil, Theophrastus, maintained that there were both male and female diamonds. During the Middle Ages these opinions were enlarged upon but not altered. In 1350 Sir John Mandeville wrote that diamonds "grew" in India and multiplied by shedding drops that became small diamonds. These ideas remained unaffected by the Renaissance. Early in the sixteenth century Jerome Cardan asserted that diamonds could not only procreate, but, like other mortals, were subject to illness, old age and death. In 1566 Francisci Rueus wrote that he knew of two diamonds that had actually produced offspring. Well into the seventeenth century, Johannes Bustamantius reported that two "married" diamonds had done so, and Anselme Boetius de Boot of Bruges, the personal physician of King Rudolf II of Habsburg, recorded that when Indian mines ceased to yield, the diggers closed them for thirty years, to allow new diamonds time to grow there.

Dressed here in the costume for summer, the Emerald Buddha is adorned with typical items of royal attire, including the Mongkut, a multi-tiered conical crown of gold, set with diamonds and rubies, culminating in a tapering spire that, in the manner of the Great Crown of Victory of the Thai kings, has a large diamond at its tip.

The Ubosoth, or ceremonial hall, of the Wat Phra Kaeo temple, in the grounds of the royal palace in Bangkok. The gentle lines and detailed ornamentation of Buddhist temple architecture are reflected in the design of traditional Thai jewellery.

NO ENTRY

It was evident, he said, that one of the two diamonds owned by the Duchess of Luxembourg was pregnant.

Clearly the mystique of the diamond was at work throughout that time; why else should the stone have been set apart from all other inanimate objects as an entity with life? But as objects of beauty, diamonds were for a long time not highly regarded in Europe. Their exceptional durability and rarity qualified them as precious stones, and in the Christian symbolism of the Middle Ages they came to represent the purity, steadfastness and strength of the Creator, but for beauty they were rated lower than pearls, rubies, emeralds and sapphires. It was only as cutting and polishing techniques improved, releasing the fire within and enhancing their surface lustre, that diamonds attained pre-eminence among gemstones.

Diamond jewellery began appearing more frequently in the royal courts of Europe during the fourteenth century. In 1319 French courtiers observed that the wife of Louis X was wearing a diamond necklace. The crown of King John II of France, captured by the Black Prince at the battle of Poitiers in 1356, was set with diamonds, rubies and sapphires. A century later, gifts from the French diamond merchant, Jacques Coeur, to Agnes Sorel, mistress of King Charles VII of France, placed her in history as the first commoner known to have worn diamond jewellery.

The growing popularity of diamond jewellery accompanied the rapid progress in cutting and polishing diamonds made under Burgundian patronage in Bruges during the fifteenth century. "As the Burgundians were great traders and bankers, all the best things somehow gravitated towards Flanders. Unfettered by income tax, they developed a luxurious standard of living, which they expressed in the wearing of precious stones," says English art historian and writer, Diana Scarisbrick, whose field of historical research is jewellery design. "The Burgundians had great taste and a desire for magnificence in clothing and jewellery. They could afford the best stones and were able to employ the best people to work on them."

By far the largest number of pieces of jewellery that have survived from that period are rings. "Rings were more often lost than other pieces," she explains. "They tend to turn up again, still intact, sometimes centuries later, long after the precious stones that had been set in other pieces have been removed by subsequent generations and reset into more modern designs. The surviving rings provide us with little mirrors of the prevailing artistic styles of different periods."

Through the centuries rings have perpetuated the talismanic role of the diamond. "In the Middle Ages and Renaissance every ring that was set with a precious or semi-precious stone was not so much a piece of jewellery as an amulet, which, by sympathetic magic, conferred the virtue of the stone upon the wearer," she says. "The virtues of particular stones enumerated by Pliny in the Roman period, were again listed by late-Antique lapidaries and taken up in a major way during the Medieval period. Belief in them persisted right through to the eighteenth century, and even today is by no means dead. One of the finest diamond talismanic rings I've seen is a fifteenth century specimen, set with a point-cut diamond, and with the Biblical inscription *Jesus altum transit* exquisitely engraved on the hoop. The diamond, because it could not be overcome by steel or fire, was believed to render the wearer invincible, and the inscription made the ring doubly talismanic in protecting a traveller against thieves."

This talismanic tradition continues today in the custom of presenting a diamond engagement ring, to symbolize that the relationship, like the stone, is forever. A ring, originally a plain iron hoop, was given as an earnest of betrothal by Romans in the first century AD, and was replaced by a plain gold ring in the second century. The earliest record that Scarisbrick has traced of a diamond ring being associated with betrothal or marriage is a manuscript she found in the Vatican. "It has an illustration representing the pageantry associated with the marriage of Costanzo Sforza and Camilla d'Aragona at

Pesaro in 1475," she says. "Hymen, the god of marriage, is portrayed in a tunic painted with diamond rings, standing beside an altar on which a diamond ring unites two blazing torches. By the diamond ring, two flaming wills, two passions, are united. The unifying symbolism of the ring, linked to the invincibility attributed to the diamond, made it an emblem of enduring harmony in marriage."

All the diamonds depicted in the illustration were either uncut or point cut, but the ring used in the marriage of Mary of Burgundy to the Archduke Maximilian of Austria in 1477 was set with hog-back diamonds forming the Gothic letter M. "And with the development of the table cut, diamond rings became an essential part of royal weddings in the sixteenth century," Scarisbrick says. "When the infant Mary Tudor was married by proxy to the baby Dauphin of France at Greenwich in 1518, a diamond ring was placed on her finger by Cardinal Wolsey, who performed the ceremony. Marguerite d'Angouleme, when she married Henri II of Navarre in 1527, took the diamond ring as her personal emblem, symbolizing a king and a queen bound together in everlasting love. The wedding ring of Albrecht V of Bavaria was set with sixteen lozenge-cut diamonds in the form of a rosette. A diamond ring was used also in the marriage of Mary Stuart and Henry Darnley at Holyrood in 1565. The diamond was widely regarded as the ultimate emblem of fidelity in love. Sixteenth century lapidaries actually recommended the use of diamonds as a chastity test, claiming that if a husband placed a diamond on the head of his sleeping wife she would turn towards him if chaste, and away from him if faithless."

A 1938 Egyptian stamp shows Queen Farida wearing a diamond tiara made for her by Swiss jeweller Teddy Horovitz, whose business at the time was based in Alexandria.

Jeweller Teddy Horovitz, now of Geneva, examines the 56.07-carat Tavernier Pear, first described by Tavernier in 1665, believed to have been part of the loot taken from Delhi by Nadir Shah in 1739.

As the table cut and later the rose cut enhanced the diamond and it became more sought after in jewellery, diamonds assumed greater importance as symbols of wealth and status. Probably the most conspicuous symbolic use of diamonds is in coronation regalia. Brigadier Kenneth Mears, CBE, who is entrusted with the security of the British Crown Jewels in the Tower of London, is the acknowledged authority on the Crown Jewels and a prolific writer and lecturer on the subject. "Jewels, from the young girl's engagement ring to the sovereign's crown, signify the status of the wearer," he says. "The Crown Jewels symbolize the wealth of the nation and indicate the status of the person wearing them. When the Queen wears her jewels on a big occasion it is not merely for self-adornment, but to show that she represents a nation of consequence."

In England the coronation ceremony dates from the crowning of Edward the Confessor in the eleventh century. But as Oliver Cromwell sold off or melted down most of the Crown Jewels during the Reformation, the present Crown Jewels have accumulated since the restoration of Charles II in 1660. Although many (uncut) diamonds were set in the Holy Crown of Hungary, presented by Byzantium to the Hungarian Royal Court in the eleventh century, they were not prominent in the British Crown Jewels until relatively modern times. "The major jewels were emeralds, rubies and sapphires," says Mears. "Most of the smaller diamonds date from the crown made for Queen Victoria in 1837, which now has 2800 diamonds in it. The three big diamonds have been in the collection for only a comparatively short while: the Koh-i-noor since the middle of the last century, and the First and Second Stars of Africa since early this century."

He sees the rise of the diamond to prominence as being broadly contemporaneous with the evolution of The Diamond Trading Company, with its considerable marketing resources, and the development of the modern fifty-eight-facet brilliant cut. "The modern cut gave diamonds a distinction and a glamour they had not had before," he says. "Only an expert eye could have told the difference between the Indian-cut Koh-i-noor and the very good crystal facsimiles we have of it. But cut as a modified brilliant, the Koh-i-noor in Queen Elizabeth the Queen Mother's crown couldn't possibly be mistaken for the crystal in Queen Mary's crown that was cut to resemble it. The modern cut brings out the vast difference there is between cut crystal and cut diamond."

Diamond historian and composer Ian Balfour pages through the manuscript of his latest operetta. The provenance of famous diamonds interests him more than their beauty, and he deplores the recutting of historic gems.

In the course of his work, Mears sees the Crown Jewels every day and handles them periodically. "I'm one of the very few people who have put the great First Star of Africa and Second Star of Africa together to form a brooch," he says. "It was last worn as a brooch on the thirteenth of June 1914, by Queen Mary, who really knew about diamonds and how to wear them."

As a result of his interest in the British collection and the fascination of the three great diamonds in it, he has found opportunities to examine several other royal collections, including the Turkish, remnants of the French, and the Russian. "The collection in the Hermitage, in Leningrad, and in the so-called Diamond Fund of the USSR, kept in the armouries of the Kremlin, encompass a display of treasures for which there is no equivalent anywhere else in the world," he says. "In addition to a range of uncut diamonds, such as only De Beers could produce in the West, large polished diamonds that display the cutter's art and modern jewellery of the million-dollar kind, the Fund includes the historic jewellery of Catherine the Great and Elizabeth of Russia and diamonds of particular interest, such as the Orlov and the Shah, a flat diamond, inscribed on three faces, which was cut to serve as a transparent covering for a miniature." His ambition is to examine the Iranian collection – which has not been seen by outsiders since the fall of the Shah – because "Iran was where, after the sack of Delhi, most of the famous Golconda diamonds, including the Darya-i-nur and diamonds allied to the Koh-i-noor, ended up."

British constitutional practice, in forbidding the removal of the English crowns from the country, so that kings cannot sell them abroad to finance military adventures, tacitly acknowledges the attraction of diamonds as a highly compact and easily portable store of wealth in periods of need. Often the sparkle of a diamond has been the only glimmer of hope for people in troubled times. Excluded from other trades and professions, many East European Jewish families who engaged in diamond manufacturing and dealing were in a position to flee the ghettos and pogroms of the Tsarist empire because they had diamonds with which to fund their flight and finance a new start elsewhere. Among the diamantaires of Antwerp, Tel Aviv and New York are many who can tell of how they or their families escaped the Nazi Holocaust by using diamonds to facilitate their passage across frontiers. Diamantaires in Hong Kong and Bangkok say that the political vicissitudes of South-East Asian countries are often reflected in the trade in certain types of diamonds, as people start putting their money into a form of wealth they will easily be able to take with them if forced to become refugees.

While a large body of lore expresses the mystique of the diamond in popular terms, the feelings that people have for diamonds are often subjective and personal. Different aspects fascinate some more than others. Diamond historian and composer of operettas, Ian Balfour, describes himself as being "slightly heretical". Having done a stint as a diamond sorter during his thirty-odd years in the industry, he is excited equally by exceptional rough and exceptional polished diamonds. Against the prevailing fashion for white or colourless diamonds, he prefers the fancy colours. He recalls seeing the dark-blue Hope diamond placed beside a magnificent sapphire at the Louvre. "There was no comparison," he says. "The sparkle of the diamond was fifty times as powerful." Believing that "square lines should be in the diamond and the curves on the female figure", he prefers the emerald and square cuts to the modern brilliant.

Attaching more importance to provenance than to excellence, he deplores particularly the recutting in recent times of the Golconda diamonds. "In India they valued the size of the stone more than anything," he says. "They gave stones a few facets, rather than cut them. The Nizam diamond, a semi-cut diamond with a few odd facets on it, was shaped as a paperweight. The Darya-i-nur, a very interesting pink slab diamond, last heard of in Teheran, is a semi-cut diamond too. The old Koh-i-noor was Mogul cut before they recut it, and there is a very good example of the Mogul cut in the Crown Jewels of Teheran. It may not appeal to Western eyes, which seek brilliance and symmetry, but it is to my mind a lovely cut. Brilliance isn't everything; sheer size is fascinating. History should be allowed to take precedence over brilliance and symmetry."

People involved in buying and selling rough diamonds often seem somewhat indifferent to polished stones. "For me the real excitement is in seeing something in the rough and wondering what it has the potential to become," says Roy Fitch, diamond valuator for the Botswana government. "But once it has been polished, there is nothing more to be added to it; the interest and the fun are gone." Rogan Maclean, who heads the diamond purchasing division of the Central Selling Organization in London, says that he is drawn to the mystery of the rough diamond – something that is lost when it is polished. The CSO's chief diamond man, Alex Barbour, finds that "looking at a piece of rough is like looking at a landscape and seeing the painting that could be made of it."

Jack Young, head of sorting for the CSO in London, is also excited more by the potential of the rough stone than the polished product. "The excitement really starts at the time the goods come off the recovery plant at the mine or the old digger turns over his sieve and, scratching about, finds something glistening there," he says. "And that same excitement is carried right the way through to the diamond manufacturer when he opens a parcel and something in it really catches his eye."

Master diamond cutter and polisher Gabi Tolkowsky describes diamonds as the passion of his life. For him the mystique is in the art of working with diamonds, the unique challenge that each of them presents to the cleaver, the sawyer, the bruter and the polisher.

"Throughout history, we have sought to discover new qualities and enhance them by creating faceted transparent surfaces and reflective internal surfaces. The quest didn't end when my great-uncle Marcel Tolkowsky calculated the 'perfect proportions' for the brilliant cut in 1914," he says. "The conventional cuts have all been perfected, but there are an infinite number of possible shapes, for each of which the best proportions could be calculated. Diamonds also have aspects and qualities that go beyond measurement. Each is a unique combination of characteristics – grain, inclusion, stress, colour, fluorescence – which determine its behaviour on the wheel. No two are the same. Every polisher is an individual, an artist, who cares for the material he is working with and has his own personal approach to each individual stone. Every diamond presents a new challenge to the craftsman. Not only in the physical sense are diamonds forever; their challenge to the craftsman is eternal."

The sixth generation of his family in the diamond business, Gabi Tolkowsky recalls being enthralled as a young boy in Tel Aviv by the conversation of his father's colleagues. "The smell of burnt oil and diamond powder in the workshop was part of my life from the start," he says. "In working with diamonds I have since found that I am continually entering new areas of discovery, learning more about them and what can be created from them. Legend has it that the Queen of Sheba, hoping to persuade King Solomon to marry her, presented him with seven diamond crystals of perfect colour, one of which he entrusted to each of seven sons, whose descendants have preserved them throughout the

Diaspora. I like to believe that anyone attempting to trace them may be able to locate six, but that the seventh will always elude them, because the story cannot end; the quest for the seventh diamond, like the quest for perfection, must continue. It absorbs me totally, and I feel compelled to discover their secrets, bring out new qualities, create new forms, knowing that I can never exhaust the possibilities that the diamond has to offer." On the CSO's behalf Tolkowsky has in recent years designed a whole new series of cuts for off-colour stones, maximizing their brilliance and colour, giving new life to diamonds that, owing to their dull appearance, were unpopular in the standard fancy cuts.

Bitten by the diamond bug, Sunday diggers at the Crater of Diamonds State Park wash their gravel (left), perhaps hoping to find another Star of Arkansas, but as most of the stones they find are of little value, they seem motivated more by the desire to participate in the quest than the prospect of financial reward.

The challenge, the quest, are powerful currents in the lives of diamond people, be they merchants on the lookout for exceptional stones, artists and craftsmen seeking to perfect new forms, or jewellers striving to create designs that will display diamonds better. If, as Jack Young suggests, the excitement a digger feels when he sees the sparkle of a diamond in his sieve passes with the diamond to those who subsequently handle it, perhaps the quest originates with the spirit of the men who through the ages have been driven by an inner compulsion to find diamonds to choose a hard life in inhospitable places.

Some seventy-five thousand Americans flock each year to the Crater of Diamonds State Park, on the Little Missouri River, in Arkansas, to sift through the surface detritus of the best-known mineralized diamond pipe in North America. The seventy thousand diamonds found there since 1906 have included such distinguished gemstones as the 40.23-carat Uncle Sam, the 34.25-carat Star of Murfreesboro and the 15.33-carat Star of Arkansas. But the three stones a day that are found there are generally under a quarter of a carat and of industrial quality; little more than souvenirs. Yet there are regulars who have been coming there to fossick for diamonds every weekend for more than fifteen years, and there are some who in autumn take home bags of soil to sort through at leisure during the winter months. The park authorities plough the soil once a month in spring and summer, charge diggers four dollars a visit, and issue them with certificates if they find a diamond.

Diamonds of contrasting colours (right) drawn from a De Beers selection of uncut "fancies".

They too participate in the quest, though perhaps not as ardently as the extreme example, reported to the Royal Society in 1677, of an unnamed Portuguese adventurer who in 1610 went to search for diamonds at Waijra Karur, in the Bellary district of India. After spending all he had on his fruitless hunt, he sold his few remaining possessions, in order to pay his workmen for one more day's work, and prepared a cup of poison to take that night if no diamonds were found. Just before nightfall, when he was about to end his life, his workmen brought him a stone weighing more than four hundred carats. Instantly his mood changed from despair to optimism, and he rushed off to sell the stone in Goa, where, before returning to his mine, he set up a stone tablet inscribed in the Telegu language with the exhortation:

Your wife and children sell, sell what you have,
Spare not your clothes, nay, make yourself a slave,
But money get, then to Karur make haste,
There search for mines, a prize you'll find at last.

CHAPTER 2 DREAMS OF RIVERS

Dawn in the Mato Grosso, and already a small party of *garimpeiros*, the wandering diggers of Brazil, are abroad. Their canoe a minute speck on a wide reach of the Juruena River, they pursue rumours that diamonds have been found in the gravels of a tributary.

Before kimberlite pipes were identified as the primary source of diamonds towards the end of the last century, all discoveries were alluvial. When men dreamt of making their fortunes by finding diamonds they dreamt of rivers.

Although today the major mining companies concentrate chiefly on finding the kimberlites in which the river diamonds originated, countless small-scale operators in inhospitable corners of the world still dream of rivers.

In their quest for diamonds and gold, well over a million *garimpeiros* roam through the vast tropical rain forests (left) of the Amazon and its tributaries. Reports of activity at Itapena Mine on the Sao Luiz River in Mato Grosso brought Antonio José dos Santos to search for diamonds in the surrounding drainages. Working close to the boundary of Itapena's legal mining concession, he sorts through gravel he has concentrated in his sieve (right). Initially he found a few quite large diamonds, but now most of his pickings are small stones (below right) and he considers moving elsewhere. The mine has since been driven to closure by *garimpeiro* activity.

Operating on the fringes of legality, *garimpeiros* are suspicious of strangers. Angelo Rocha de Amorim, now in his eighties, came as a *garimpeiro* to Tepequém, near the Venezuelan border in 1949. The small general-dealer's store and *cantina* he opened almost forty years ago to supply fellow diggers has become a regular meeting place for these clannish people.

Whenever *garimpeiros* concentrate, hordes of camp-followers move in with them, and temporary shanty towns spring up in the jungle, complete with stores, *cantinas,* bordellos and scores of unplanned children – all ultimately dependent on the price of diamonds.

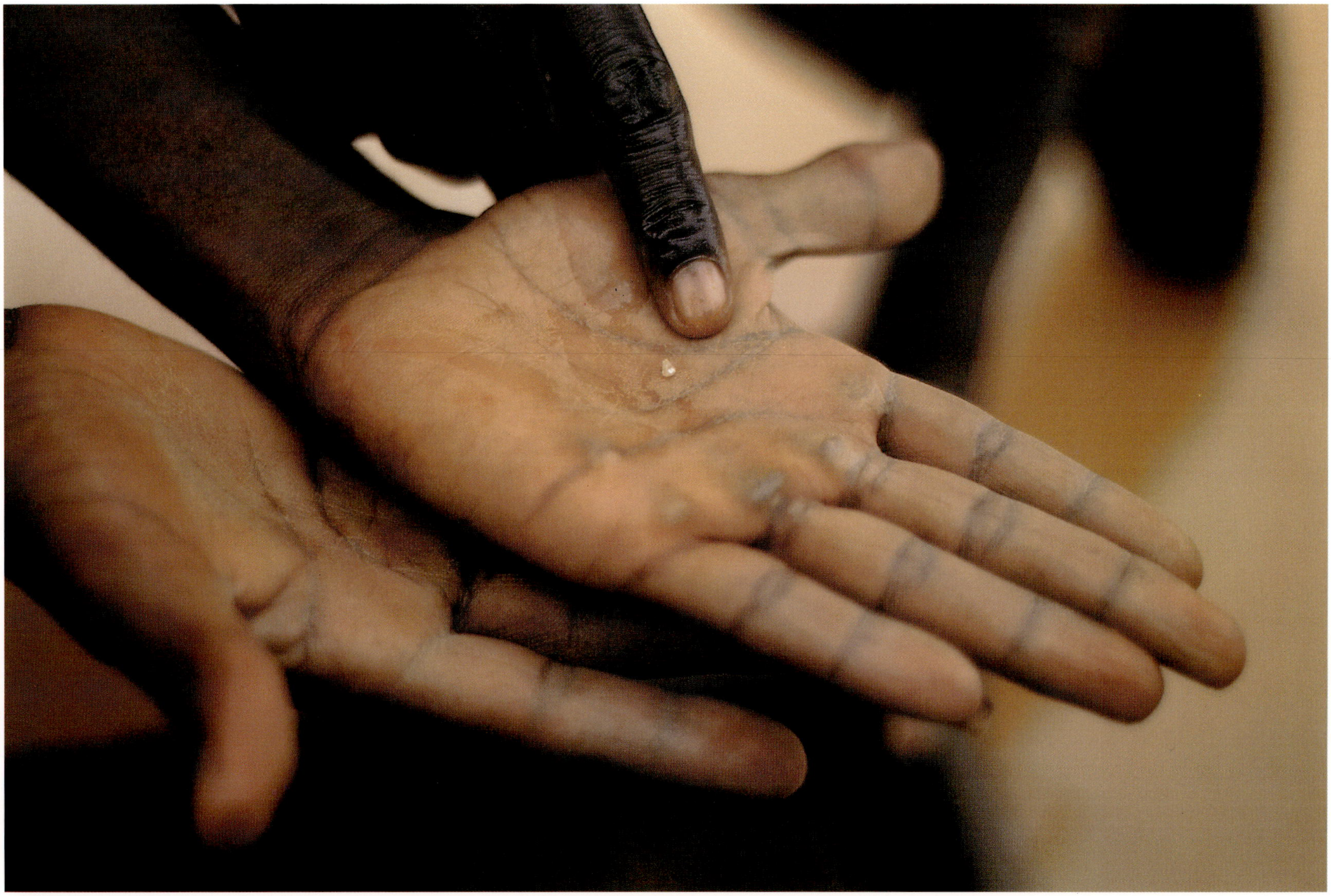

Diggers in the Tshikapa province in Zaire have written on the cliff face *"Mabe ya mbila elengi na musaka."* This well-known Zairois proverb can be literally translated as "The highest palm nuts are the best for sauce." It would be uneconomic for a mining company to exploit this deposit, but small-scale operators, with low overheads, are able to make a living from recovering such small, imperfect stones as this (above), and literally move mountains in the process.

At Gong Gong, one of the earliest alluvial diamond diggings on the Vaal River, in South Africa, the Bowers family still operate in much the same way they did forty-odd years ago, re-working the tailings left by diggers at the turn of the century. Nicholas Bowers picks through the concentrate from the last sieve of the day, watched by his wife Katie and brother-in-law Kleinjan McKay Bowker.

Remnants of dreams – blasted by wind and sand, the "ghost town" at Bogenfels, one of several on the desert coast of Namibia, remains as a monument to the dreams of the Germans who thronged there during the early years of this century to seek their fortune mining for diamonds among the dunes of the Namib desert.

A PARTY OF *GARIMPEIROS*, CAMPING OVERNIGHT on the bank where a small river entered a larger headwater of the Amazon, fired a shot in the air and brandished their machetes to warn an approaching boatload of geologists to keep to the far side. Rumours of a gold find some two hundred kilometres upstream had over the past three weeks brought a flood of these wandering diggers, who roam the remote areas of the Brazilian rain forest in search of gold and diamonds, up the river on foot and in small boats. A police checkpoint downstream had not prevented over two thousand of them from getting through, and the diamond geologists were worried that if the gold find proved disappointing a reverse flood of disconsolate and hungry men would threaten the security of their camps. There was also the danger that they might inadvertently stumble upon some indication of what the prospectors were after, and the legal limitations and cumbersome procedures involved in registering claims and establishing mining areas would give the *garimpeiros* plenty of time to pre-empt them.

Far from civilization, on the frontiers of development in a densely forested country the size of the United States, the *garimpeiros* operate in a world that is largely beyond the effective reach of the authorities, a world in which self-help provides a more impressive form of redress, and where the services of a professional gunman bring speedier, more certain retribution than due process. On the outskirts of Juina, a clapboard town that sprang up recently in the Mato Grosso jungle, roadside crosses mark where two drifters suspected of killing a local taxi driver were lynched, after being dragged from the police cells by a combined mob of townsfolk and itinerant truck and taxi drivers.

"Life is cheap among those who have little to lose," says Jeff Watkins, who has travelled these jungle byways himself for almost a decade as a field geologist for the Brazilian diamond mining company Sopemi. "The *garimpeiros* have a rough code of ethics and a code of honour among themselves. If one of them is found to be cheating or stealing from his companions they will summarily execute and bury him on the spot. He will not be left to cause problems elsewhere. This is the law of the *garimpeiros.*"

"The profession of *garimpeiro* has long been honoured in Brazil," says Tony Carrington, another senior Sopemi geologist. "It started with the *bandeirantes*, the *paulistas*, who spread out from São Paulo into Bahia and the central northern parts of Brazil in search of gold and slaves in the seventeenth century, and pioneered the country in the process."

Diamonds were first found in Brazil early in the eighteenth century by *garimpeiros* who were washing for gold in the beds of the Jequitinhonha and Ribeirao do Inferno rivers in the Minas Gerais district, not far from the town of Tijuco, which is today called Diamantina. Not knowing what they were and little realizing that they had intrinsic value, the diggers used the shiny stones as counters in card games. A friar, who had been in India, recognized them as diamonds, but kept his knowledge to himself, the better to collect all he could of these interesting but "worthless" stones. In 1726 some fell into the hands of Dom Lourenço de Almeida, the Portuguese governor of Minas Gerais, who, having lived for a time at the centre of the diamond trade in Goa, certainly knew what they were, but remained silent and lined his own pockets. After a year or two the secret slipped out, however, and some forty thousand adventurers poured in to wash the gravels of the many streams in the Serro do Frio range around Tijuco.

A party of *garimpeiros*, on their way to a rumoured gold find in Brazil's Roraima state, fire a shot in the air and brandish their machetes to warn off a boatload of diamond geologists.

The town has retained its association with diamonds for over 250 years. Shops facing onto steep, cobbled streets stock the pans, sieves, pumps and other equipment needed by the *garimpeiros*, who still work the streams in the vicinity with some success. Diamonds are traded openly in the streets, in taxis and on public benches, and workshops in the town cut and polish the local product. On the Jequitinhonha River, where it all started, Mineraçao Tejucana, a Brazilian interest of the Société Générale de Belgique subsidiary, Sibeka, has been dredging 120 kilometres of concessions in the river and adjoining flats since 1977. Five dredgers, the largest of which displaces 2500 tonnes, move some eight million cubic metres of alluvium a year to recover at best one carat of diamonds in a hundred cubic metres. The diamonds are small, but over ninety per cent are gemstones, and a small quantity of gold recovered with the diamonds makes the operation profitable.

Yolanda Adelaide Vieira, general manager of the Mineraçao Tejucana dredging operation on the Jequitinhonha River, in Brazil, is responsible for processing eight million cubic metres of low-grade alluvium a year to recover on average less than a carat of gem quality diamonds in a hundred cubic metres of waste.

"Historically, the *garimpeiros* have been in the forefront of geological exploration in Brazil, and have been responsible for identifying many areas of gold and diamond mineralization," says Carrington. "In recognition of their part in opening up the country for development, the Mines Department has long had a favourable attitude towards them, allowing them to dig pretty well anywhere, if they pay a small licence fee to the local authority and, where the land is privately owned, obtain permission from the owner."

Officially, there are today some eight hundred thousand *garimpeiros* registered with diggers' unions and syndicates, but there are believed to be twice that number in all, wandering about Brazil in search of noble metals and precious stones.

"The traditional *garimpeiro* is a man of the forest, a rugged frontiersman, operating alone or with a partner, who goes out with a pan, a sieve and a mule to look for gold and diamonds," says Carrington. "Some may be driven to it by economic circumstances, but most of them are natural loners, who are disinclined to settle in one place and find the wandering life of the *garimpeiro* suited to their temperament. They are eternal optimists, forever dreaming that tomorrow the big stone, the big nugget, will appear in their pans. Even when the geological criteria are unpromising, they have an unshakeable faith in the place where they have chosen to dig. They will say that because of something or other that happened on the journey there they know it to be a lucky area. Their dreams are encouraged by the fact that a small proportion of them do strike it rich, and that a few of them have actually become extremely wealthy."

"We come across these traditional *garimpeiros* in many parts of Brazil, living simply and working with very rudimentary equipment, and have found them to be people with an incredible sense of decency and correct behaviour," says Watkins. "I remember one old fellow in the Mato Grosso being so upset because he couldn't offer us coffee that, just as we were about to leave him, he went off to his grass hut and came back with a polished agate: the one thing of value he could give us as a memento of our visit."

At Tepequém, in the hills north of Boa Vista, close to where Roraima territory borders on Venezuela, *garimpeiros* have been working the gravels of the Cabo Sobral River for diamonds since the 1940s. Angelo Rocha de Amorim, now in his eighties, arrived there from Bahia as a *garimpeiro* in 1949. He married there, and in 1953 he stopped digging, set up a cross on the hillside to mark a place of permanent settlement, and opened a store to supply the other *garimpeiros*. "There were about three thousand digging here for diamonds in 1949," he says, "but when the gold price went up most of them went away to pan for gold, and there are only about two hundred left in the area now."

Waltemar Ferreira da Silva, an Amazonian Indian otherwise known as Teco, operates four gravel pumps with sluice boxes on the river, and finds the rewards sufficient to employ twenty-four men to rework river gravels that were worked through by hand in the forties. There are several other small parties operating with pumps and boxes, but many of the *garimpeiros* on the Cabo Sobral still work in the old way, using three round-bottomed sieves of different gauges to sort and concentrate the gravel by hand. One of them is Anisio Teixeira dos Santos, who found a 5.6-carat stone soon after arriving there in 1949, and has been trying ever since to find a bigger one. So too is Raimundo Saraiva, who wants to sell a fifty-five pointer to Joaquim Gomes, who has been coming up twice a month for the past eight years to buy from the *garimpeiros* and resell to dealers passing through Boa Vista. "The largest stone I've ever bought here was five carats; but, ah, such quality, such excellent colour!" Joaquim Gomes says, waving an arm in the direction of where the river disappears into the forest that fills the plain below to the horizon. "Besides, it is worth coming up here just for the view – to get above the forest."

The main street of the makeshift *garimpeiro* town that sprang up on the São Luiz River, in Mato Grosso, after word of activities at the Itapena mine got around. In six months the number of inhabitants grew to three thousand.

"Unfortunately, but inevitably, a new type of *garimpeiro* has emerged and become dominant in the last decade or so," says Carrington. "They no longer work as individuals but as large groups, usually backed by people financially and politically more powerful than themselves, who provide them with motor-driven pumps, washing boxes and other equipment. Operating with only a digging certificate, they undertake the mechanized exploitation of mineral deposits, for which legally they should have a licence and mining lease. This has become a serious problem for the mining companies."

The situation parallels that which existed thirty-odd years ago in Sierra Leone and elsewhere in West Africa, where small operators swarmed onto alluvial diggings before the deposits could be systematically exploited by suitably equipped mining companies. While removing the more easily found larger stones, they mixed up the diamondiferous gravels with the barren overburden, diluting the grade of the ore and making it uneconomical for the companies to recover the smaller diamonds they left behind.

Years of toil in an inhospitable climate are recorded in the lines on Raimundo Saraiva's face. The $150 he receives from buyer Joaquim Gomes for a half-carat diamond he recovered from the Cabo Sobral River will pay his debts at the Tepequém store.

In Brazil a number of companies that have undertaken costly exploration and identified interesting alluvial deposits, have applied for and been granted the exclusive rights to exploit them, only to find that their claims have been overrun by hundreds, and in some cases thousands, of semi-mechanized *garimpeiros,* who had in the first place been alerted to the prospect of good pickings by the company's application for a mining lease.

There had been no diggers or history of diamond digging on the São Luiz River, in Mato Grosso, when Sopemi discovered payable alluvial deposits. The company cut 150 kilometres of roads and developed the Itapena mine; then the government established an area of rural reform there and brought in settlers. Word of Sopemi's activities reached the *garimpeiros,* and they began arriving to work the drainages outside the claim. One of the settlers who owned the surface rights to land within the claim had the idea that if he invited the *garimpeiros* onto it he could strengthen his hand with Sopemi by saying that unless they gave him a good deal he would rather take the ten per cent from the *garimpeiros.* Now the *garimpeiros* were encroaching on Sopemi's operations, and the landowner was powerless to get rid of them.

In six months their number rose to over three thousand, and their camp grew into a town of makeshift dwellings, the main thoroughfare lined with open-fronted *cantinas,* where rows of unattached young women wait on benches for diggers to come and buy them *caninhas* and engage them in opportunities to participate in the profits of their diamond sales. Here and there newly arrived diggers offload their digging equipment, their families and materials for erecting shelters at sites allocated to them by the man the *garimpeiros* recognize as their leader. Articulated brewery trucks groan through the rutted tracks of the settlement, delivering quantities of beer to the shops hastily established by traders who follow the *garimpeiros'* movements and are quick to exploit the commercial potential wherever they concentrate.

Armed guards patrol the fences at the Itapena mine. The invasion of concession areas by illicit diggers is a delicate problem for the mining companies, which have to try to protect their interests, without precipitating open hostility.

Luiz Barbao was a *garimpeiro* for eight years before deciding he would do better by selling them their supplies. Jeremias Borges, who has shops in camps all over the country, came there to sell gravel pumps to the *garimpeiros,* and took the opportunity to establish a pharmacy when he noticed that the settlement lacked one. After digging for five years, Julio Pereira Leite decided there would be more money in opening a *cantina,* where his customers pay in cash or diamonds. "I operate only in diamond areas," he says. "With diamonds you don't have a fixed commercial price, as you have with gold, and so there is always the chance of picking up something really good." He keeps a diamond balance under the bar counter for weighing any stones they may want to convert into cruzados. His customers seldom give him any trouble in the bar. "We find bodies outside occasionally," he says, "but they are the result of private disputes that have nothing to do with us."

"They are a tough race of people, accustomed to violence. They know we will not use force against them, and feel that they can take their chances, as they consider us to be soft," says the chief geologist of Sopemi, John Oglesby. "We are under pressure from the Mato Grosso state Mines Department to take action, because this type of thing is becoming a major problem. But we have learnt from the experience of others. Three months ago, a para-statal mining company, with all the political clout in the world, called in the Federal Police and the army, who drove the *garimpeiros* off the property, but killed a few in the process. Three days later the *garimpeiros* returned in force and shot the geologist, the administrator and a security guard, bringing the mine to a standstill."

Salustiano Porto, a recent arrival at the São Luiz River diggings, has spent twenty of his thirty-six years on diamond *garimpos* in various parts of the country. His father was a *garimpeiro,* and although Salustiano tried working for a while as a clerk, he prefers, as he puts it, to risk his life on the *garimpos,* because it is the sort of life he knows best. But only with some is digging a family tradition, says Manoel José de Sousa; most are first-generation *garimpeiros* who have been drawn to digging by the prospect of wealth. Although none of his family were diggers, it seemed to be the best way of making money that was open to him. He has been digging for twenty years, doing everything himself by hand to begin with, and then in partnership with an associate who had a pump. Now he has his own pump and only supervises the work. Here a pump can produce about a hundred carats of diamonds a week, which sell for perhaps twenty US dollars a carat. He gives the landowner ten per cent, and, as owner of the pump, takes sixty-five per cent of the residue. The balance is divided equally between the seven men working on the pump.

The dreams of the Indians who dug for diamonds on the tributaries of the Krishna cannot have differed greatly from those of the *garimpeiros* working the tributaries of the Amazon, and their methods of treating the gravels were essentially the same as those that have been used by alluvial diamond diggers everywhere, modified by the technologies of their times. In India, as in Brazil, the first diamond discoveries were probably made by alluvial gold diggers, as they were too in China, where the first recorded discovery of diamonds was made in West Hunan province during the Qing dynasty, by a farmer who was panning for alluvial gold. Considering that until late in the last century nothing was known of kimberlite, and that before then all the diamonds in circulation had been found in alluvial deposits in association with gold, Plato's inference that they are a transparent form of the noble metal was an informed opinion twenty-four centuries ago. Indeed, the association of diamonds with gold and rivers goes back almost to the dawn of time. Thousands of metres underground in the gold mines of the Witwatersrand, miners find diamonds embedded in the gold-bearing conglomerates deposited in a river estuary 2700 million years ago.

Tavernier's description of the Golconda mines in the seventeenth century as being worked by a rabble of fanatics guided by a wizard, whose wand was said to point unerringly to places that were rich in gems, seems to have been a culturally loaded account of what he saw, for by then the "wizards" had certainly acquired some knowledge of practical geology. At many of the mines the diggers worked the recent sediments of the riverbed during the dry season, and during the rainy season moved back onto higher ground, to work in pits, where they extracted diamondiferous material from a single stratum of much older sediments in an ancient conglomerate of rounded pebbles.

In much the same way, diggers on the Vaal River, in South Africa, today still migrate seasonally between the riverbed and higher ground, not far from where the discovery of diamonds in 1866 led to Africa replacing Brazil as the major producer, just as Brazil had replaced India a little over a century earlier. Here, when heavy rain and melting snow in the highlands cause the Vaal to rise, the diggers strip overburden from the banks to get at the old underlying terraces. When the river is low they throw breakwaters out into the stream, and work the gravels in which the diamond industry in Africa first took root. From here, men who came from Europe dreaming of making their fortunes on the Vaal, went on to find the "dry diggings" at Kimberley and discover that volcanic pipes of a material they called kimberlite are the primary source of diamonds – a discovery that was to transform the industry world-wide. But the Vaal still has its dreamers.

Growing up in Kimberley, Pat Mason has naturally been aware of diamonds for most of his life, but he was thirty-five before regular contact with diggers through his mining supplies business prompted him to give it up and start digging for diamonds himself. "Now I feel that I am part of a romantic tradition," he says. "I have a great affinity for the Vaal, and diamonds are the Vaal. Although I'm working old terraces several hundred metres from the river at present, I like being as close to it as possible. The water is low at the moment, and I should've been there already."

The old terraces were first worked by Cornish miners at the turn of the century. Lacking the equipment to strip off the overburden, they honeycombed the whole area, digging shafts, three metres wide and up to ten metres deep, from which they tunnelled into the terraces in all directions, linking up with the tunnels radiating from neighbouring shafts.

"Diamonds are found here in fossilized streambeds, called runs," says Mason. "The old-timers who tunnelled here put a man on top to hand-treat the gravel in a sieve as it came out. When he saw in his wash that the ground they were into was weakening, he could tell them to change the direction they were tunnelling in, to stay with the run. Because they worked slowly, they could follow a run, even if it was only two metres wide. Having the machinery to strip the overburden, we can get down to working the pillars the old-timers left between their tunnels to support the roof. But we work too quickly and remove too much ground – about a hundred tonnes an hour – to be able to follow the wash as closely as they did."

Alluvial diggings are too unpredictable for one to be able to plan ahead, which is probably why De Beers has left them to the small diggers and concentrated on kimberlites, he says. "You can be sitting on a run and yet not find a single diamond for the next hundred metres. Diggers believe that if your name is on a diamond you'll find it, and that's pretty well right. You can leave a piece of ground, and somebody else can start there and find in a week what you had not found in two or three years. It happens all the time. And then you have people coming back to ground they've worked previously and making a big success of it the second time. The unpredictability means that you can always do better, in a different place or the same place; if you find a forty-carater today, it doesn't mean you won't find a 140-carater tomorrow."

One small diamond was all they found in the concentrates that day at Moonlight on the Vaal (left), where Coenraad "Franky" Fraenkel, assisted by his brother Annatt, on right of picture, works his claims. Among discarded boulders and old tailings dumps at Gong Gong on the Vaal (right), the Bowers family have pegged claims to glean the diamonds that earlier diggers may have left behind.

Amichai Shmuely, a hotelier in the area, has lived among the diggers since 1947 and was himself a digger for twelve years. "When you are working a pipe or fissures you can calculate what you are likely to get, but with alluvium you can work a hundred tonnes and find nothing, and then work another hundred tonnes and find a hundred carats," he says. "In one patch here on the river I found 320 carats in a month. On another occasion I went four months with the same process, the same scale of work, and didn't find a single carat. You can't plan ahead, because you may go blank."

There is nothing quite like finding a good river diamond, Mason says. "The first one I found hooked me for keeps. I had been battling for seven months, finding only small stuff, when it turned up: a six-carat yellow. It wasn't a fancy yellow, but to me it was a wonderful diamond, and I wanted the world for it. Most diggers do."

In twelve years on the Vaal a 39.8-carat stone that he took from the gravel of the river itself is the largest diamond he has found. "This is the only life for me," he says. "It's the excitement, the feeling of anticipation every time I turn the sieve over. They found a 300-carat stone here back in the 1800s, and it can happen that one day I'll turn my sieve over and find a really big one."

"A lot of people used to come to the diggings with the idea of finding a big stone and becoming rich overnight," says Shmuely. "But you have plenty of time to think when you're sitting out there on the river, and very soon you realize that only by an extraordinary and unforeseeable stroke of good luck will you become an instant millionaire, and that the more pressing concern is to improve your equipment and become more cost-effective. Diggers who can't find enough diamonds to finance their operations have to leave the game, but the only digger I know of who gave up digging after finding a lot of big diamonds stopped because he had become too old to dig. Those who have made a lot of money stay in the game because they enjoy it. But it's a tough game. In summer it gets so hot that you can't touch your equipment, and in the winter you have to light fires to unfreeze your pipes before you can start in the morning. You can be up to your ears in debt today, and tomorrow you can turn the sieve over and not owe anybody a penny, and still have money in your pocket. I'm a gambling man, and I see it as a great game of chance. No matter how bleak things may appear to be, the digger is always optimistic. On the next turn of the sieve he could be up half a million."

At van Wyk has been digging on the Vaal for over forty years, and his association with

N.H. BOWERS
2 CLAIMS
GONG-GONG

diamond digging goes back to 1924, when his father forsook farming to try his luck on the diamond fields. He remembers running, as a boy of eight or nine, to peg claims for his father in the 1928 Lichtenburg diamond rush. "After school I used to collect sacks of *bantoms* (discarded concentrates from the sorting tables) and resort them at home," he recalls. "One could make a living out of sorting *bantoms* in those days because many of the diggers were new to the game and didn't know how to run their equipment properly. We'd go through their tailings and find quite a few diamonds they had missed."

The river has been good to him, he says. "Costs are high, but I've always come through all right. The profits aren't so great that one can make big investments, but we have lived well. My sons and I all have our own houses. I drive a good car and don't owe anybody anything. Even my bank manager seems to like me. It's hard work, but I'm my own boss. I've never really thought about doing anything else."

When he started on the river Van Wyk had to do everything by hand. "Thirty years ago I built the six-foot pan that I am still using, and it's been a very lucky pan for me," he says. "I've taken a lot of diamonds out of it. The biggest was 103 carats, but I've also found stones of 34 carats, 27 carats and quite a few of 12 and 13 carats. Carat and half-carat stones turn up every week."

He has seldom taken a holiday away from the river. The eldest of his six children is forty-three, the youngest two and a half. His three eldest sons are diggers, working their own claims, and they form a country-music band, which has recorded a number of songs. A self-taught musician who was himself recorded playing the banjo in the thirties, Van Wyk would rather stay home and play the concertina in his sons' band than take a holiday elsewhere. At an age when most men seek retirement, he prefers to keep on digging, although he now processes only forty tonnes a day compared with the 150 tonnes he handled formerly. "Digging keeps me young," he says. "I will never retire, because I enjoy the work and want to spend all my time beside the Vaal. If I look at all the places here that I've worked, I remember them as if it was yesterday. It is my life. I like to come down to the river on a Sunday and sit here alone or with my wife. She also knows all the places. It's her life too."

His eldest son, Attie van Wyk, grew up on the river and has been digging for fifteen years on a fairly large scale. "It is in my blood; I have always been a diamond man," he says. "There are good times and bad times, but on balance I do well. Hard work and the belief that one day I'll find a really big one keep me in business. But when you do get a big one, you start believing you will find another, and another... That's the way it is with diamonds."

Francois du Rand, who dives for diamonds in partnership with Hector Bergstrom at Koingnaas, on South Africa's west coast, surfaces to check his bearings. The two men work under licence inside the De Beers concession area and share the diamonds they recover with the company.

Diamond trawler owner Davy Clark (above) looks over the shoulder of sharp-eyed fisherman Edward Engelbrecht, who on his first day aboard the diamond vessel, operating off South Africa's west coast, caught a 53.9-carat diamond that nearly got away because it was too big for the screen classifier and would have been dumped overboard with the oversized waste. West coast diamond trawler *Western Jupiter* operating in twenty metres of water about three kilometres offshore (left). Divers guide the suction hose on the seabed, and the gravel that is pumped up is separated on board from the waste and concentrated ashore.

CHAPTER 3 RE-CREATING THE EARTH

But for the great volcanic disturbances that emplaced kimberlites and lamproites in the earth's crust, diamonds, which are formed in the mantle more than a hundred kilometres underground, would never have reached the surface.

The devastated landscape surrounding Mauna Ulu volcano on Hawaii Island gives some idea of the scenes that must have accompanied the emplacement of diamond pipes.

Over many millions of years the pipes have been eroded down to the level of the surrounding countryside and covered with water-laid sediments and windblown sands, and diamonds carried away by water have been deposited in surrounding drainages.

In searching for these pipes earth scientists often have to track the diamonds in alluvial deposits back through contemporary and ancient drainages, combining modern techniques and their knowledge of earth history to locate hidden pipes. In a sense, they mentally re-create the earth.

Working from a major river in Brazil's Roraima state, Sopemi geologists (left) have followed the trail of indicator minerals up a tributary stream to where their results justify laying out a grid and sampling the adjacent forest floor. Under conditions of extreme humidity, the wet, concentrated soil samples have to be back-packed by field assistants (right) many kilometres through trackless jungle to the nearest road.

When in the short Arctic summer the tundra of northern Ontario is briefly accessible, float planes fly teams of Monopros diamond geologists to base camps on the shores of unnamed lakes (left), from which geological teams go out by helicopter to sample rivers and streams.

In the People's Republic of China, where alluvial diamonds have been found in twelve provinces and kimberlites containing diamonds in three, the sampler washing gravel (above) is part of a geological programme aimed at assessing the diamond resources of this vast country.

A "soldier" termite (left), one of several forming a defensive circle while additions are made to their home, stands on a minute Cape yellow diamond that "worker" termites have hauled, together with other building materials, from many metres below the surface. Termites, which for thousands of years brought grains of indicator minerals to the surface in this way, provided De Beers geologists with their first clues to the existence of the rich Jwaneng pipe under fifty metres of Kalahari sand and calcrete in Botswana. Flying low over the desert (above), geologists trail a "sting" that picks up the magnetic impulses emitted by some kimberlite pipes. The magnetic record is synchronized with a photographic record to assist later in identifying the magnetic anomalies on the ground.

Near where Botswana borders South Africa, a small herd of Greater Kudu browse in the bushveld of the northern Transvaal, ranging over the ground in which De Beers geologists discovered the Venetia pipe, now being developed into a major new diamond mine.

PROSPECTING GEOLOGISTS EXPLORE ancient landscapes, which might have existed many thousands or many millions of years ago, but of which often only the merest traces, perhaps no more than inferences, remain today. They are, in a sense, adrift in time: dealing in the present with the practical demands of living far from civilization in jungle or desert, yet working within visions of the past that they conjure from clues afforded by the rocks and landforms about them. A geologist hacking through bush on a hillside a thousand kilometres from the sea may perceive himself as walking along a shoreline on which the surf ran high two billion years ago.

The landscapes they explore today are generally far older than those inhabited by alluvial diamond diggers. While river diggers look directly for diamonds in recent sediments, the geologists seek their primary sources, the kimberlites and lamproites that brought them to the surface from deep in the earth's mantle many millions of years before erosion released them into streams and rivers. But they use the alluvial deposits too. In the beds of contemporary and defunct rivers, sediments containing minerals commonly associated with primary sources are often the places where prospectors pick up the scent that enables them to back-track up tributary drainages, following the trail of garnets, ilmenites and other kimberlitic minerals to the source rocks.

"We prospect stories, many different stories," says field geologist Jeff Watkins. "The fascination of our work is that each day we read a little more of a story in the landscape, and each story is a fragment of a larger story, which itself is at most a paragraph in earth history. Our final reports, our versions of the story, are only final in the sense of being the best we can do within present technical, financial and legal limitations. As these conditions change, many reports will be rewritten."

Once the violent volcanic activity that accompanied the emplacement of a kimberlite pipe had subsided, the crater and cone of the new pipe would have looked something like this dormant volcano on Hawaii Island.

Reflecting the wider order of nature, in which atmosphere, earth and living organisms form a unit, the natural history of diamonds is grander, more complex and infinitely more amazing than any conjectural account of their origin dreamt up by the philosophers of antiquity. Yet the speculative element remains. Most educated people know that diamonds crystallize naturally from other forms of carbon at high temperatures and pressures far beneath the earth's surface, but where did the carbon come from and how did it get there? Many diamonds are so old that the source carbon must have been present in the mantle from the beginning, derived probably from gases that composed the solar system, such as methane, which has been spectrographically recorded in the atmospheres of other planets, and accumulations of carbon atoms could have crystallized as diamonds. The formation of diamonds in the mantle being, it is believed, a process that has continued throughout earth history, source carbon may also have come from surface organic material, such as the shells of countless marine creatures, compacted into limestone and then, at places where the continental plates of the earth's crust meet, taken down hundreds of kilometres into the mantle, to depths at which temperatures and pressures favour conversion to diamond.

By dating the minute inclusions of other minerals that were encapsulated in diamonds at the time of their formation, earth scientists are now able to tell when that happened. Thus they have established, for example, that some diamonds from the Kimberley mines, in South Africa, were formed three and a half billion years ago, but remained in the earth's mantle until a mere ninety million years ago, when the kimberlite picked them up and carried them through the crust and to the surface.

"A kimberlite is like a train that took the diamonds aboard at the diamond station," says Alex van Zyl, chief geologist in charge of prospecting operations in South Africa for the diamond mining giant, De Beers. "The condition in which they reached their destination depended on what happened on the journey. If the train stopped at a station where the pressure and temperature were unfavourable for diamond preservation, the diamonds would have been destroyed. In some situations a short stop might not have damaged them, whereas a stop of say five million years might have done so."

Knowledge of this kind narrows down the area in which geologists can expect to find *diamond-bearing* kimberlites to the very old, stable cratons, or continental shield areas, because these enormous masses of rock have rooted into the near-fluid mantle, and the cooler medium they provided for a greater part of the journey gave the diamonds a better chance of surviving the trip. Kimberlites in the less stable so-called mobile belts around the edges of the cratons are generally not diamondiferous, although lamproites, another type of intrusive mantle-derived rock that occurs in these belts, including the prolific Argyle pipe in Australia, sometimes are.

Chief geologist in charge of De Beers' prospecting operations in South Africa, Alex van Zyl, among others, spent several years methodically tracking indicator minerals up the dry watercourses in the bushveld that led eventually to the Venetia pipe. Here (left) he examines a handful of gems recovered from bulk samples at Venetia.

Understanding of the cratonic connection was still at a speculative stage when De Beers, spurred by the need to stay ahead in the face of new competition, embarked in the mid-1950s on a quest to learn more about kimberlites. It began by sending teams to seek the primary sources of alluvial diamonds coming out of West and Central Africa, and went on to prospect much of the continent over the next two decades. Its exploration was still governed largely by the distribution of alluvial diamonds, however, and its major discoveries, the Orapa and Jwaneng pipes in Botswana, were made when the techniques it uses today for selecting target areas and evaluating samples were still in their infancy.

"We simply divided our grant areas into quarter-degree squares and then systematically sampled thousands of square kilometres, using prismatic compasses for direction and bicycle wheels fitted with cyclometers to measure distances," recalls Dr Gavin Lamont, who began prospecting for De Beers in Botswana in 1955, and was chiefly responsible for finding Orapa in 1967 and Jwaneng in 1973. "We looked for kimberlitic minerals in streambeds, and where there were no streambeds we took samples of the top centimetre of sand, in which the wind concentrates particles of heavy minerals, leaving them to accumulate on the surface, while blowing the lighter material away."

Samplers in Botswana (left) systematically sample thousands of square kilometres of desert using prismatic compasses for direction and bicycle wheels fitted with cyclometers to measure distances.
In the featureless open spaces of the central Kalahari (right) the trail of indicator minerals in soil samples has led to where a field geologist has decided to set up a prospecting drill to probe beneath the mantle of sand. By these methods the great pipes at Orapa and Jwaneng were found.

Selection Trust geologists prospecting in the dry Motloutse River found three diamonds, but no deposits, and after they left the area in 1962 De Beers took over their grant. Sampling up-river from the diamond sites for about eighty kilometres, the De Beers geologists found a few diamonds themselves, before the river course petered out. "We covered the entire headwater area, using every sampling technique we knew of, and found nothing," says Lamont. "Studying the geomorphology, however, I eventually realized that the river had been decapitated by an ancient upwarp in the land surface, and that the source of the diamonds, like the original source of the river, must lie on the other side, to the west of it."

But extensive sampling to the west produced nothing of interest, and, growing impatient, he and his assistant, Jim Gibson, went much further west and, over a period of three days, drove along all the roads and tracks marked on their maps, taking samples every four kilometres. Back in camp they concentrated these down to seventeen bags, and found garnets and ilmenites in fourteen of them. Knowing that they were onto something big, they followed up with conventional sampling, which led to the discovery of the Orapa pipe, some two hundred kilometres from where the first diamonds had been found in the Motloutse River.

"Manfred Marx, who was leading our prospecting team up there, called me on the radio at my office in Lobatse and said they had found eleven hundred ilmenites in their latest samples and were still counting," says Lamont. "I immediately went to look at the aerial photographs at the Geological Survey office, and there the pipe was, although until we knew it was there it was indistinguishable from the many small pans in the area. We outlined the pipe with a magnetometer, put down prospecting pits and started washing the kimberlite, and the diamonds came rolling out."

Whereas Orapa had been discovered under less than a metre of calcrete, the Jwaneng pipe was completely hidden beneath up to fifty metres of desert sand and calcrete. It might never have been found without the assistance of termites that lived in the Kalahari many thousands of years ago, when there was still sufficient rainfall to support them. For millennia the termites had burrowed down through the sand to collect moist clay in the kimberlite for building their mounds, and for millennia rain and wind had broken down the mounds, removing the lighter materials in the clay and concentrating the heavier minerals in the surface sand.

"We began picking up garnets in our samples a fair distance out from the pipe, and knew we were getting close when we started finding ilmenites, which, owing to their higher specific gravity, don't disperse as far," says Lamont. "We had to outline the pipe by drilling. As our own drill couldn't cope with the thick overburden, we hired a contractor who was drilling for water in the area to do it with his jumper drill. Then, because we couldn't put down a prospecting pit through that much sand, we fitted fifteen-inch bits and did the evaluation with the drill to a depth of about two hundred metres."

Following their success at Orapa, De Beers initiated a more scientific approach to prospecting in the early seventies under the leadership of the late Dr Louis Murray, then consulting geologist to and a director of De Beers, and deputy technical director in charge of geology for Anglo American Corporation, which provides technical and geological management for the prospecting and mining operations of De Beers.

"We set about assembling and correlating every scrap of information we could gather about every kimberlite we had access to," recalls Barry Hawthorne, who now occupies the position at Anglo American then held by Dr Murray. "We supplemented our analytical facilities in Johannesburg by establishing a research laboratory in Kimberley to examine the samples sent in by our prospecting teams from around the world, and there we began a very detailed study into the nature of kimberlites, as a result of which we acquired considerable skill at assessing the potential of any diamond-bearing rock anywhere in the world." The vast body of information built up over the years, systematically stored and continually added to, has helped keep De Beers in the vanguard of diamond research and exploration.

Like other volcanic pipes, kimberlites are solidified remnants of fluid material, called magma, that was forced up through the earth's crust. "But kimberlites come from much deeper in the mantle than the basalt lavas commonly associated with volcanoes," says Dr John Bristow, a De Beers research geologist. "Their chemistry and the work we've done on temperature and pressure relationships point to the origin of diamondiferous kimberlites at depths of 150 kilometres or more. Because their magmas differ in composition, basalt lavas tended to well up and flow, whereas kimberlites behaved more like

Sampling the soil at the base of termite mounds (left), has become a standard technique for diamond prospectors in Botswana. Heavy mineral grains in the moist material that termites bring from beneath the sand are cemented into the walls of their mounds, and the process of weathering concentrates them in the surrounding soil.

"LGM's corner" – a hand-lettered sign (right) nailed to the bunkhouse wall at Itapena mine in Brazil pays tribute to Dr Louis Murray, consulting geologist to De Beers and a deputy technical director (geology) of Anglo American, who modernized the approach of both companies to diamond prospecting. Dr Murray, who customarily chose this quiet corner to sip a beer at sundown, was killed in a helicopter accident while visiting prospecting operations in the Andes.

bottles of Coke uncapped after being shaken up. As they neared the surface, the volatiles stored in them at depth were suddenly released, and they blew out as enormously explosive volcanoes. The sudden release of energy drastically lowered the temperature, and instead of oozing lava they rained ash and kimberlitic debris, which formed cones around the rims of the pipes."

While kimberlite pipes have much in common with one another, they do not conform equally to a simple conceptual model. "Owing to the complicated and cyclical interplay of subsurface and volcanic processes involved in their formation, they are complex geological structures," says Dr Roger Clement, consulting geologist to De Beers for South Africa and Namibia. "The surface craters resulting from explosive outburst are underlain by carrot-shaped bodies, called diatremes, which at depth grade into irregular root zones, where the pipes often split into several channelways. After their emplacement, crater lakes formed and were infilled by sediments, including diamonds and other mineral particles, eroded from the surrounding cones. The kimberlite in the diatremes below the craters is considered to have been emplaced by explosively induced gas streaming processes, whereas the kimberlite occupying the root zones has crystallized directly from the intruded kimberlite magma."

"Although a pipe that has not been eroded at all has never been found, it is estimated that the diatreme zones of some pipes probably went down to depths of over a kilometre," says Hawthorne. "In some parts of Africa the last vestiges of the original cones are reflected in deposits of diamondiferous gravels that were washed outwards from the pipes into surrounding drainages. In Botswana, the Jwaneng pipe, which has long been protected by a thick covering of sand in the Kalahari basin, has lost perhaps only a couple of hundred metres through erosion, and is being mined in the crater zone. The present surfaces of the Finsch mine in South Africa and many of the pipes in Siberia are in the upper part of the diatreme zone. At Kimberley, however, the original surface was probably a kilometre above the present ground level. Here early mining was in the lower part of the diatreme, and we are now working in the root zone."

Kimberlites have been emplaced at many different times in earth history and in many different parts of the world. In Africa they range in age from fifty million to 1600 million years and are often contemporaneous with great mountain building periods and the break-up of the southern proto-continent, Gondwanaland. Similar ages have been recorded in other continents.

Many kimberlites have been found in the Soviet Union and southern Africa in areas where there has been little relatively recent geological activity, says Hawthorne. "Where the geological history has been turbulent for long periods there is less chance of finding a primary source. In West Africa, Burma, Thailand, Borneo and Brazil the primary sources of most of the alluvial deposits may be so old, and tropical weathering has been so thorough, that they could have been completely eroded away or deeply buried." Furthermore, many of the alluvial diamonds in these areas could have been transported to their present locations long ago from distant sources; perhaps even sources that lie in other continents today.

Little is known outside the People's Republic of China about the diamondiferous kimberlites that have been found in the country in the last twenty-five years. Alluvial diamonds have been discovered in twelve provinces and kimberlites containing diamonds in three, according to Zhang Peiyuan, the senior geologist in the Ministry of Geology and Mineral Resources responsible for diamond prospecting projects all over China.

At the Kimberley and Johannesburg laboratories, and to a lesser extent satellite laboratories since established in other countries where De Beers geologists prospect for diamonds, high-tech instrumentation is used to produce very quickly accurate analyses of the characteristics of individual mineral grains, with a view to a more precise evaluation of prospecting samples. "We simply took the view in the old days that if we found kimberlitic minerals in our samples there must be kimberlites around and that we should look for them and see whether they were diamondiferous," says Van Zyl. "Now that we know how to look at our samples more scientifically, we waste less time and money chasing off after red herrings. As the events that affected the diamonds during their ascent from the mantle presumably left their imprint also on the other minerals that accompanied them, it is possible to obtain from the indicator minerals some idea of the potential of the ore bodies that shed them."

By placing its prospecting on a more scientific basis when it did, De Beers anticipated future necessity, for diamond prospecting today must necessarily be more selective. The sort of labour-intensive sampling that was done in past decades in Africa became too expensive in the eighties, making a shift from Third World to First World prospecting techniques imperative – a shift that was within the capabilities of only the larger companies.

A joint prospecting venture undertaken in the seventies by De Beers and the Angolan diamond mining company, Diamang, was in many respects the last of the old and the first of the new. On the one hand they had five hundred field assistants taking samples every two hundred metres over an area of three thousand square kilometres and examined thirty-five thousand samples a month at their laboratory in Angola. On the other hand, under pressure of limited time imposed by the revolutionary war, they developed new techniques for covering large parts of a country quickly.

Rising costs made target selection increasingly important everywhere. Kimberlites were, in fact, too abundant to go chasing off after every one of them in the hope that it might be diamondiferous. As it was neither practical nor economic to high-density sample millions of square kilometres in Australia, Brazil or Canada by combing the countries from end to end with long lines of samplers spaced at regular intervals, it was essential to identify the most likely areas and start prospecting where the chances of success were greatest. Once again the research geologists were able to assist in determining the broad geological and mineralogical characteristics that indicate whether kimberlites in a region could contain diamonds and to build conceptual models to assist in identifying the types of terrain that would make the best targets.

"Target selection is based on a good understanding of many facets of geology: on detailed knowledge of continental structure, tectonics, petrology, geomorphology and sedimentation, which together guide one to start in places where there is a relatively good chance of success," says Roy Edwards, who after extensive field experience in East Africa, Angola, Brazil and Canada is now the consulting geologist responsible for De Beers' international prospecting activities world-wide. Target selection therefore requires the combined efforts of highly qualified specialists in many different areas of geology. But, Clement cautions, it has not as yet achieved the status of an exact science.

Geological considerations are not the only ones, however. It is not simply a matter of finding diamondiferous kimberlites, but of finding ones that can make money. As a rule, the further away one goes from infrastructure the bigger and richer a pipe must be for it to be payable. Accessibility, costs and climate are consequently crucial criteria for target selection, particularly in the unmapped tropical rain forests of the Amazon, the Australian and African deserts, or the Northern Territories of Canada, where the thermometer remains well below freezing for half of the year. In such places one needs to have a model, not only of the best places to look for pipes, but the sort of pipe one needs to find – the sort that could profitably be mined in that environment.

"There may be similarities, but each environment you work in is geologically, geographically, infrastructurally, socially, culturally and politically unique," says Edwards. "Each therefore requires a prospecting strategy that takes all these factors into account. Outside experience and specialist input are valuable, but the working model for an area must be evolved in that area, and local people must be involved in generating a prospecting strategy that is applicable to that environment."

Failure to appreciate such differences, and too much reliance on principles and techniques developed elsewhere, partly explain why geologists were for many years unable to find a primary source in Australia, although some of them actually covered the ground where in 1979 the Argyle mine – now the world's biggest producer in carat terms – was discovered by relative novices in diamond exploration, the Ashton Joint Venture consortium.

The granite foothills of the Kimberleys, in north Western Australia (right), where in 1979 Ashton Joint Venture geologists discovered the prolific Argyle pipe. Field geologist Maureen Muggeridge (below right) found what proved to be the first Argyle diamond in a bulk sample of river gravel a few months before the pipe itself was discovered.

"We accepted uncritically the generally held view at the time that lamproites do not host diamonds," says Manfred Marx, who after participating in the discovery of Orapa was seconded to prospect for Stockdale in Australia. "Our prospecting techniques were therefore geared specifically to looking for kimberlites, which as a rule are easier to find, because lamproites often do not shed the usual indicator minerals."

Although in the part of north Western Australia where the Argyle and Ellendale lamproites were eventually discovered lamproites outnumber kimberlites twenty to one and in places form hills that stand proud of the plain, they were ignored by geologists, who had twice prospected the area unsuccessfully for diamonds. High-density sampling, in which a large number of small samples are taken, was an appropriate technique for tracking garnets and ilmenites back to kimberlites, but to find the Argyle lamproite it would have been necessary to take bulk samples of twenty or thirty tonnes and look directly for diamonds in them.

Anglo American geologists had in fact found lamproites containing diamonds in Zambia some thirteen years earlier. "The problem was that, because we had not yet established a sophisticated petrological laboratory, we thought they were kimberlites," explains Clement. "Had we recognized them as lamproites they could well have directed us to the Western Australian lamproites, which had been described in the literature as long ago as 1941."

"Since the discovery of the Argyle and Ellendale lamproites in the so-called mobile belt in this region, we have found diamondiferous kimberlites in the cratonic nucleus," says Marx, who is now diamond exploration manager for Freeport, one of the smaller diamond exploration and mining companies in Australia. "They weren't found earlier because they too don't shed the usual garnets and ilmenites, although they do shed spinels."

In Canada the advanced state of the earth sciences made it possible for Edwards to adopt a strategy suitable for prospecting with very few staff a vast country, in which costs are high and access is often difficult. "This, together with the results of high-quality, low-density sampling done right across the country by our predecessors, Hard Metals Canada and Diapros, has enabled us to construct a model of the whole shield area, as a basis for target selection," he says. "Using specially written computer software to re-examine this data, we have been able to draw up an inventory of targets and give them priority ratings, so that we can put our money on the best chance. Our strategy then is to go into a good geological environment and either

look for a pipe and see if it has diamonds in it, or look for diamonds and see if we can find their source. An understanding of glacial movements during the last Ice Age gives us an idea of the provenance of the minerals we find in glacial tills, outwash gravels spread over the countryside and under glacial clays deposited in lakes that formed in front of the retreating ice."

Sopemi geologists (left) discussing a prospecting programme at a base camp deep in the Brazilian rain forests are, from left, John Oglesby, João Franke, Nilo Barbosa and Homero Silva. On a river in Roraima state, a Sopemi prospecting team (right) head their flat-bottomed aluminium skiff towards camp.

"In Brazil, as a result of uplifts in the cratonic areas over a billion and a half years ago, coarse-grained sediments, including diamonds that must have come from very old pipes in these areas, were deposited around the edges of the cratons," says Sopemi's research manager, Tony Carrington, whose main task is to identify the best target areas for exploration. "The diamonds have been transported and deposited many times during the deposition and erosion of these old sediments. This has happened so often over a long period that when we try to trace alluvial deposits back to their primary sources the trail simply becomes weaker the further back we go and eventually disappears."

While it will be very difficult to find the primary sources of the diamonds in the ancient sediments, if indeed the pipes have been preserved, the prospects are better in several areas where the alluvials appear to have come from younger kimberlites that date back eighty million to 130 million years. "But outcrops are rare," says Sopemi's chief geologist, John Oglesby. "Rocks often weather to a depth of two hundred metres or more in the humid tropical environment and are hidden by soil, a thick layer of humus and dense vegetation – and we are looking for a diamondiferous kimberlite with a surface of perhaps only ten hectares in a prime target area of a million square kilometres."

The cratonic areas are chiefly in remote parts of the Amazon basin, where they can be reached only by river. "As there are many rapids on rivers in these areas, often we have to use light, motorized canoes to get in men and supplies, for distances of perhaps five hundred kilometres," says Oglesby. "In one area it takes us two days by road to reach the point where we launch our canoes, and then eleven days by water to get to the target area. So we have to spend almost a month travelling – there and back – in order to work there for one month."

"Today's diamond prospector uses a combination of techniques, with a changing emphasis from place to place, depending on which technique is more useful in an area," says Van Zyl. Airborne geophysics has been successful in penetrating the thick sand cover in many parts of the world. Satellite imagery provides prospectors with working maps in areas that have not been geologically mapped adequately. Although kimberlites are too small to be identified directly on satellite images, conventional aerial photography sometimes helps in identifying ground features that may be kimberlites. However, the prospector's best tool remains the recognition and analysis of heavy minerals derived from kimberlites.

A freelance navigator, whose skill when flying at tree-top height is rated among the best in the world, Karoline van Dunk (below right) has worked on geomagnetic surveys in many parts of Africa and Australia. Engaged here on a survey for De Beers Botswana, she gives precise directions to the pilot Nols Harding, as they pass low over the ground at two hundred kilometres an hour.

"There is no such thing as a rigid system in prospecting," says Jeff Watkins. "There is always room for innovation and lateral thinking." As an example he cites diamond prospectors in China, who are said to have gone from village to village exchanging new grass sandals for old, which they then burnt to analyse the residue of what had been picked up in the course of the wearer's day in the fields. "Basically, we are looking for and investigating anomalies. We may find them through airborne magnetics, structural analysis or gravity measurement, get a look at them on aerial photographs, and then follow them up on the ground with strategic sampling, to see if we can find any of the right minerals in the area."

Prospecting geologists must have an eye for anomalies of all kinds, he says. "In Angola we found a kimberlite because an observant prospector noticed that the anthills, instead of being out in the open, as they usually are, were all around tree bases. We didn't know why, and never found out what caused it, but we hadn't seen it anywhere else in the world; it was an anomaly, and it proved to be a kimberlite. We had an anomaly in Minas Gerais we named the 'cow anomaly'. Someone noticed that all the cows were grazing in one small area in a huge field, although the grass everywhere was nice and green. We looked and found that just in that spot the grass was more succulent, because it was in richer soil, which proved to be over a kimberlite."

Not the smallest clue should escape the eye of the prospecting geologist, whether expressed in major geological features or the distribution of plants and animals and the fragments of rock that armadillos, rabbits, ants and other burrowing creatures bring to the surface. In reading maps he is not merely looking at them, but studying them until he can "feel" the geology. He must immerse himself in the area he is going into, to the extent of absorbing the local culture and speaking the language of the countryside. While exploring the past, he must be alive to the present. If he hankers after the comforts he left behind, everything ahead will seem an insurmountable obstacle, instead of a welcome challenge, and he will not be sufficiently in the present to see the things he should be seeing.

Prospecting geologists occupy a world that is far removed from their academic preparation for it. "At university you deal only with fresh rock samples, which ring when struck with a hammer, whereas in Brazil, owing to tropical weathering, your hammer is more likely to sink into the rock with a dull thud," says Watkins. "When I started prospecting in Angola, the ink barely dry on my degree certificate, I quickly had to learn a lot of things they hadn't taught at university, such as what to do when a bushfire is approaching along a broad front at twenty kilometres an hour and your vehicle can only travel at ten kilometres an hour over rough terrain. I had to learn how to build bridges, dig deep pits and administer first aid. We were up to three days' drive from the nearest small village, so we had to be independent. Often we couldn't get fresh meat, and when we became tired of eating sun-dried fish, we hunted for the pot. After eleven months under canvas, we'd have a few days off at Christmas, and then go back into the bush for another year."

Prospecting has developed into a high-tech activity. Seated on the left in a DC 3 aircraft that is being fitted out by Anglo American's geophysics department, Anglo's deputy technical director (geology) Barry Hawthorne discusses modifications with chief geophysicist Eddie Kostlin, independent electronics engineer John Holst and divisional geophysicist Phil Klinkert.

Before going to Brazil he spent five and a half years in Angola, and ended up working in a buffer zone between opposing forces when the civil war flared up in 1974. "We decided to pull out in mid-1975, and began winding down our operation and getting all our people out of the area," he says. "Another chap and I were the last to leave. I was on the radio to the office in Nova Lisboa when a shell went through another part of the building and a bullet shattered the window, showering me with glass. I told them we were under fire and said I'd get back to them when I could. As we drove out of the village I saw the dust kicking up in the road and thought it was raining. Then I realized that somebody had opened up on us with a machine gun. We just put our heads down and kept going. It was not until we were up in the highlands three days later that we were able to string out our antenna and radio back to Nova Lisboa." Going to Angola at that time was a calculated risk, he says, but adds that a young man looking for adventure is almost immortal.

In addition to good health and professional expertise, Van Zyl lists a number of qualities necessary in a prospecting geologist. "He must possess the usual Boy Scout capabilities and must understand his environment and be able to live with it," he says. "Above all, while maintaining a sensible approach to the financial side of his activities, he must combine more than normal drive with optimism that borders on the unrealistic."

Watkins draws an analogy between prospecting and fox hunting: the thrills of the chase, motivated by the belief that you will make a kill, which for the prospecting geologist is when he discovers a mine. "All the kimberlites I've found have been tantalizingly interesting, although they ended up being uneconomic," he says. "That would be very disheartening if I didn't always feel that the next one will be a mine. At the start of a hunt you have to believe it will be a good fox, that the animal will be worth the hunt. Once you pick up the scent you want to get to the fox as quickly as possible, but if when you find a good footprint you realize you are chasing a five-week-old cub, you break off and look for another fox. Making the kill, finding the mine, is the thing. Afterwards you don't want to sit around dissecting the fox. You leave that to the mining geologists, the engineers, the metallurgists – all you want to do is go out and find another fox."

Dr Don Fraser, the Anglo American Fellow at Worcester College, Oxford, chats about diamonds and other minerals of the earth's upper mantle with recipients of Oppenheimer travel grants, geology students Elizabeth Hide and Roger Walling.

CHAPTER 4 INSIDE THE VOLCANO

For a moment it is as if a volcano that has been extinct for 250 million years has suddenly been re-activated.

With a display of force reminiscent of the volcanic disturbances that emplaced the kimberlite, seventeen tonnes of liquid explosive tear 120 000 tonnes of ore from the side of the pit at Jwaneng, releasing dense clouds of dust and acrid smoke, hurling rocks and boulders high in the air.

All natural diamonds were formed in the earth's mantle and reached the surface by way of kimberlite and lamproite pipes.

Whereas the traditional river diggers recover diamonds that nature has washed from exposed pipes and deposited in alluvial gravels, the miners who work these pipes descend into the craters and cores of the extinct volcanoes themselves.

The discovery of the Mir (peace) diamond pipe in Siberia in 1955 by geologist Yuri Khabardin heralded a new era in the history of diamond mining – an era in which the Soviet Union emerged as a major diamond producer.

The copious Argyle pipe in Western Australia, where the capacity of lamproites to yield diamonds was first recognized, protrudes above the valley floor between two ranges of hills.

Ore truck operator Helen Guest takes a "smoko", smoke break, at Argyle mine with loader operator Nick Anderson and fellow truck operator Doug Soames (above) in the grounded bin of a loader – the cleanest and coolest place in the pit.
Only five per cent of Argyle's production is in gem quality stones, but these include pink diamonds with a melted appearance (right), which on world markets are considered rare.

Sir Russel Madigan, who represented CRA, Australia's biggest mining company and principal participant in the development of the Argyle diamond mine, in the negotiations with Harry Oppenheimer that led to the agreement to market most of Argyle's production through the Central Selling Organization.

Botswana's Minister of External Affairs, the Hon Dr G.K.T. Chiepe (right), who, as Minister of Mineral Resources and Water Affairs when the Orapa and Jwaneng mines came into being, took a leading part in negotiations between the government and De Beers. "The talks were tough, but fair," she recalls. "It was fantastic to feel that I was helping to shape the future of my country. Today the diamond mines are the backbone of our economy, providing the people with clinics, schools, roads, employment and new skills, and they finance drilling all over the country for water – our scarcest resource."

Springbok fossick for green shoots at Airport Pan Game Reserve (left). Established by the mining community at Orapa and financed by the mine, the reserve is a haven for desert species, including the rare cheetah and brown hyena.

In a room behind the town hall at Jwaneng, assistant production manager Sean Daly, on the right, and computer operations supervisor Alpheus Setico, on the left, trained Botswana's first Olympic boxer, mines stores assistant Magare Tshekiso, who represented the country at the Seoul Olympic Games in 1988.

Working in more than a hundred metres of water (left), the diamond mining research vessel *Louis G. Murray* "vacuums" the seabed for diamonds deposited off the Namibian coast by the Orange River.

Closed-circuit television cameras in a deep-sea diving module relay colour images of the seabed to the control cabin on the *Louis G. Murray* (top). When the water is clear, artificial lighting gives the camera visibility for up to ten metres.

Sharks' fossilized teeth, fish vertebrae, pebbles, shells, corals and a few small diamonds in a sample (above) taken from the continental shelf off the coast of Namibia.

AT TWO O'CLOCK THE EARTH MOVED beneath the feet of the watchers near the rim of the man-made crater in the Kalahari desert, at Jwaneng. They had waited half an hour, the warning siren had sounded for fifteen minutes and they had known when to expect the blast, yet it took them by surprise. They experienced a series of shocks, but afterwards it was impossible to say in what order they had been: the loud crack of the explosion that seemed to burst from the sky, the tremor underfoot, or the dull boom 150 metres below, where seventeen tonnes of liquid explosive tore 120 000 tonnes of kimberlite from the side of the pit, sending up a great cloud of blue-grey smoke and yellow-brown dust reminiscent of the volcanic eruptions that emplaced the kimberlite there some 250 million years ago.

Sheltering in the scoop of an electric shovel from the blast (left), Emanuel Rapelang and Richard Mooketsi have just detonated high explosive charges to dislodge over a hundred thousand tonnes of kimberlite in the pit at Jwaneng. Soon the massive trucks are rolling again (right), hauling the ore to the primary crusher on the surface.

Scrub birds resumed their song, cicadas took up the chorus, the blast foreman checked for misfires and the red flag that had flown all morning was lowered. Soon the huge electric shovels were clearing up, loading seventeen tonnes with every scoop, and before long the fleet of sixteen 85-tonne trucks was again spiralling up the concentric benches of the open pit, hauling the ore to the primary crusher on the surface.

From that point on the whole process of diamond recovery was a matter of reducing the size of the material hauled from the pit and systematically rejecting waste, discarding 3.6 million parts of the ore treated for every one part of diamond retained.

In the primary crusher the ore was broken into fragments smaller than 150 millimetres, which then went to the scrubbing and screening plant. There everything finer than one millimetre was washed out and discarded, and everything coarser than twenty-five millimetres was sent for recrushing. Material sized between one and twenty-five millimetres went on to the DMS (dense media separation) plant, where it was mixed with ferrosilicon solution, the dense medium. The less dense material, which "floated" off the ferrosilicon, was deposited on the tailings dump; the denser material, which sank, was collected as a concentrate of heavy minerals on a screen at the bottom, washed and mixed with a slightly denser solution of ferrosilicon. The material that floated off at that stage was returned to the DMS plant for re-treatment, while the concentrate was washed, dewatered and separated into four sizes. After being tumbled in hot-air driers it passed through X-ray machines that used the fluorescent property of diamonds to separate them from the other heavy minerals. Again the material rejected by the machines was set aside for re-treatment, while the final concentrate was sorted by hand.

"Of the more than twenty thousand tonnes of ore we process a day, between forty and fifty per cent is rejected in the scrubbing plant," says Bob Walker, superintendent of Jwaneng's treatment plant. "And in the DMS plant the rejection is almost total, except for between .1 and .2 per cent. Twelve to fifteen tonnes of concentrate go to the X-ray machines, and from them each day we get about six kilograms of diamonds – nine million carats a year."

The mine was brought into production by De Beers Botswana (Debswana), an equal partnership between De Beers and the Botswana government, in 1982, ten years after the kimberlite was discovered there under some fifty metres of Kalahari sand and calcrete. By then an enormous amount of work had been put into evaluating the deposit: 249 large-diameter boreholes had been drilled to define the ore body to a depth of two hundred metres, and six shafts had been sunk to an average depth of 158 metres, in order to obtain a parcel of diamonds large enough to make possible an accurate valuation of the stones and a reliable estimate of the mine's economic potential.

The geologists had found that the top of the ore body, extending over fifty-two hectares, consists of three lobes that merge near the surface but separate at depth into three pipes. About sixty metres of the original crater zone had been preserved against further erosion in a depression caused by downfaulting of the encasing rock. The top of the kimberlite had been altered to calcrete, but it still contained indicator minerals and diamonds, and deeper probes disclosed reddish, oxidized kimberlite and light-green kimberlite – representing different stages of weathering by a fluctuating water-table – and finally pristine blue kimberlite.

Power for the people – powerlines span the desert (left) between Jwaneng and Gaborone, the capital of Botswana. The supply of electricity to remote communities is one of the more obvious benefits from an economy enhanced by diamond mining.

In reaching the decision to mine the deposit, the developers, before spending millions of dollars on testing the viability of a mine, had to consider first whether there would be a market for the type of diamonds found in the prospecting stage. They then sampled the deposit in phases, so that it could be abandoned at any point if the results did not warrant further expenditure. "When looking at a new deposit we normally first do some sampling to see if there is any chance of its being economic," explains Tinus Oosterveld, who heads the ore evaluations department of Anglo American Corporation, technical consultants to Debswana and De Beers. "If it is, we move to the next phase, and so on until we have enough information for a preliminary feasibility study. If the results still look good we do a final feasibility study."

The thick sand and calcrete overburden was a major obstacle, physical and financial, to taking large enough samples of the ore body. Whereas with gold a half-kilogram sample of material finely disseminated in a narrow vein is sufficient, diamonds are relatively large particles scattered throughout a massive body, and the number of carats yielded by twenty-tonne samples is barely sufficient to determine the diamond content. At Jwaneng ore evaluators were initially limited to four-tonne borehole samples, and had to devise new techniques that, while saving on the cost of sampling, still produced reliable results. Owing to the major contribution that big stones make to the value of a deposit, it was necessary also to forecast the number and value of big stones the mine would produce, and because the large stones are often not represented in the parcels of diamonds obtained from samples, the information had to be extrapolated from the experience gained of other deposits.

"In working out whether diamonds found at a new prospect will support a mine, a twenty-carat sample of diamonds is a long way from being enough to go on," says Oosterveld, "but over the years we have developed statistical models, and if we compare the sample with perhaps a hundred twenty-carat samples drawn randomly from the production of known mines for a period of two or three years, we can see where it fits in."

"Apart from the size, grade and potential of the ore body, we also have to take into

In the final recovery area at Jwaneng (right) chemist Gerald Fryer, then general manager Mike Wittet and assistant general manager Dave Harries survey the production, watched by security personnel – former Botswana policemen, who work under chief security superintendent Bill Phaphe, arms folded at the rear.

Oxford graduate Louis Nchindo, director of Debswana and head of the company office in Gaborone, was instrumental in establishing the National Stadium. His country's growth is epitomised for him in the view from his high-rise office window, when he recalls that as a boy in Gaborone he had reason to fear being attacked by lions while walking between the railway station and his home.

"At the time of Independence sceptics gave us little chance of economic survival," says Botswana's Minister of Mineral Resources and Water Affairs, the Hon A.M. Mogwe. "The diamond mines were a godsend, and rapidly transformed the economy, increasing the revenue of the country from less than ten million Pula a year at Independence to over a billion today."

account the most suitable method of mining it, the infrastructure necessary to support the operation, personnel requirements, capital outlay, running costs and the tax formula applied by the government," says Anglo American consulting engineer Ken Trueman. "A single factor, such as taxation, may be critical in deciding whether or not we mine a deposit."

At Jwaneng it was clear from the start that, as at Debswana's other major mine at Orapa, which was also situated in a wilderness where until then the only inhabitants had been at a few widely scattered cattle posts, an entire town would have to be laid out. A thousand housing units had to be built for married employees and accommodation for another thousand had to be provided in single quarters. Schools, clubs, a large hospital, sportsfields and other amenities had to be built, equipped and staffed. Water for domestic and industrial use – some three hundred thousand cubic metres a month – had to be piped from fifty kilometres away.

Jwaneng recovery plant superintendent Bob Walker visits the orphaned kudu bull, named Ore, he "recovered" from the wild and bottle-fed until it was old enough to release in the mine's nature reserve.

Having spent a great deal on evaluating the deposit and establishing the mine, treatment plant and town, the developers regarded revenue generation to recover their outlay as a priority in the short term, and because the grade of ore in the centre lobe was far higher than in the other two, it was there that initially they concentrated the mining operation. Wanting to start processing the high-grade ore as quickly as possible, they removed the upper layer of low-grade material and set it aside, to be blended back with the high-grade ore later. They then mined the centre lobe down to 130 metres while stripping overburden from the other lobes and gradually bringing them into production, blending the ores so that the grade delivered to the treatment plant would be close to the average grade for the whole ore body.

"Our intention is to get all three lobes down to the same level and then mine them together, which is less expensive than mining on different levels," says Jwaneng's general manager Mike Wittet. "What was originally a roughly circular pit over the centre lobe will become an eliptical mine, 1200 metres long and 750 metres wide, with three blue or grey hearts. If current tests confirm that there is, as we believe, the volume and grade of ore below the top 200 metres that we have already proven, this could continue as an opencast mine down to 350 metres, with a life of forty to fifty years, and then continue underground, as the Kimberley mines have done, for much longer."

When mining men speak of the "life of mine" they are talking about a mine's projected life based on currently determined ore reserves that would be payable at current market prices. It is not fixed. In the light of technological improvements that enhance the rate of extraction and reduce the cost of mining and treatment, ore reserves are continually reassessed, and when what was classified uneconomic becomes payable it is added to the reserve and extends the life of the mine.

Ore evaluation is therefore a continuing process. The types of diamonds, as well as ore grades and size distributions, differ from one mine to another, and often from one part of a mine to another. The differences may relate to the type of kimberlite, the geological zone of the pipe, or the dilution of parts of the kimberlite by raw rock that fell into it at the time of its emplacement. Geologists gather information about the types of kimberlite in a pipe; the ore evaluators process it, using specialized techniques and statistical methods to calculate the ore reserve and forecast the type and quantity of diamonds that will be produced over a period. Information of all kinds is used to construct geological, statistical and metallurgical models, and classify ore in terms of what is possibly, potentially or probably economic, with a view to putting the right parameters into production planning and control. "We need a picture of the total asset in order to provide management with information on how best to mine it to ensure that there will be no waste of resources," says Oosterveld.

Tele Modikwe, chief sorter in the final recovery section at Jwaneng, examines a batch of diamonds under a microscope to ensure that no stones that are not diamonds are passed on to the size-sorting section.

Market conditions also have to be taken into account in deciding a mining strategy. The sales arm of the industry needs to know what it can expect the mines to produce over a period of years to be able to tailor its promotional campaigns to the sort of goods it will be receiving. This is another reason for not high-grading a mine: when a mine reaches the point of no longer being able to supply a certain type of diamond the result is an undesirable change in the selling mixture offered by the sales arm, which prefers any changes it makes to be part of a well controlled process. If a specific type of diamond is selling particularly well, however, the sales arm may ask for more of it. The ore evaluators, who keep an inventory of diamonds still in the ground and know where the different types are "stored", then consult with the mine planners and operators to try to find ways of altering the mining emphasis to meet the requirement.

At Jwaneng the entire pit has been divided into fifty-metre squares, twelve metres (one bench) thick, and bulk samples of about two hundred tonnes taken from each of these 60 000-tonne blocks furnish information on which the geologists advise management about the best way to handle the ore reserve. "We keep an eye on the mining to see, for example, that they don't mine more waste than necessary in the areas of contact between ore and other rock," says resident mine geologist Leigh Harrison. "Density measurements and other tests we do on the bulk samples enable us also to determine the strength of the kimberlite for design purposes. We build up the information about the angles of wall contacts, about the dips and joints and strengths of the wall rock, on which new cuts will be made as the mine expands. Because it will have to last for a good many years, we need to know that the angle of the pit is right; if too steep it could collapse; if too gradual we end up having to move too much waste."

Computer software specially written for opencast mining is used to devise annual, five-year and thirty-year mine plans, which form the basis of the mining budget and are updated yearly. The plans cover the shape of the pit and how it will develop over the period, the basic parameters being the number of tonnes the plant is able to process in order to recover a given quantity of diamonds, the tonnages of ore and waste that have to be moved, and the costs.

"When we get down to 350 metres the cost of taking an enormous slice of waste off the top in order to get a small slice of ore deep down will have to be weighed against the cost of going underground, bearing in mind that an opencast mine can deliver purer ore to the plant than an underground mine, in which the contamination is generally greater," says assistant production manager Frank Grobler. "At present, to mine close on six million tonnes of ore a year we have to move another seven million tonnes of waste, and we estimate that over the life of the opencast mine we will remove three times as much waste as ore."

To metallurgists working on the Jwaneng treatment plant it was obvious from the outset that many of the larger fragments rejected by the DMS plant must contain diamonds which, while well worth recovering, were too small to raise the specific gravity of the whole fragment enough for it to sink through the dense medium and be collected in the concentrate. They calculated that if they crushed the tailings to finer than eight millimetres they could increase diamond recovery substantially. "The feasibility of introducing a third crushing stage was discussed early on, but postponed because of the state of the market and the size of the debt that the developers would have had to incur," explains Wittet.

The delay of a few years before designing a re-crushing plant enabled the developers to incorporate crushers that were capable of doing a better job than any additional crushers they could have installed in 1982. Costing ninety million dollars to build, and another eighteen million dollars to supply with water, the new crushing plant at Jwaneng is designed to treat six hundred tonnes of currently produced tailings an hour, while the revaluation of tailings dumps from former years, which now represent ten per cent of the total ore reserves for the opencast operation, has added years to the life of the mine.

"A lot of our thinking concerns the future," says Trueman. "We are continually involved in the long-term planning of the mine, taking all factors into account. We incorporate improvements in mining and metallurgy, and try to steer the mine in such a way as to ensure that it has the longest possible life and that we extract the maximum possible number of diamonds from it. Even when market conditions require us to slow down on production, as happened in the early 1980s, we do it in such a way as to give a maximum return for what we put into it."

Advances in crushing technology have been intimately bound up with the growth of the diamond mining industry. Over a century ago the small-scale miners in Kimberley worked through the so-called "yellow ground" of the weathered zone with pick and shovel and spread the ore over large cleared areas, where it weathered to sand that they could treat in their rudimentary plants. Crushing became necessary when they struck harder ground at thirty-five to forty metres, and at fifty to sixty metres they ran into the "blue ground" for which the crushing equipment available to them at the time was inadequate. This, combined with their financial and practical inability to sink shafts or construct inclined roads into their small claims, compelled them to sell out to larger combines, setting in motion the process of consolidation that led eventually to the formation of De Beers Consolidated Mines in 1888.

A century later the original Kimberley mines that date from that time are approaching the end of their productive lives. In terms of current life of mine, underground mining will cease there before the year 2000, although the re-treatment of the dumps will continue longer. This does not take into account the reserves of ore beneath the current levels that have hitherto been regarded as uneconomic. "If these reserves become payable, as they well may, underground mining could continue into the next century," says Jack Forster, general manager of the Kimberley mines.

Eight hundred metres underground in the old De Beers mine the pipe has shrunk to three narrow root bodies, only one of which is payable. Future development will take Wesselton down to a thousand metres, and at the Bultfontein and Dutoitspan mines, which are served by a common shaft, an infrastructure is being created at 820 metres to enable them to be mined at deeper levels.

"Our main challenge is to keep the mines running profitably for as long as possible," says Forster. "To do this we naturally have to make use of new technology and develop the competence, expertise and training of our staff so that they can use it most effectively. In the old days, when a jack-hammer broke down it took only one of many operators out of production until it was fixed; today, if one of the big jumbo-rigs we use for drilling breaks down the loss to production is dramatic. This has created a new category of specialist maintenance planners who ensure that our equipment doesn't break down. The new technology requires fewer, but more highly skilled, people."

Men who have worked on various types of mines describe diamond mining as a different "culture" and "a gentleman's game" compared with, for instance, gold mining where the miners work under cramped conditions in narrow stopes. Perhaps because the workforce and organization are smaller in diamond mining, the management style is more personal, more intimate. "There is more concern for the individual because, being more mechanized, we don't have to get the productivity out of the person and there is less pressure on him to physically do the mining," says John Walls, general manager of Premier mine, in the Transvaal.

"The different types of ore body exploited on diamond mines encourage the use of diverse highly mechanized mining methods, and this motivates technological innovation and creates opportunities for self-actualization on the job", says Forster. Opencast mining is suited to mechanization on a massive scale, whereas underground mines that have descended into the root zone of kimberlite pipes and are working small, variegated ore bodies scattered at depth, provide opportunities for experimenting with new mining methods.

A consideration in choosing the method to be used is the sort of ground being mined, which may range from rock so soft that it will break down to sand within half an hour if placed in water, to rock so hard that it is impervious to weathering. "Where it doesn't fracture easily we might decide to blast instead of using the block caving technique," says Walls. "On the other hand we wouldn't want to put a lot of tunnels into very friable, easily fractured ground. The rock mechanic needs to know the geological background, what the original rock was, how the kimberlite broke through it, whether it was a single or multiple occurrence. All this gives us an understanding of the stresses that developed in the ground we are working through and an idea of how best to support it."

Block caving works something like a tin of sugar with a hole in the underside through which the sugar is running out and the sugar inside continually closing in on itself. Horizontal extraction tunnels, called scraper drifts, are driven under a block of ore perhaps a hundred metres thick and bounded by the rock walls enclosing the pipe. These tunnels connect with the bottom of a V-shaped vertical trough that undercuts the ore body. The trough is blasted, but the undercut block breaks up under its own weight and slides down into the drifts below, from where it is removed by mechanical scrapers. As ore drops out below, ore above closes in to take its place. Where the ore doesn't break cleanly at its contacts with the enclosing rock a technique called sub-level block caving may be used to blast slices off the hanging wall.

Vertical crater retreat, a method currently used at the De Beers and Wesselton mines, involves drilling a series of large-diameter holes through the ore body from above and then detonating simultaneously explosive charges placed in the lower two metres of each. As successive blasts retreat further up the holes a dome-like inverted crater is formed, from which the broken ground is removed through tunnels to the main shaft.

Several methods may be used in one mine during its productive life. At Premier mine a single fifty-hectare pipe the size of the three major Kimberley pipes together was first worked as an opencast mine, from which the original developer took the better grade material, ignoring the very low-grade areas. When mining from the surface became too expensive the mine went underground. For a long time it was thought that it would end at four hundred metres, where a seventy-metre gabbro sill – a later geological intrusion through the pipe – cuts the ore body in two, but engineers found that they could establish what was virtually a new mine underneath it. First they attempted sub-level open stoping, mining backwards from a central slot, leaving pillars at intervals to support the sill, but they failed to prevent it from collapsing into the open stopes, and so went over to block caving.

Premier processes over seven million tonnes of ore a year, about a third of them from old tailings dumps that contain enough diamonds to be payable using modern recovery techniques and can be "mined" at low cost, because the material has already been brought to the surface and crushed. The ore body sampled to date gives the mine a life of another twenty years, but lower levels that have yet to be evaluated could extend it by many more. Of some two million carats of diamonds extracted each year, about eighty per cent is industrial grade, and includes rare types that have unique qualities highly valued in the electronics and other high-tech industries. The remainder are gems, many of them extraordinarily beautiful stones of superb quality, and a number of them exceptionally large.

A 163-carat diamond (right) from Premier mine, which is renowned for having produced many large stones, including the biggest ever found, the 3106-carat Cullinan diamond.

Since mining began in 1903 this aging yet enduringly serendipitous mine has produced almost three hundred stones of over a hundred carats, among them the largest gem diamond ever mined, the 3106-carat Cullinan, which yielded the peerless First Star of Africa and Second Star of Africa in the British Crown Jewels. Among them too are the Niarchos, cut from a 426.5 carat rough stone, the flawless Premier Rose, cut from 353 carats of rough, the Taylor-Burton, cut from 240.8 carats, and the recently recovered 599-carat Centenary Diamond unveiled at the De Beers Centenary banquet in Kimberley on 11 March 1988, reckoned to yield a top-colour polished stone of over three hundred carats.

Owing to the mine's propensity for producing very large stones, ore for treatment at Premier is crushed to a maximum size of sixty millimetres, compared with twenty-five millimetres at Jwaneng, and the fraction between thirty and sixty millimetres is examined by X-ray machines, which remove the larger diamonds, before the material is crushed finer. It was at this point in the process that the Centenary Diamond was found, but the Cullinan, had it arrived in the treatment plant today, would have been shattered in the first crush. "The risk of crushing another Cullinan is one we have to take," says Walls. "There has to be a maximum crushing size. Every pipe has a characteristic distribution, and one has to determine the range in which one gets the best return in diamonds against capital invested in the plant. It would be crazy to put another stream through the plant to handle a coarser fraction, in the hope of finding a larger diamond every five or ten years."

Since it was emplaced 1700 million years ago the upper two kilometres of the Premier pipe have been eroded away, and over a period of ninety million years the Kimberley pipes have similarly lost more than a kilometre. Diamonds liberated by nature from these and an unknown number of other kimberlites, of which little or no trace may remain today, were deposited in alluvial sediments dispersed throughout the Western Transvaal and Northern Cape, where they are still mined by small, independent operators. Many more diamonds ultimately found their way through the drainage system of the Orange River and perhaps other smaller west-flowing rivers to the sea, where Atlantic currents distributed them and wave action concentrated them in beach gravels along the coast of Namibia and Namaqualand. Owing to major fluctuations of the mean sea-level associated with Ice Ages and other natural events of global proportions, these beach deposits are found at various levels, from well inland of the present coastline, where they were blanketed by the windblown sands of the Namib Desert, to far out on the continental shelf.

The first of these deposits was discovered near Lüderitz in 1908, and several German companies worked concessions on the coast north and south of Lüderitz until Germany

Some fifteen kilometres inland from the present coastline just north of the Orange River is the last remaining section of fossil beach that has still to be mined. As it is so close to the river that carried the diamonds to the coast, geologists expect that excellent quality stones will come from this ancient beach.

The new frontier – the active surf zone, the strip of wild water between the furthest out that the land-based foreshore operation can go and the closest in that the large recovery vessels can come, poses the ultimate challenge to marine diamond mining engineers. Several million years ago, before the sea-level settled at its present position, the fossil beach shown in the upper picture would have looked something like this.

lost control of the territory in World War I. In 1920 Sir Ernest Oppenheimer bought the concessions and formed Consolidated Diamond Mines of South West Africa (CDM), which to this day continues producing diamonds from these gravels. With the establishment of the company township of Oranjemund in 1936 the focus of mining activity moved south to marine terraces found a few years earlier in a narrow strip of coast extending a hundred kilometres northward from the mouth of the Orange River, following Dr Hans Merensky's discovery of diamonds south of the estuary. This wild stretch of surf-pounded coastline became the scene of one of the biggest earthmoving operations ever undertaken, in which more than thirty million cubic metres of sand a year were stripped off to get at the diamondiferous gravels and conglomerates. On the foreshore, between the tides, the overburden removed was used to build great walls of sand against the sea, behind which mining was undertaken to depths of twenty metres below sea-level. Although the proportion of waste to diamonds at CDM is two hundred million to one, virtually the entire production is of gem quality, and annual recovery increased from less than half a million carats in 1951 to a peak of a little over two million carats in 1977.

In the early 1960s a Texan oil man named Sammy Collins obtained marine rights for his Marine Diamond Corporation and, using a vacuum sweeping technique, began mining the seabed in concessions adjoining CDM's land-based operations. Fearing that wild-catting might ruin the deposits before they could be properly prospected and evaluated, De Beers, after much negotiation and legal disputation, gained control of Marine Diamonds in 1965. Mining stopped in the early 1970s, when these particular reserves were exhausted, but De Beers Marine, under contract to CDM, continued prospecting, taking its probes further and further out into deeper water, developing increasingly sophisticated techniques, including robots that crawl on the seabed, to define and evaluate deposits and explore the feasibility of mining the old submerged beaches on the continental shelf.

"The life of the land-based mine here has always been ten years," says CDM's general manager Keith Whitelock. "We have been able to keep going only because we found cheaper ways of doing things, but there is an end to it. We are mining very superficial beach deposits in a narrow strip that becomes narrower as we go north. The quantity of diamonds in it is finite, and for the past few years our production has slipped to just on a million carats a year. Ten years from now there'll be hardly anything left that can still be mined in the way we are mining now."

Before taking over at CDM, Whitelock was for six years general manager at Orapa, mining the biggest payable pipe outside the Soviet Union, producing five million carats a year, with ore reserves that could last for centuries. But he does not see himself as having come to Oranjemund to preside over its demise. "I picture the next decade as the time for exploring the potential of the whole delta region, including the site of the town itself, which is built on an old channel of the Orange. Loops of the ancient diamond-bearing channel that we've prospected could support two smaller mines for quite a few years, and there are areas north and south of Lüderitz that were not as thoroughly worked in the old days as they can be using modern technology. Throughout our mining area thin bands of gravel in the overburden challenge us to find ways of extracting diamonds economically from such low-grade material, perhaps by adapting our method of removing overburden – with dredgers operating on artificial ponds behind the sea wall."

But perhaps the greatest challenge is the active surf zone, a strip of turbulent water lying between the furthest out that the land-based operation can reach and the closest inshore that large recovery vessels are able to come. "There are more carats out there than are left on land," says Whitelock, with a sweep of his arm in the direction of the ranks of Atlantic rollers advancing towards the shore, and beyond to where De Beers Marine pursues diamonds from the mouth of the Orange River to the outer limits of their dispersal on the continental shelf. "That's our next horizon."

CHAPTER 5 THE NEW ALCHEMISTS

Where Medieval metaphysicians pondered how many angels could dance on the point of a needle, modern physicists are able to make diamonds that dance on the point of a finger.

Here a diamond synthesized at the De Beers plant in Springs, South Africa, dances for production superintendent Kobus Koen on the finger of Tony Moore, executive in charge of diamond synthesis.

The alchemists of old attempted vainly to transmute lead into gold; the new alchemists are able to transmute graphite into diamond, using high-pressure diamond presses that replicate conditions and processes that occur in the earth's mantle.

Synthesized, rather than natural, diamond grit is now the dominant material over a wide range of uses, and in the industrial diamond business a diamond press has become as important as a diamond mine.

In the Italian town of Marmo, near the marble quarries of Carrara, is the studio (left) of Carlo Nicoli, where internationally acclaimed sculptors, such as Stella Shawzin, transform the local marble into art, using tools tipped with industrial diamonds. Pieces that Stella Shawzin has sculpted from Carrara marble with these tools, like this fine reclining figure (below), are exhibited in galleries around the world.

New York at dawn (left) – the centre of a mighty industrial machine that could not operate without industrial diamonds and diamond-tooled products.

Only diamond is hard enough to polish a diamond. The 407.43-carat Golden Giant (above) is held here by Hy Kessler, whose hand rests on the scaif, or wheel, impregnated with diamond dust, on which he polished the stone in the New York diamond cutting works of the Samuels family.

Diamond tools enabled Naoyoshi Toyama (left) and other Japanese monumental masons to cope with the post-war demand for headstones of granite, which is most easily cut with diamond saws. The use of industrial diamond was taken up so eagerly by other industries that Japan in time outstripped the United States as the principal user.
A live Japanese reed frog (above) poised to spring from the granite head of its decorative garden likeness.

The fishermen of Hiuchi Nada (left) find shelter for their boats under the Seto-Oh-Hashi bridge, spanning thirty-eight kilometres between Shikoku and Honshu islands in southern Japan. The central piers were erected on seabed rock that first had to be shaved perfectly flat using diamond tools. Yukinori Hina, a contractor, and engineers Hisayoshi Naito and Susumu Torin (above), of Shibuya Dymodrill, used diamond bits to drill holes in the concrete for all the light standards, guard rails, drainage pipes and for bolting the concrete beams to the piers.

The Shin Kansen, bullet trains, on which millions of Japanese commute daily (above). Diamonds are used to cut the armour-plate glass windows to form airtight seals with the window frames, and to tool the brake-pad surfaces to the degree of precision essential when braking at over two hundred kilometres an hour.

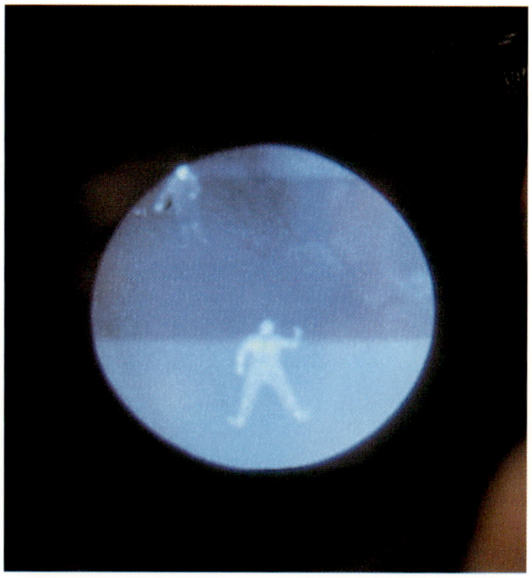

London Fire Brigade station officer Dave Berry (left) enters a smoke-filled room, concentrating on the viewing screen of his Thermal Image Camera, which records the radiant heat emissions it picks up through the dense smoke as a thermal image (above) of a prone figure and someone approaching to assist.

The germanium infra-red optic of the camera has to be protected by a thin film of diamond, formed by chemical vapour deposition, instead of the usual glass lens.

TEN THOUSAND YEARS AGO, and probably very much earlier, Stone Age people who hunted over the savannahs of southern Africa around present-day Kimberley engraved exquisite fine-line petroglyphs of roan antelope, zebra, ostrich and other creatures on stone tablets and the smooth faces of kopjes and free-standing dolorite boulders. Using a pecking technique, they made stippled engravings too, but it was in their fine-line work that they revealed their eye for form and detail, surely incising precise, unbroken lines in the hard surfaces, with a confidence that suggests that they worked with exceptionally hard tools and possibly employed a chiselling technique similar to that used today by steel engravers. The lines they cut in the black-patinated dolorite are so delicate that they are not easily seen in the field, except in low sunlight, and then only if one knows what to look for. The points of their tools must have been tough and fine indeed, for until the engravings were photographically enlarged many of the details were invisible to students of rock art.

A Bushman "gallery" of rock engravings (left) at Springbok Oog, in the arid Karoo region of South Africa. Testing the hypothesis that Bushmen used diamonds to incise their fine-line engravings, archaeologist Peter Beaumont (right) tries his hand at engraving a stone tablet with a thirty-millimetre dog-tooth diamond (below right). His verdict: they could have, but whether they did is still an open question.

"We have been so busy trying to interpret this art and what motivated the artists that we have neglected to investigate how it was done and what tools were used," admits Peter Beaumont, the archaeologist at the McGregor Museum in Kimberley. "I am attracted to the hypothesis that diamond points might have been used to draw these fine lines, and it is scientifically proper that I should test it. An experiment with a dog-tooth diamond certainly proved that diamonds could have done the job."

The Griqua shepherd who found the first recorded diamond in South Africa cannot have been the first person to pick one up, he reasons. A hundred thousand years ago Stone Age cave-dwellers were mining specularite – a crystalline iron ore that in transmitting light shines blood-red – to decorate their bodies and taking back to their living sites shiny pieces of mica they picked up in the veld. White quartz being one of their principal materials, they would always have been on the lookout for glittering white stones, and many a diamond must have been found in this way. "Someone finding a diamond would have experimented with it, and might have discovered that he could engrave very fine lines with it. A possible reason why we haven't identified any gravers at engraving sites is that diamond, not being readily replaceable and having a longer use life than other materials, would not lightly have been cast aside, as other tools were in great number once they became blunted. So it is quite conceivable that diamonds were used."

Beaumont worked with the renowned physical anthropologist Professor Raymond Dart in proving that, some seventy thousand years before there were mines of any kind in Europe, mining for specularite was undertaken in southern Africa by Middle Stone Age people who were ancestral to the Bushmen and are the earliest representatives of Modern Man, *Homo sapiens sapiens*, known to science. He believes that the engravings made over the last ten thousand years belong to the oldest and longest artistic tradition on earth, which began with body decoration over a hundred thousand years ago and ended with the demise of Bushman rock art in recent centuries. If future research confirms that the fine-line petroglyphs on the South African veld were in fact engraved with diamonds, the use of diamonds as tools has spanned archaeological and historical time, from the Stone Age to the age of the silicon chip.

In Asia and Europe too, the first "industrial" application of diamonds was as engraving points. Diamonds were used to engrave metal in India during the fourth century BC, and diamond-tipped tools made in India and the Middle East for engraving and carving jade were regularly exported to China during the second century BC. The Roman Pliny, writing in the first century AD, noted in his monumental *Naturalis Historae* that gem engravers worked with diamond fragments hafted to iron. Although the properties of diamond were valued by the ancients and have been utilized through the ages, it was not until well into the present century that their use in industry became widespread.

Nearly all the Brazilian diamonds reaching world markets during the eighteenth and nineteenth centuries were of gem quality; there was no abundance of inferior quality stones in search of industrial applications. Premier mine, in the Transvaal, was the first to produce a large proportion of industrial quality diamonds, followed by the Belgian Congo, which began producing during the early decades of this century, and in time released, in addition to some gem and near-gem stones, a flood of boart, suitable only for crushing to make abrasive grits and powders.

Realizing that disposing of huge quantities of boart might become a daunting problem, Sir Ernest Oppenheimer in 1934 formed the Diamond Development Company in London, to develop new uses for industrial diamonds and conduct research into the manufacture of tools. Events moved more swiftly than anticipated. Stimulated by World War II, the demand for high-precision grinding of hard materials placed diamonds among the strategic minerals and gave a powerful fillip to their use in industry. De Beers went to considerable lengths to assure supplies of this commodity, so critical to the Allied war effort, says John van Itallie of Saddle Brook, New Jersey, a distributor of General Electric industrial diamonds, "and no production line in the US was ever stopped for lack of a diamond tool." Indeed a strategic reserve, supplied by De Beers, was in time established in Montreal in terms of an agreement which his father was instrumental in securing between the British, US and Canadian governments.

Within a year of the war ending, Sir Ernest separated industrial diamond sales from the activities of the CSO and established Industrial Distributors (1946) Limited to market industrial diamonds more aggressively world-wide. To head it he appointed E.T.S. (Ted) Brown, a former diamond sorter, whose business skills and enthusiasm for marketing lower grades of diamond profitably had attracted his attention.

By then it had become too big an industry to be without a research base. At Sir Ernest's request, his old friend Sir Francis Simon, who was then Professor of Physics at Oxford, had organized a group of leading scientists, chiefly from Oxford and Cambridge, to advise Sir Ernest on developments relating to the physics of diamonds. On Professor Simon's recommendation, Sir Ernest in 1947 established the Diamond Research Laboratory in Johannesburg, also under Brown's leadership, and the research resources of the Diamond Development Company were transferred there from London.

"Ted Brown was an applications man, not a mining man," recalls Dr Henry Dyer, who was recruited by the laboratory while completing his PhD at Cambridge in 1951 and is today a director of De Beers and head of its Industrial Diamond Division. "Although we did some early work for the mines on improving recovery methods, the real motivation was that diamonds and their uses needed research to sustain them, broaden their applications and generally protect their parish."

A Harwell researcher's report that he had turned diamonds blue by placing them under a high-energy electron beam led to a rapid broadening of the laboratory's scientific base in the early fifties. Previously, radiation had produced unattractive colours; blue diamonds, on the other hand, had always been at a premium, and the gem trade was deeply perturbed. Dyer was dispatched to lead a research team at Reading University to investigate radiation damage to diamonds and the colours produced. And then, as they were nearing the end of their work in 1955, General Electric announced that it had made diamonds synthetically in the United States. Modern physicists had realized the age-old alchemist's dream of transmuting the base into the noble.

This gave fresh impetus and a new direction to De Beers' research, and Dyer was recalled to assist in setting up the Adamant Research Laboratory in Johannesburg to intensify research into diamond synthesis. Diamond synthesis had long been recognized as a theoretical possibility. The Swedish company Allmana Svenska Elektriska Aktiebolaget (Asea) had in fact synthesized diamonds two years earlier, but had deferred announcing it until it perfected the process. General Electric's process was commercially viable, however, and the United States regarded it as having such strategic significance that it was classified under the Atomic Secrets Act. Patents could not therefore be filed in foreign countries, as this would have meant disclosing the process, and General Electric was limited to filing secret papers at home and in Britain and Canada, with whom the United States pooled its nuclear secrets.

"Professor Simon and his co-worker, Dr R. Berman, calculated theoretically the equilibrium line between the stability fields of carbon as graphite and carbon as diamond, establishing categorically the pressures and temperatures necessary for making diamond under stable conditions," says Dyer. "That set our target; the technological problems were to create those conditions and have the right reactance materials to make it work."

Under the pressure conditions that we consider normal, graphite is the stable form of carbon and diamond is the unstable form, Dyer explains. Instability is relative, however, and diamond is unstable only to the extent that if raised to and kept at a temperature of about 500 degrees centigrade it would invert to graphite over a period of ten billion years – a few hundred million years more than twice the age of the earth.

"Diamond is like a ball in a billiard table pocket: less stable than on the floor because, without the restraint of the pocket, it would naturally fall to the floor, where, unable to fall further, it would be graphite," he says. "If we set up the right vibrations by shaking the pocket – heating the diamond – we can pop the ball out onto the floor, convert the diamond to graphite. What we have to do is reverse the process and convert graphite to diamond. This is a lot more difficult, because the vibrations necessary to get the ball up from the floor and into the pocket would *a fortiori* cause it to jump straight out and back onto the floor. The trick is to create, by applying pressure, conditions in which graphite is the unstable form. When the denser form, the diamond, is subjected to pressure, it is more inclined to remain in the denser form than go over to the less dense form, graphite. Thus, as the pressure is increased, the instability of the diamond relative to graphite diminishes, until the Berman-Simon line is crossed and diamond becomes the favoured form."

Simply creating conditions in which graphite is unstable does not necessarily cause it to change, just as diamond, when it is the unstable form, may nevertheless remain diamond forever. But if the graphite is dissolved in iron, nickel, cobalt or manganese, to break up its organized structure, the carbon will, under pressures at which diamond is stable, recrystallize as diamond. Synthesized diamonds are thus made from carbon in a metallic matrix placed at the focus of high temperature and pressure. The resulting mass is broken down with acid to separate it from the diamonds that have grown inside it. During synthesis the environment inside the reaction vessel is too hostile for the internal temperature and pressure to be measured from outside; the art lies in using inferential methods to determine what is happening inside and controlling the process to produce different types and sizes of diamonds.

Another method of growing diamond, first suggested at the turn of the century but still largely experimental, is by chemical vapour deposition (CVD). "Even under normal

The kibbutz at Toolgal manufactures stone-cutting diamond-toothed saw blades that are among the finest in the world (below). Diamonds embedded in flexible wire saws are used to cut blocks of marble from the mountainside at Carrara (right) and reduce them to manageable sizes for shipment to destinations in Italy and abroad.

pressure conditions, separate carbon atoms, converging individually to a surface can assume other forms, though graphite is the more stable," Dyer explains. "If they can be induced to stick to spots where there is already diamond there is a good chance that they will conform to the existing structure and grow as diamond. To pursue the analogy, if individual billiard balls are dropped from above with skill, they may be dropped into the pockets – caught halfway – and not end up on the floor. We have made crystals of diamond in this way, but it is a temperamental process: if a maverick atom refuses to conform to the existing structure, the next atom deposited beside it will probably be a maverick too, and pretty soon they will all be mavericks. Little cells of improper growth come to dominate the whole process. CVD does, however, represent a major technological advance, with potentially far-reaching consequences. It holds out the possibility of being able to coat things with a continuous film of diamond – which already has a few applications – and eventually it will find a commercial niche, but in new products rather than replacement products."

When the Adamant Laboratory started out in 1956 it was still a long way from achieving synthesis, let alone developing the techniques for fine-tuning the process. Brown assembled a team of scientists under J.F.H. Custers, which developed apparatus that incorporated a press that had been built originally for briquetting gun cotton. Instead of trying to leapfrog directly to the main objective, they concentrated first on discovering more about generating high pressures. To their surprise, in what was purely a calibration experiment, they in 1958 produced their first diamond.

"It was a fluke," says Dyer, who was then assistant director in charge of research. "In fifty attempts to repeat it we managed to do so only three times. We were not quite there. Then Dr Pete Wedepohl, a brilliant young physicist on our staff, suggested that we use a conical rather than a cylindrical reactance vessel, and in September 1959 we got our repeatable system."

Coincidentally, General Electric, freed of official secrecy, filed its overseas patents world-wide next day, and it was found that the two companies had independently arrived at solutions to the problems of synthesis that were very similar in terms of both equipment and process. This raised legal issues which, after protracted negotiations, were eventually resolved by De Beers agreeing to manufacture under licence from General Electric, but with no transfer of technology, De Beers having developed its own.

"We on the scientific side were fired up with enthusiasm, but were given no specific mandate," says Dyer. "General Electric was becoming a force in sectors of the market, but the philosophy of De Beers at that stage was to combat their competitive thrust by taking up cudgels for natural diamond." Sir Ernest's former private secretary, John Rudd, a great-grandson of C.D. Rudd, Cecil Rhodes's original partner in De Beers Mining Company, was working with Brown at that time. He confirms: "We went into action to defend our whole industrial diamond position against assailment by synthetics."

Management's interest in synthetics was quickly rekindled, however, when Belgium's sudden withdrawal from the Congo seemed to threaten supplies from the Sibeka mines, then the world's largest producer of boart, and endanger De Beers' own sales commitments. "Almost overnight we were under pressure to go over to commercial production," Dyer remembers, "and in 1960 we formed Ultra High Pressure Units in Springs, outside Johannesburg, where we went into operation the following year with seventy-five 500-tonne presses. By then Sibeka had become investors in the venture. When the political transition from Congo to Zaire passed without any immediate disruption of the supplies of natural industrial diamonds, management's interest in diamond synthesis again ebbed. The presses we started with, twice as big as we needed at the time, soon became too small for us, but we were unable to convince management that this prevented us from matching the new products that General Electric was coming out with, and particularly its advance towards producing the small but very well grown

In a part of Ireland that was threatened with depopulation and economic stagnation, Fran Ryan and Jean Murphy enjoy some of the benefits of a regional economy revitalized by the industrial revival of Shannon, where they sell handmade Irish woollens at a croft they converted into a boutique.

crystals needed for saws used in cutting rock, then still the preserve of natural diamond, but now the biggest single application of synthetic industrial diamond."

On the distribution side of the operation, Brown had in the interim selected Shannon, on the west coast of Ireland, for setting up a base from which to supply Europe and North America with industrial diamonds and tungsten carbide.

Overlooked by Bunratty Castle, an ancient O'Brien citadel, the whole area had been a swamp known as Rineanna, meaning point of the birds. In the ninth century, Norsemen coming up the River Shannon to lay siege to Limerick had passed that way, and it was from there that Brian Boru had gone up to Dublin and defeated the Danes at the Battle of Clontarf in 1014. It had always been the poorer side of the country, from which people emigrated in search of a better life elsewhere. To moderate the exodus, the government had established the Shannon International Airport, and from 1945 until 1958 it had been a refueling and maintenance stop for eighty per cent of North Atlantic air traffic, providing direct employment for two thousand people and substantial indirect employment in the area. Since the introduction of jet passenger aircraft, however, most of the traffic had been overflying Shannon. The government, wishing to ensure its continuance as a major international airport, had created an industrial and warehousing estate within a duty free zone bordering the airport, and was offering tax concessions, freedom from import and export duties, grants for purchasing manufacturing equipment and other incentives to induce international companies to install themselves there.

Brown at once recognized its advantages, situated on the doorstep of his major markets. Shannon Diamond and Carbide was opened there in 1960, and Industrial Grit Distributors (Shannon) was incorporated the following year to market natural diamond grit. With the inauguration of International Diamond Products in 1963 Shannon became a centre for crushing and grading natural industrial diamond. At about the same time Ultra High Pressure Units (Ireland) was formed and a third of the Springs synthetic manufacturing capacity was moved to Shannon.

De Beers contributed greatly to the success of the Irish government's scheme to halt the depopulation of Shannon, says Don Walshe, a native of the area, who joined the company in 1964 and is now its Shannon-based manager of information systems. "De Beers displayed its confidence by buying twenty-three acres and erecting its own buildings, when other companies were only leasing land and premises. The number of local people it employed directly grew to about eight hundred, while its demand for engineering expertise in the products and services supplied by local enterprises stimulated the growth of a large infrastructure that gives employment to probably an equal number. Tool makers using De Beers products found it convenient to establish themselves there too, so as to be close to their source of supply."

In 1962 Brown dispatched Rudd to open a new marketing offensive in Europe, starting with the De Beers Diamonds for Industry exhibit at the Paris Fair. "It was felt that we had to show producers that we were prepared to spend money on promoting their industrial diamonds," says Rudd. "We had also shown that we were capable of delivering reliable synthesized and natural industrial and of supporting the diamond-tool maker. The trouble was that in many countries our distributors were diamond-tool makers who were themselves buying from our competitor. To sort this out and be able to compete effectively with General Electric, Ted Brown sent me to open offices to promote industrial diamonds for De Beers in Munich, Paris, Barcelona and Stockholm." Then came a spell in the United States, and in 1969 Rudd rejoined De Beers, moved to Japan and established offices throughout the Asia-Pacific region over the next eighteen years, during which Japan, from being a minor user of industrial diamond, grew to be the world's major consumer, outstripping even the great industrial machine of the US.

"There were a number of reasons for this," says Rudd. "The Japanese had felt too remote from the source to become dependent on natural diamond, but their fears were

Tsukasa Gondoh – poet, potter, artist and president of De Beers Industrial Diamonds in Japan. Diamond tools, valued at more than $650 million, account for almost twenty-five per cent of all machine tools manufactured in Japan each year.

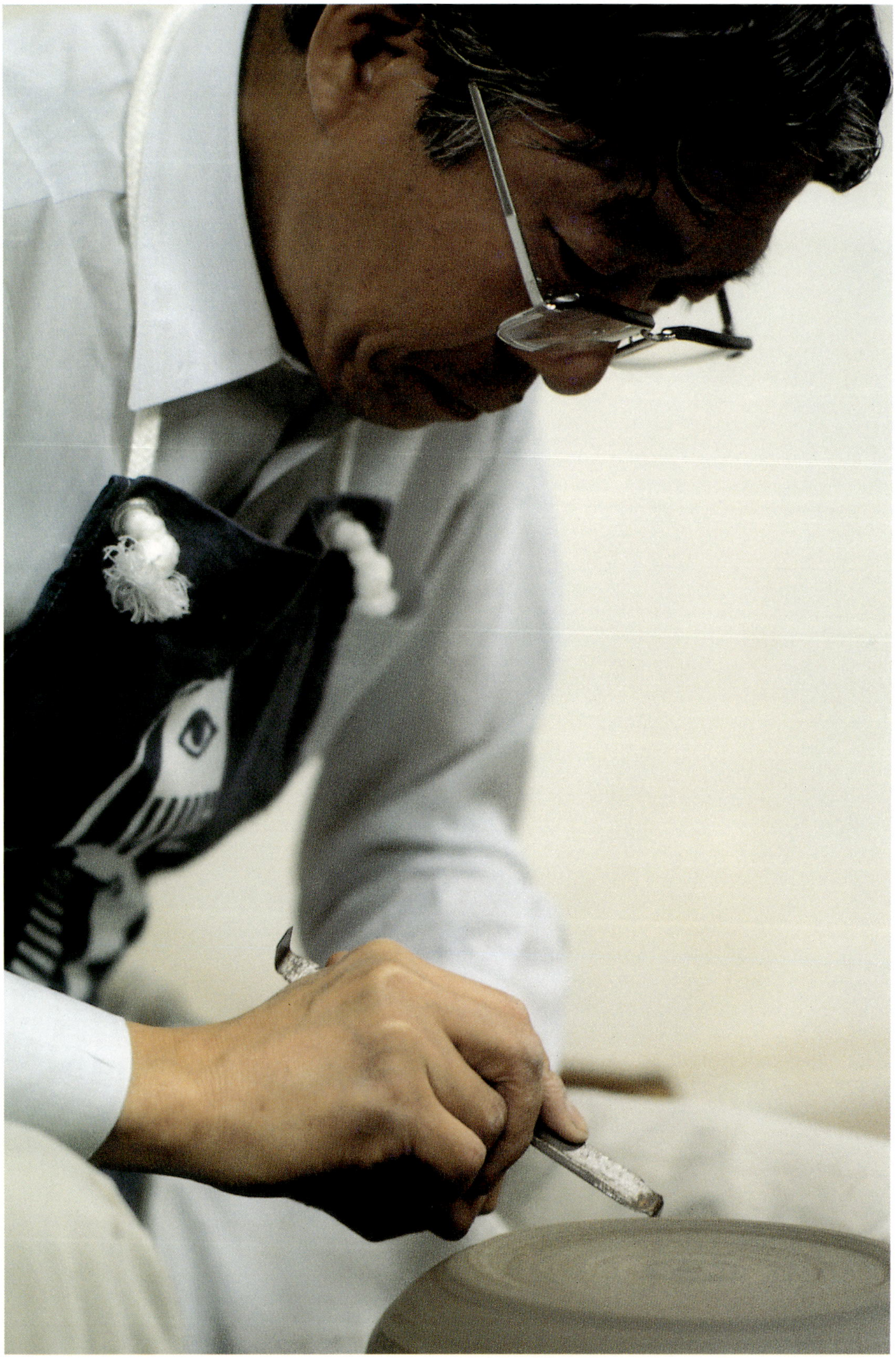

allayed by the advent of synthetics, and the greater use of diamond went hand in hand with the enormous growth of what were essentially new industries, based on new technologies. Another reason was that it became *de rigueur* in post-war Japan to have granite gravestones, which must be cut with diamond saws."

Meanwhile, Dyer established the De Beers Industrial Diamond Division in London in 1966 and set up a technologically orientated marketing and advisory support section to assist tool makers. In Sweden, the system that Asea had perfected was making little impact on the market, and an approach to De Beers resulted in the two companies forming a fifty-fifty partnership to combine De Beers' technology with Asea's facilities. "I was particularly keen on the arrangement because I'd set my heart on Asea's three 10 000-tonne presses as a means of overcoming the limitations of our small presses," says Dyer. "And with them we were able to develop the technology to produce our first SDA (Saw Diamond Abrasive) and counter General Electric's advances in this field. Our success enabled me to persuade management that we should have larger presses at our other factories. We built our first new block at Shannon and set up our first three large presses there in 1970. Since then we have continually upgraded and installed bigger and better presses."

Two Japanese craftsmen, using diamond tools, engrave a polished granite memorial tablet, listing several generations of a family that has lived in the same village for centuries. When complete the tablet will be erected as a gift from the family to the village.

Nowadays all De Beers' sales of industrial diamonds to the world market are executed through Shannon, where all the natural boart – almost entirely of Australian, Botswanan or Zairean origin – is crushed and processed, and the entire synthesized production of its three manufacturing plants in South Africa, Ireland and Sweden is processed and packaged.

Sales of synthesized diamond outstripped those of natural industrial in the late seventies and today constitute more than eighty-five per cent of the 160 million to 180 million carats of industrial consumed each year. In the industrial diamond business a diamond press is now more important than a diamond mine.

"The Argyle mine, in Australia, was an aberration when it came on stream in the early eighties and began generating enormous quantities of natural industrial that hadn't been there before," says Dyer. "Previously the total output of natural was static and the available supply was actually diminishing, because improved technology in the gem business enabled it to absorb qualities that formerly had been classified industrial. Natural could never have coped with the demand, which was growing ten to fifteen per cent a year. The Argyle production caused a little temporary indigestion but, at the rate at which demand is increasing, it will be absorbed until natural is again the same percentage of the total market as before."

"The great advantage of synthetic diamond is that tool makers don't have to risk dependence on a finite resource," says Walshe. "With natural diamond there was always the spectre of there not being enough available for their needs; with synthetic that danger doesn't arise – if needed it can be made. In a few specific areas natural diamond is more suitable or the user is satisfied with its performance and wants to stay with the product he knows, but in most applications the synthetic finally gets the edge, because if the product isn't quite right you can go back and twiddle the numbers in the pots and bring out something slightly different, tailored to the client's needs."

Although diamonds are industrial necessities, they are a hard sell. There is constant day-to-day confrontational competition with other producers. But product preferences are not irrational; the principal concern of both competitors and customers is the technical merits of the product. Ultimately, if the product is good enough the industry takes over and provides the momentum. A lot of effort is consequently put into technical

research and developing new products for new applications, and in this the two major producers, as Dyer puts it, "push and pull each other along". There is also an interaction with the tool makers using the products, who come back to have the performance of their tools evaluated.

To facilitate this interaction the De Beers Technical Service Centre was moved in 1975 from London to Charters, an old country estate at Ascot, nearer Heathrow Airport, where clients could visit without the traffic delays of getting in and out of the city. It was effectively a move closer to the main markets of Europe.

At Tochigi, in the Japanese countryside, Nikon manufactures lenses for its top-quality cameras, using "soft" synthesized diamond pellets in special tools that generate the curves of the lenses, which have been set out here (left) for inspection. Afterwards they are fitted into their housings (right) and inspected finally before being shipped to photographic suppliers all over the world.

Horst Wapler, manager of the centre, is a graduate of Hanover University who worked in De Beers offices in Munich and Dusseldorf before being transferred to London in 1975. "Developing new products or improving an existing product are the work of the laboratory in Johannesburg, but once a product exists, matters pertaining to the market, how it can be expanded and what can be done to assist clients in developing tools that make the best use of the product, is our function here," he says. "The purpose of our service to tool makers is to assist the distributors and sales offices in their selling. They refer a customer of theirs with a technical problem or a new set of diamond tools he wants assessed before putting them on the market, and we assess performance with regard to grit type, size, concentration, bond type and machine parameters to determine the optimum specifications."

Synthesized diamonds range from drilling sizes, which are set individually in bit heads, down through the sawing range and grits to micron powders. They have to be made not only to the sizes, but also to the shapes and textures required for different applications and the different types of bonds that unite them with the working surfaces of tools. The points of the diamonds protruding from the bond either break away or wear down during use, and the idea is to obtain a balance between the wear on the bond and on the diamond, so that the tool will work in a constant way throughout its life. Because the attack on the diamond is not the same in machining say optical glass as when cutting granite or grinding tungsten carbide, the strengths of the bonds vary, and the bonds – resin bonds, metal bonds, vitreous bonds, ceramic bonds – differ according to their application. Resin bonds, for example, are used principally in carbide grinding, where the bonding material should wear faster than the grit, which must continually present a cutting edge. The diamond grit is also deliberately made to an irregular shape by growing what are called mosaic crystal structures. Metal bonds are more suitable for grinding glass and ceramics, because the grit and the very hard matrix wear away together. Most suitable for drilling and sawing are sintered metal bonds, in which the diamond particles are mixed with a metallic powder and can be cold-pressed into the required shapes and sizes before being sintered together through the application of heat slightly below the melting point of the metal constituent. For instruments such as dentists' drills the diamond is bonded by electrolytically deposited nickel.

A new product that finds its biggest single application in oil-well drilling is polycrystalline diamond. It consists of small diamond particles sintered together under high pressure with the addition of a bonding agent, usually cobalt metal, which promotes inter-growth between the diamond crystallites. It is made in biscuit shapes, a layer of pure diamond on a backing of carbide or another suitable material which may be clamped or brazed onto a tool. It may be cut into required shapes using lasers and electric spark erosion techniques.

The major limitation on the use of diamond as an abrasive is in grinding ferrous metals. Carbon being soluble in these metals, diamond has a strong chemical affinity to them, and the chemical reaction set up between the carbon and the metal when the tool becomes hot quickly destroys the diamond. High-pressure technology made it possible to produce a substitute material for dealing with ferrous metals: cubic boron nitride, which is second to diamond in hardness. The strength and hardness of diamond are due to its crystal structure. Atoms of carbon have six electrons, four of which are available for making chemical bonds. This high ratio of bonding electrons to the total results in very strong bonds. In diamond, each atom bonds with its four neighbours, which in turn bond with their four neighbours, each sharing one electron with each of its neighbours. This produces a tetrahedral structure, which is the strongest known structure. Cubic boron nitride is an analogue of diamond. Nitrogen has five bonding electrons and boron has three; the two together can behave like carbon, because boron "takes" one electron from nitrogen, so each ends up with four and, under the temperature and pressure conditions that would produce diamond, alternate boron and nitrogen atoms can produce a diamond-like structure.

Ever since the first diamonds were synthesized the question asked probably more than any other has been whether gem diamonds could be made synthetically. "Yes, in terms of quality and colour we could create gemstones, but they wouldn't be exactly the same thing," says Dyer. "The synthetics we make are yellow. In nature this coloration, which is caused by nitrogen, is removed by diffusion over millions of years. We obviously can't remove the colour in the same way; to produce a colourless stone by synthesis we have to leave nitrogen out of the process, in the absence of which it is more difficult to grow diamond. The point is that if we aren't duplicating nature's process we're not really duplicating nature's product. People don't want replicas, they want the real thing. There would be no sense in embarking on such a costly high-tech venture to produce something for which there isn't a market."

Industrial applications for diamond extend from the heaviest types of drilling equipment down to the finest scalpel blades used by eye surgeons. "With the demand for higher technology and better tools, working to finer tolerances with harder materials, the place of diamond as the ultimate machining element is assured," says Dyer. "Pure technological research keeps us ahead in the range and quality of our products. Ceramics, optics and computer and information technology are the industries that will lead the world into the next century, and we are involved in all of them."

Dick Swann (right), wartime RAF Spitfire pilot, inventor, and managing director of Engis, a British company that has developed a diamond polish for the perspex windows, windscreens and canopies of aircraft that become pitted and fuzzy owing to chemical and hard-particle damage. Where formerly the windows had to be removed and cleaned under factory conditions, all the windows of a jet airliner (below) can now be cleaned in position in a fraction of the time.

CHURCH

CHAPTER 6 THE FAMILY BUSINESS

A century after Cecil Rhodes founded De Beers the company remains what it immediately became at its inception: the undisputed leader of the world diamond industry.

In the Kimberley board room in which Rhodes formed the company, directors assembled on 11 March 1988 for the historic Centenary meeting of the board.

The founder was represented by the equestrian statuette of Rhodes on the table. Looking down on the gathering was a photograph of Sir Ernest Oppenheimer, who became chairman in 1929 and was the creator of the Central Selling Organization (CSO), which today regulates the sale of some eighty per cent of the world's rough diamond production.

In the foreground on the left the chairman of De Beers, Julian Ogilvie Thompson, talks to the retired chairman, Harry Oppenheimer, and Harry's son, bearded Nicky Oppenheimer, chairman of the CSO.

Other directors present are, from left, Peter Leyden, Bertie Lincoln, Henry Dyer, Fred Hodgson, Monty Charles, Anthony Oppenheimer, Sidney Spiro, Teddie Dawe, Grey Fletcher, Gavin Relly, Sir Evelyn de Rothschild and Sir Philip Oppenheimer. Alex Barbour and Baron Edmond de Rothschild were absent.

For sixty years the Oppenheimer family has given continuity to the direction of the company, which, despite the scale and complexity of its international operations, has preserved many characteristics of a traditional family business.

Now in his mid-nineties, retired De Beers director Jim Joel (right), great-nephew of the renowned Barney Barnato, started in the diamond business as a trainee sorter in Kimberley in 1919 and still has an office at Barnato Brothers in London.

Henry Rudd, great-great-grandson of Rhodes's friend and original partner, Charles Rudd, with great-grandsons John and Robin (right), at Rudd House, the family home at Kimberley, which was donated by De Beers and restored by the Cape Provincial Administration as a museum.

Early in the eighteenth century the discovery of diamonds in Brazil around the town of Tijuco, now Diamantina (left), led to the imposition of strict controls by the Portuguese Crown, including the total suspension for several years of all mining in the district, to protect diamond prices in Europe.

Georgina Harwood (right) displays a necklace of eleven uncut perfect diamond octahedrons that her grandfather, "Matabele Thompson", selected to buy as a gift to her grandmother from a bucket of diamonds that Barney Barnato habitually kept behind his office desk in Kimberley.

While some of his students chat in the background (top), Professor Laurie Ackermann, Rhodes Scholar, former judge and first incumbent of the H.F. Oppenheimer Human Rights Chair established at the University of Stellenbosch in 1988, sits in the courtyard of the Law Faculty.

Coming from Australia, Canada and South Africa, recent recipients of Rhodes Scholarships, of which some two hundred are awarded each year, discuss their studies in Milner Hall at Rhodes House, Oxford (bottom). They are, from left, Tony Deitz, Malcolm Brown, Andrew Rolfe, Alec Cameron, Ian Jackman, Tim Evans, Xiyanda Lekalake and Dan Crowley.

With Nicky Oppenheimer at the controls of the company helicopter, natural scientists Dr Richard Liversedge and Dr Rudi Bigalke pass low over a herd of eland as they carry out the annual game count at Rooipoort, De Beers' private game reserve near Kimberley, which supplies surplus animals for restocking national parks and public and private game reserves in southern Africa.

Before going to be hung at the University of Western Australia as an Australian Bicentennial project, the bells of St Martin-in-the-Fields (top above), which rang out over Trafalgar Square for some 250 years, were, in response to an appeal by the Australian and New Zealand Association of Bell Ringers, retuned and refitted at the CSO's expense at the Whitechapel Bell Foundry in London. Lou Hagopian, chairman of N.W. Ayer, which handles De Beers' public relations and advertising in the United States, heads a meeting of his New York staff who are working on a public service campaign against drug abuse (above). At the table, clockwise, are Lou Hagopian, Sirge Helder, Janet Kraus, George Eversman, Jim Murphy, Ken Sausville, Lee Rubin and Earl Shorris. Pope John Paul celebrates evening mass in the Independence Stadium in Gaborone (right), which was constructed with assistance from De Beers Botswana as a gift to the nation.

In the waiting room of the diamond buying office in Tshikapa, Zaire, diggers and their agents (far left) weigh their goods on finger balances using matchsticks and bottle tops as weights.
On a purchasing expedition in Zaire (left), Land Rovers belonging to Sediza, a buying associate of the CSO, cross the Loange River between Kinshasa and Kananga.

At Barkly West a river digger, Boet Sonnenberg (far left), draws the attention of buyer Warren Symcox to the merits of a 20.7-carat stone in a parcel of 66.6 carats he is offering to De Beers.
John Gie (left), head of buying for De Beers at Harry Oppenheimer House in Kimberley, having fun with a yellow diamond of more than three hundred carats.

Leaving his sandals at the door of Joaquim Gomes's buying office at Tepequém, in the far north of Brazil, *garimpeiro* Raimundo Saraiva (far left) shakes the tube in which he keeps his finds to indicate that he has a diamond to sell.
In his office in Pelikaanstraat (left), Tim Redston negotiates a purchase with Moussa Tchiam, a Gambian client who acts as a broker in Antwerp for West African diggers.

FOR A CENTURY DE BEERS has remained pre-eminent in the world of diamonds. Its stabilizing influence on the market is felt throughout the industry, by producer, dealer, manufacturer, jeweller and retailer, right through to the end user, the value of whose investments it protects. Reliant on this stability are hundreds of thousands of diamond diggers and miners in Africa, South America, Australia and the Soviet Union, nearly three-quarters of a million diamond cutters and polishers in India, thousands more in Antwerp, New York, Tel Aviv and countries of the Pacific Rim, and an untold number of people associated with diamond jewellery manufacture and sale in Japan, South-East Asia, North America, Europe – indeed, everywhere. To a developing country like Botswana, which has emerged as the Western world's largest producer of gem quality diamonds, the stability of the international diamond market is vital to the national economy.

Although today its activities as a producer, purchaser and purveyor of diamonds extend over the face of the earth, De Beers retains its head office in Kimberley, the small provincial city in the northern Cape that in the 1880s became the cradle of industrialization in southern Africa. When the focus of industrial development moved to the Rand after the discovery of gold in the Transvaal, it was natural for De Beers to remain in Kimberley to manage its mines, and today the directors of this multi-billion-dollar international company still meet formally in the board room at 36 Stockdale Street, where Cecil Rhodes, Barney Barnato, Alfred Beit and F. Philipson-Stow shaped the future of the diamond industry a hundred years ago.

The preservation of this tradition, when it might have been more convenient for an international business of that size to have the head office in a world capital, seems to be largely a matter of sentiment, but it is a sentiment that reveals the company's sense of commitment to its place of origin and the community it has been linked with for generations, and says much too about the "culture" of the company itself. Part of it also is the sense of history that is so important to the company in a business that will always be to some extent cyclic. "None of the problems we encounter from time to time is ever really completely new," says Robin Crawford, De Beers director and one of the chairman's management team. "If we have a difficulty grappling with what seems to be a new situation, the solution can often be found in our history."

While it is true that Cecil Rhodes saw his achievement in Kimberley as part of his greater vision of what could be accomplished in southern Africa under the aegis of Great Britain, his consolidation of the mines a century ago and the evolution subsequently of a central selling organization in London, in tandem with De Beers, were motivated less by sentiment and historical reflection than the compelling practicalities of mining and marketing.

Although the first authenticated diamond discovery in the Cape Colony in 1866 had attracted some diggers to the alluvial deposits on the Vaal, Orange and Hartz rivers, it had been treated with disbelief by the outside world. The finding of the 87.5-carat Star of South Africa three years later had engendered some enthusiasm among speculators, and a "new rush" of small-scale diggers in 1870 had led over the next two years to the establishment of several major "dry" diggings in what turned out to be the weathered upper layer of kimberlite pipes: the Bultfontein, Dutoitspan, De Beers and Kimberley (Big Hole) mines at Kimberley, and the Koffiefontein and Jagersfontein mines nearby in the Orange Free State.

At the age of seventeen, Rhodes had come to Africa in 1870 in search of adventure, and to Kimberley a year later to seek his fortune. With the profits he made from selling ice and hiring steam-driven water pumps to the diggers he bought his first claim, in the De Beers pipe, in 1873. The need to consolidate production and regulate distribution was soon obvious to him and others. It was becoming physically impossible to continue mining the pipes as a multitude of small individually held claims and, as previously noted, the harder ground encountered deeper down required mechanized treatment that individual diggers could not afford. The need for the regulation of distribution was equally evident, for the volume of production from the South African mines – six times the Brazilian production – had by then caused an international recession in prices.

After legal restraints on the number of claims an individual digger might own were lifted, Rhodes and his friend Charles Rudd in 1880 combined their claims in the De Beers pipe to form De Beers Mining Company Limited. The number of individual claims was dwindling fast, absorbed by syndicates and larger companies, and by 1885 only a handful of major players was left, of whom the principals were Rhodes and Barnato.

The struggle between these two enterprising Englishmen, so different in background and personality, for control of the Kimberley mines has been recounted too often for all its colourful, sometimes amusing, details to bear repetition here. In March 1887 the Barnato Diamond Mining Company was placed in voluntary liquidation and the shareholders' shares exchanged for shares in the Standard Diamond Mining Company, which was amalgamated a few months later with the Kimberley Central Diamond Mining Company. This made Barnato the largest shareholder in the Kimberley mine. Backed by the London merchant bank N.M. Rothschild and Son, however, Rhodes was able to outbid Barnato for claims adjoining Barnato's in the Kimberley mine. The upshot was that Barnato capitulated to Rhodes's inducements, and on 12 March 1888 De Beers Consolidated Mines Limited was founded, with Rhodes, Barnato, Beit, and Philipson-Stow as the major shareholders. Its assets were the whole of De Beers mine, seventy-five per cent of Kimberley mine and controlling interests in Bultfontein and Dutoitspan mines. When Kimberley Central shareholders threatened to prevent Barnato from merging his interest in the company with De Beers, Rhodes persuaded him to put Kimberley Central into voluntary liquidation, thus enabling De Beers to buy its assets from the liquidators for £5 338 650 and assume undisputed control of Kimberley mine. Over the next few years De Beers acquired the remaining shareholdings in Dutoitspan and Bultfontein mines and bought the newly discovered Wesselton mine.

In Europe, Amsterdam and Antwerp had for centuries been the main cutting and polishing centres and the cities in which the bulk of the trade in polished diamonds was conducted. But London had been the chief distribution centre for rough diamonds from the mid-seventeenth century, when the dominance of the English East India Company had enabled English Madras to supplant Portuguese Goa as the major entrepôt for diamonds from the Indian mines. Several London diamond merchants of Portuguese and Dutch Jewish origin, who had proved more skilful at purchasing diamonds than the East India Company itself, were permitted by the company to do business in Madras and transport their goods in its ships. As a result, in 1732 it was possible to affirm in the preamble to an Act of Parliament abolishing customs duties on precious stones that "this Kingdom is now become the great mart for diamonds and other precious stones and jewels, from whence most foreign countries are supplied." And although at about that time Brazil replaced India as the major producer, so well entrenched had London's position become that most of the traffic in the new production passed through the hands of London merchants.

Towards the middle of the last century successors to these merchants began concentrating in Hatton Garden, in the commercial area around Holborn Circus that became London's diamond district. Here, following the consolidation of the Kimberley mines, a group of ten merchants and brokers with agents in Kimberley formed the London Diamond Syndicate to buy the De Beers production and divide it among themselves for sale to the trade. And with De Beers in control of production and the Syndicate handling sales, they were between them able to preserve a degree of market stability.

The death of Rhodes in 1902 coincided with the formation of a rival company to mine the newly discovered Premier pipe in the Transvaal, and it was left to his successors at De Beers to cope with the threat to market stability posed by the flood of new productions that were to bypass the Syndicate from Premier mine and alluvial deposits discovered in German South West Africa (Namibia) six years later.

At first the Premier company rebuffed the advances of De Beers and the Syndicate, but when the market was seriously weakened by the American financial crisis of 1907 it agreed to limit its production. Another ten years passed before De Beers was able to buy Barnato Brothers' stock in Premier from Barnato's nephew Solly Joel and gain the control it deemed essential for the efficient regulation of production and sale. It was less successful in South West Africa: the German Regie reneged on an early undertaking to sell the whole production through the Syndicate, and a subsequent agreement to "pool" production for marketing was aborted by the outbreak of World War I.

The years after the war were marked by chronic instability in the diamond market, owing largely to the pressures of over-supply. The danger to the security of the diamond industry, as Sir Ernest Oppenheimer said some years later, was not the discovery of a new rich diamond field, but the irrational exploitation of it.

For an efficient mechanism that would bring together for sale the productions of new producers with those of De Beers and enable the producers to regulate sales, the industry had to wait until Sir Ernest was in a position to take command.

Born in Friedburg, Germany, less than a month after Rhodes and Rudd had formed the original De Beers Mining Company, Ernest Oppenheimer had in 1896, at the age of sixteen, joined the firm of Anton Dunkelsbuhler in Hatton Garden as a trainee diamond valuer. He had displayed such acumen for the business by the time he was twenty-one that in the year of Rhodes's death he had been posted to Kimberley as the firm's agent.

Diamonds were his first interest, and to someone with his ability and ambition, control of De Beers was the obvious plum, but the road to its attainment was long. Although during his first fifteen years in South Africa he was chiefly occupied in buying diamonds for his firm, he became involved, through Dunkelsbuhler's Transvaal mining interests, in the development of gold mining on the East Rand, and by the time he was ready to make his bid for De Beers, he had built his financial base in gold.

In 1917, combining British and American finance, he founded Anglo American Corporation of South Africa to mine gold on the East Rand, and in 1919 Anglo American bought the South West African alluvial concessions held by German companies before the war. A year later Oppenheimer, who was soon to be knighted for his services to the British war effort, formed Consolidated Diamond Mines of South West Africa (CDM) to acquire and consolidate these assets. The acquisition of an important diamond producer, which provided him with a direct role in shaping diamond policy, was a major step towards realizing his ambition.

By then there were other African producers in the market. Deposits found in Angola in 1912 were being mined by Lisbon-based Companhia de Diamantes de Angola (Diamang), in which Anglo American, in association with Barnato Brothers, was able in 1923 to obtain a small interest, with representation on the board and a contract to purchase the production. Further north, in the Belgian Congo, the world's largest industrial diamond deposits – alluvial and pipe – had been discovered in 1918 by Compagnie du Chemin de Fer du Bas-Congo au Katanga (Bécéka), on whose behalf they were being mined by Société Internationale Forestière et Minière (La Forminière).

Events moved swiftly after Anglo American was admitted to the Syndicate in 1924, and the same year Sir Ernest nailed his colours to the mast at Anglo's annual general meeting. His experience, he said, had taught him that "only by limiting the quantity of diamonds put on the market, in accordance with the demand, and by selling through one channel, can the stability of the diamond trade be maintained." A few months later the resignation of Anglo American and Dunkelsbuhler precipitated the disintegration of the Syndicate, and the next year, after becoming a partner in Dunkelsbuhler, Sir Ernest formed a new Syndicate, in which Anglo and Dunkelsbuhler shared forty-five per cent, Barnato Brothers had forty-five per cent and its associate Johannesburg Consolidated Investments held the balance. Assisted by Solly Joel of Barnato Brothers, which was a major shareholder in De Beers, Sir Ernest was appointed to the board of De Beers in 1926, and in 1929 he was elected chairman.

A Sunday afternoon at home in the Surrey countryside for Gary Ralfe (left), an executive director of the CSO and director of De Beers.

Sir Ernest's actions after being elected chairman displayed a creative singleness of purpose. The twenties had been a period of disintegration in the industry, of prices destabilized by producers fighting each other for a larger share of the market, and he was determined to restore the balance. At his urging, De Beers acquired concessions and shareholdings that gave it control over all the major diamond mining interests in southern Africa. The most important of these was CDM, which in 1930 De Beers bought from Anglo American in exchange for redeemable debentures – a transaction that gave Anglo influence in De Beers and strengthened Sir Ernest's position in the De Beers boardroom. At the same time he began replacing the Syndicate with a structure better adapted to the purpose of orderly distribution.

"Putting that together was my father's greatest business achievement," says Harry Oppenheimer. "The Syndicate had simply bought diamonds, giving the producers no say in its affairs, and there was a clash of interest. During those early years of the Great Depression it was clear that the whole system would break down unless the producers and merchants could work together."

Sorters at 2 Charterhouse Street prepare to sort productions from various countries – marked with their national flags – and blend them into the CSO's London selling mixture.

In 1930 Sir Ernest formed The Diamond Corporation (Dicorp), to buy from outside producers, and The Diamond Purchasing and Trading Company, to buy the productions of De Beers' mines in South Africa and South West Africa, and in 1934 he incorporated The Diamond Trading Company (DTC) to buy from both companies and sell to the trade. Thus he created a single sales channel, controlled by the major producers. Then, in an exchange of shares with Barnato Brothers and Anglo American, De Beers obtained the entire share capital of Dicorp in 1938. The structure, which came to be known as the Central Selling Organization (CSO), was in place.

"The CSO is something of an enigma," admits Gary Ralfe, one of its executive directors and a director of De Beers. "The producers, the trade and the international press know what it is, yet it doesn't exist as a legal persona. We see it simply as an association of companies that buys in the world's major productions, assorts them, values them and finally makes them up into boxes for sale at regular sights to its clients in the trade."

Diamonds being a luxury product, the demand for them is more erratic than for necessities, and consumer confidence would be shaken, even lost, if prices were allowed to fluctuate wildly. It is, therefore, a basic principle of the CSO never to lower its selling prices, and its chief function has been to sustain and protect them. "To do this we try to reconcile supply and demand," says Ralfe. "When demand is stronger we have an inventory from which to add to the supply, and may at the same time increase prices; when demand is weak we curtail supply."

De Beers director Sidney Spiro (right) in the office of his colleague and friend Charles Hambro at Hambros Bank in London.

"Balancing supply and demand from sight to sight is not so difficult," says Sir Philip Oppenheimer, Harry's cousin, who headed the CSO for some thirty years. "But when you come to what should be mined, and what quotas you should have, and what the sales are likely to be over the next two to three years, it is extremely difficult." The CSO does its best to forecast production, says Alex Barbour, deputy chairman of the CSO and a director of De Beers, "but we never really know what the mix will be until we actually get it out of the ground and onto the sorting table."

"In the days before even my memory of it, you had a sort of natural monopoly, because De Beers was the only very big producer of diamonds, but it's very far from being like that now," says Harry Oppenheimer. "Today it's a question of having an organization which can buy diamonds from all over the world and stock them in bad times and sell out the stocks in good times, and in that way preserve the stability there wouldn't otherwise be. It has been possible to do this with diamonds because it is a comparatively small industry, and we've had not only the ability, but also sufficient finance to handle the diamond business. Nowadays the system can only be maintained so long as all sorts of different producers in many different countries think that we render a service which is worthwhile to them."

"From the moment that Premier mine started out in opposition to us our history has been one of trying to get selling control over the diamonds we don't produce ourselves, of persuading other producers to sell through the CSO," says Ralfe. "We have been successful to the extent that eighty per cent of the rough gem diamonds now produced in the world passes through our hands."

During the years that Sir Ernest was creating the CSO structure, however, the diamond industry was experiencing the full impact of the Depression. Although De Beers closed all its mines, and outside producers cut down production, Dicorp built up large stocks, which it was still holding when World War II broke out. After the war it was able to sell them for a windfall profit of forty million pounds, half of which went to the newly formed De Beers Investment Trust, which invested substantially in the new goldfields in the Orange Free State and on the Far West Rand, and half to recapitalize the CSO. "It was policy to invest outside the industry, so as to have enough funds to protect the diamond market in lean times," explains South African-born London banker and De Beers director Sidney Spiro, who worked closely with Sir Ernest. "The financial side of the business has always had to maintain a fine balance between looking after the cash needs of the industry and expanding investment outside."

"We aren't silly enough to think that times will always be good," says Harry Oppenheimer. "We knew that even in good times we couldn't just accumulate large sums in cash, because as the money depreciated the price of the diamonds we needed to buy with it would rise. We deliberately invested outside the business in order to have something which we could borrow against if diamonds were in a bad way."

Until the mid-fifties the CSO received diamonds chiefly from De Beers' own mines and privately owned mining companies elsewhere in Africa: Selection Trust in West Africa, Williamson Diamonds in Tanganyika, Bécéka in the Belgian Congo and Diamang in Angola. This orderly pattern was disrupted by developments in Sierra Leone, where illicit digging in Sierra Leone Selection Trust's concessions proliferated to the point that what amounted to a fifth of the world's illicit gem production was being smuggled by Lebanese traders through Liberia to Antwerp, seriously endangering market stability.

Three young CSO executives – Monty Charles, Teddie Dawe and Derry Turner – put forward a proposal that Dicorp open its own buying offices in Sierra Leone. It was a radical departure from anything that had been considered before. The Colonial government had not been fully aware of how much revenue it was losing and was interested in the proposal. It consequently opened up all but two of Selection Trust's concession areas to local diggers and invited De Beers to set up buying offices to purchase their productions. In response The Diamond Corporation Sierra Leone was formed in 1956 and granted exclusive export rights, and Charles, Dawe and Turner were dispatched to Freetown to open buying offices. "From the government's point of view it was guaranteed its taxes on everything that passed through our hands," says Sir Philip. "Our own purpose was to ensure, by competing with other buyers, that a realistic price was paid for the diamonds, which the Lebanese were picking up for a fraction of their value – in some areas by the cigarette tin or Coca Cola bottle."

"The main purpose of the buying offices was, and still is, not to buy up all the diamonds they can, but to buy what is necessary to forestall downward pressure on our prices," says Rogan Maclean, a London director who spent ten years buying in West Africa. "In a strong market we can afford to be less active, but when the market is weak we must buy more than we normally would."

"It changed our lives in London," says Charles, who was later to take over the diamond division and run it for twenty-five years. "For the first time, instead of sitting in our glass house in Charterhouse Street, we had to go out into the world and learn how to trade in competition with the toughest traders in the business."

The young men who went out to West Africa as buyers were thrust into a life that was not only more challenging, but utterly different from anything they had known in Charterhouse Street. Operating from out-stations, they trekked through the bush, accompanied by bearers carrying on their heads large galvanized iron boxes of British one-pound notes, the standard currency and denomination in which all purchases, no matter how large, were made. Maclean recalls a period of four days in which he bought the equivalent of four million dollars worth of diamonds and paid for them in one-pound notes. When they ran short of money they radioed for more to be dropped to them from the air. The experiences they shared united them in an informal fraternity, whose members occupy many of the senior managerial positions within the CSO today. "Working out there created a sort of inner bond between people that has been very successful in the organization, giving it a spirit that makes it unique," says Anthony Oppenheimer, Sir Philip's son and a director, who is himself a Sierra Leone "old boy".

"For the company it was a tremendous thing," recalls Dawe, who afterwards became head of the administrative division of the CSO. "Not only because we were gaining control over such a large part of what had been illicit trade, but because it was the start of our having to buy goods outside, and gave us experience that stood us in good stead when later, after West African countries and Zaire and Angola became self-governing, we had to negotiate with national governments."

The outward thrust into the competitive rough market came in the closing years of Sir

Ernest's life. He had created a company structure that was ideally adapted to the singularities of the diamond industry and perfectly suited to occupying a central position in it. He had established also the basis of its "culture", giving to its inner relationships and outward image the character of a family business. For reasons rooted deep in Jewish history the diamond business is conducted with a minimum of record and a maximum of trust, and because the fidelity of close relatives is generally a better bet than that of outsiders, it has always been a family-type business. The family trades with other families it knows it can trust. De Beers, the CSO, the "Syndicate" is perceived by the trade as a family business doing business with family businesses.

"In other industries, firms that start as family businesses may survive after there is no longer direct family involvement, but not in the diamond business," says Ben Bonas, a leading London broker. "It rarely works to delegate to other people, because it is a hands-on business like no other. It is a remarkable achievement of the Oppenheimers that they were able to engender trust in De Beers and create a management structure of people who, although not family, were treated in this highly personal business as if they were." A quite remarkable degree of loyalty to the family, on the part of both employees and clients, cements the whole organization.

"It has of course grown beyond being a family business, but we like to think that it retains something of the family character," says Harry Oppenheimer. "There has certainly been continuity. The firms that are in it today are the direct successors in title to those who were in it at the beginning. The Rothschilds, for instance, who financed the formation of the company, still have members on the board."

"No family could have produced enough people to run De Beers today on strict family lines," says present chairman Julian Ogilvie Thompson. "What both Sir Ernest and Harry Oppenheimer quite rightly did – and a lot of it arose directly out of their personalities – was to create a system in which the people working with them in the business became friends and notional partners, made to feel part of a broader family. Something of their personality rubbed off on all of us. We still like to think that our people feel themselves to be part of the De Beers family."

It was not to be simply an old-fashioned family business that managed to survive through to the third generation, however. "Its strength is that it never tried to be anything but a diamond company," says Harry Oppenheimer's son Nicky. "Through its happy association with Anglo American it was able to participate in ventures outside the industry as an investor, without getting involved in managing them. It has, therefore, been able to dedicate all its management effort to the diamond business and to staying ahead of the game."

Upon Sir Ernest's death in 1957 he was succeeded as chairman of both De Beers and Anglo American by Harry Oppenheimer, who had been active in the business since the age of twenty-three and was then forty-nine. In the late thirties he had ruffled a few conservative feathers in the CSO by launching, of all things, a generic consumer advertising campaign to promote the sale of diamond jewellery in the United States. But it had been a giant step in the growing sophistication of the company, the prototype of what in the post war world grew eventually into a world-wide promotional and informational network. The world in which he took command had changed greatly from that in which his father had grown up, and he had the freshness of outlook and flexibility of mind to cope with it. In Europe many of the old relationships between business communities had been disrupted by the war; new people, with new attitudes, had come to the fore, and Israel had emerged as a major new cutting centre. And by the time he became chairman Africa too was changing.

"The marketing system my father built was based on doing deals with large companies operating in a few colonial countries, which was quite different to having to negotiate with governments of newly independent states and deal with the productions of hosts of

On his eightieth birthday, retired De Beers chairman Harry Oppenheimer (left), in the library at Little Brenthurst. "His contribution during fifty-five years as a director and twenty-seven years as chairman made him the undisputed leader of the industry," says his successor, Julian Ogilvie Thompson, "and he remains its elder statesman today."

At his stud near Newmarket, De Beers director Sir Philip Oppenheimer (above right), who headed the CSO in London for some thirty years, reaches past his stud manager, Walter Crowe, to stroke his favourite brood mare, On the House, held by his son Anthony Oppenheimer, an executive director of the CSO and a director of De Beers.
CSO chairman Nicky Oppenheimer, who is also deputy chairman of De Beers, in the farm-yard (right) at his White Waltham home with his son Jonathan, an Oxford undergraduate who was selected as twelfth man for the Blues cricket eleven in his first year at the university, and springer spaniels Meg and Maggie.

small-scale diggers," he says. "Fortunately, I was able to keep the business together by holding to a recognizable principle and having the luck or ability to adapt it to changing circumstances."

"Harry Oppenheimer led our transition into this new era, and charted our course," says Ogilvie Thompson. "His contribution during fifty-five years as director and twenty-seven years as chairman made him the undisputed leader of the industry, and he remains its elder statesman today. Above all, he was able through difficult times to keep the CSO together as an efficiently functioning organization that continues to be privately managed."

His grasp of the changes taking place was evident in his negotiations for the Williamson mine in Tanganyika after the death in 1958 of its owner, Dr John Williamson, with whom the CSO had since 1947 had contracts to buy its production. Independence was in prospect, a new national government would have aspirations that had to be taken into account, and the colonial government was naturally concerned. "With this in mind, he came up with a solution that was way ahead of what anyone else was thinking at that time," says Crawford, "and it won the day against competition."

"We had bought the mine from Dr Williamson's heirs, but I was pretty sure that it was a position that couldn't be maintained," Harry Oppenheimer recalls. "So I offered the government a fifty per cent partnership in the mine, and because they didn't have the money, I suggested that they pay for part of it with the death duties they were going to get, and pay for the rest out of the dividends they would receive on their shares. Tanzania became independent soon afterwards, but the arrangement has continued, and it pleases me that, although our half share isn't worth much today, we are still in friendly partnership with the country."

At about the same time the Soviet Union emerged as a major producer. Large alluvial deposits had been found in the Urals in the forties, and in the mid-fifties big diamond pipes were discovered in Siberia. A contract between Dicorp and the Soviet government signed in 1959 was terminated in 1963, but the Soviet Union, which later became the world's largest producer of gem diamonds (accounting for a third of the total production), continued to market its exports in a way that would not undermine prices.

Buying operations in West Africa were expanded in the sixties and Dicorp opened offices in all the main producing and trading centres in the region. Recognition of the new African reality was again implicit in the adaptations made to accommodate political changes, first in previously British Sierra Leone, and later in the former Portuguese and Belgian possessions, Angola and Zaire.

In 1959, a year before Dicorp Sierra Leone's exclusive export rights expired, almost two years before the country became independent, Dicorp and Dicorp Sierra Leone negotiated a new agreement with the government that led to the establishment of a single official export channel for all rough diamonds, other than the Selection Trust production. The Government Diamond Office (GDO), as it was called, was managed by Dicorp, which also contracted to buy all the diamonds sold through the office, while Dicorp Sierra Leone was reduced to being merely one of many licensed diamond buyers supplying it with diamonds. "Bringing the government into our operation was a major change of approach," says Sir Philip, "and it set a pattern for future work in African countries, where conditions became more difficult as time went by."

This arrangement worked well in Sierra Leone for more than a decade. In 1970, however, the government acquired a majority holding in Selection Trust's mining operations and formed the National Diamond Mining Company to take them over, and in 1974 the government declared an open buying market, depriving Dicorp of its exclusive export rights. Ten years later a newly formed para-statal marketing company bought the remaining privately held forty-nine per cent interest in the mining operation and began selling the whole production direct to the market.

Occupying the highest position in the diamond world, Julian Ogilvie Thompson, a Rhodes Scholar and chairman of De Beers, has been described by his predecessor, Harry Oppenheimer, as "a very great business man who, in addition to his technical skills, has a great sense of and feeling for the traditions and romance attached to this unique company".

Although Dicorp continued buying in West Africa for a few years, it was symptomatic of the declining importance of production in the region that it eventually closed all its West African buying offices. Sierra Leone, in 1988, was the last to go. But it retains offices in Kinshasa, with satellite offices in the producing areas of Zaire, and in Antwerp, where it is assumed that most diamonds not bespoken under Dicorp contracts will ultimately surface.

After Zaire achieved Independence in 1960, Bécéka, with which Dicorp had long had a sales agreement, changed its name to Sibeka (Société d'Entreprise et d'Investissements) and replaced La Forminière with a new locally registered management company, Société Minière de Bakwanga (Miba), to manage its mines. With the nationalization of all foreign-owned enterprises in 1973 Sibeka lost control of Miba. Dicorp buying offices continued operating, however, and a contract was negotiated with the government for the establishment of a sorting office in Kinshasa to undertake provisional valuations of the Miba production for sale through the CSO. This arrangement proved satisfactory to all concerned and was continued after the government in 1978 restored twenty per cent of Miba and the management contract to Sibeka.

In Angola, meanwhile, Harry Oppenheimer had initiated the formation of a consortium, in which De Beers and Diamang each had forty-five per cent and the Portuguese government ten per cent, to mount a massive exploration programme, led by Roy Edwards, to prospect the concession areas lost by Diamang when its exclusive mining rights expired in 1971. Over a million square kilometres had been prospected by the time that the escalation of the anti-colonial war made it impossible to continue. After Independence in 1976 a clash between Diamang's Portuguese directors and the new MPLA government resulted in the sixty per cent held by Portuguese shareholders being nationalized. Production since then has see-sawed, with the De Beers group and other entrepreneurs at different times endeavouring, in the face of adverse conditions, to restore it to the pre-Independence level of two million carats a year. In 1986 the state holding company, Endiama, liquidated Diamang and absorbed its assets. In 1989 Endiama and De Beers issued a joint statement of intent, in terms of which the two companies would establish a partnership to prospect and mine known sources of diamond-bearing kimberlite and Endiama would market the Angolan production through the CSO.

During the sixties and seventies De Beers substantially increased its production resources. From the discoverers, Allister Fincham and Ernest Schwabel, De Beers acquired control of the Finsch pipe, north-west of Kimberley, and developed it into its biggest domestic producer. It acquired control of short-lived seabed dredging operations off the South West African coast, which, under the guidance of Louis Murray, and since his death of Peter Leyden, managing director of Anglo American's diamond services division and director of De Beers, became the nucleus of marine prospecting and mining research operations that continue to the present. In Botswana, the finding by its geologists of the rich Orapa diamond pipe created an unprecedented situation. The Botswana government argued that no developing country could be expected to permit mining of its resources on the scale that De Beers proposed without claiming a right to participate, and so obtained a minority interest in the company formed in 1969 to mine the pipe, De Beers Botswana Mining Company (Debswana). De Beers, therefore, could not simply regard the production as its own, but had to satisfy its fellow-shareholder that it was in Debswana's interests to sell through the CSO.

The Diamond Corporation Botswana was incorporated to buy the diamonds from Debswana and sell them on to the CSO, and in 1974 the Botswana Diamond Valuing Company was launched to sort the Orapa production in Gaborone and prepare it for sale in London. For some years the purchases were negotiated in London with the government valuer, but after the Letlhakane and Jwaneng mines came on stream in the late seventies and early eighties, increasing Botswana's production three-fold, the valuing company built a modern sorting headquarters in Gaborone, Orapa House, with the capacity to handle all the productions right through to completing sales to the CSO inside the country. One effect of this is that an important new skill, diamond sorting, has been developed locally.

Valuer for the Botswana government, Roy Fitch, in white shirt, and his team check the assortment made by the Botswana Diamond Valuing Company at Orapa House in Gaborone, watched by the then Permanent Secretary, Ministry of Mineral Resources and Water Affairs, Charles Tibone, wearing a jacket and tie.

All these arrangements were not achieved without difficulty, however, and in the course of protracted negotiations Debswana developed into a fully equal partnership. "The government had entered into an agreement originally which, as things turned out – although not in terms of what was known at the time – was probably too favourable to us," says Harry Oppenheimer. "When the size of the operation grew enormously, they engaged themselves in re-negotiating. We went through difficult times, but nevertheless came to solutions which both of us were reasonably happy with and developed a very agreeable relationship."

"The negotiations were tough, but both sides had to be fair. Working together for our mutual benefit, we got to know one another well, and in the end I think we were all satisfied; there were no winners, no losers," says Botswana's Minister of External Affairs, Dr G.K.T. Chiepe, who as Minister of Mineral Resources and Water Affairs at the time took a leading part in the negotiations. "It was fortunate that our then president, the late Sir Seretse Khama, in whose tribal territory Orapa was discovered, was able to convince his tribesmen that mineral resources should be, not a tribal asset, but a national asset. This set a precedent for the rest of the country, and the diamond mines are today the backbone of our national economy."

Dicorp's contracts with producers differ in detail but are in principle the same. Dicorp agrees to buy, and the producer to sell, the whole gem diamond production of a mine, at regular intervals throughout the year, for a fixed period of years. Initially, a new producer submits a month's production, which is then sorted into sizes, shapes, qualities and colours corresponding to the DTC's selling categories, of which there are some five thousand. If the producer's expert valuer agrees that they have been correctly matched, the assortment then becomes the producer's standard sample, on the basis of which Dicorp buys the current run-of-mine production at the CSO's price per carat for each category. Diamonds of more than 10.8 carats, however, are bought separately, at negotiated prices. Once Dicorp and the producer's valuer have agreed that each assortment produced corresponds with the standard sample, the diamonds go into the mixture of productions received in London from various sources.

In addition to being expert diamantaires, the valuers must be familiar with the full range of the CSO's assortment and prices, relative to those prevailing in the volatile open market. "We are there to look after the producer's interests and see to it that the total amount paid corresponds to the total value of the product," says Roy Fitch, valuer for the Botswana government. "We watch the market, keep an eye on the CSO, and if we feel they are selling anything too cheaply we will talk to them about it. We also have the right to check the contents of any DTC box against the values on the buyer's invoice and demand an explanation if they don't correspond to our valuation."

The financial resources of De Beers were fully extended during the early eighties in supporting the industry through its biggest recession since the thirties: the consequence of a "boom and bust" cycle set in motion by rampant speculation on the polished diamond market. As more will be said about this in dealing with the CSO's selling function in the next chapter, it is sufficient to say here that for a while the effects that the speculation had on market prices also bedevilled the CSO's relations with its contract producers.

One example of these difficulties occurred in 1981, when the Zaire government suddenly abrogated its agreement to market the Miba production through the CSO and announced its intention also to take over the purchasing arrangements on alluvial diggings. Viewing the proposed alternatives as inimical to the maintenance of stable prices, the CSO withdrew from the negotiations and recalled its sorting and buying office personnel. The setback turned out to be temporary, however, because the government, finding the new arrangements unsatisfactory, renewed its contract with the CSO. Yet at the time the loss of the contract placed the survival of the CSO under a good deal of speculation, just when De Beers was becoming involved in negotiating a sales agreement with the developers of the new Argyle diamond discovery in north Western Australia. It also gave the CSO a strong incentive to show that it was still the force it had been in the industry, that it had not lost its grip.

Directors representing the Botswana government on the board of De Beers: Baledzi Gaolathe (right), Permanent Secretary, Ministry of Finance and Development Planning, and (below right) Cuthbert Moshe Tebogo Lekaukau, Permanent Secretary, Ministry of Mineral Resources and Water Affairs, chairman of the Botswana Diamond Valuing Company and deputy chairman of De Beers Botswana.

"Once we knew that a major find in Australia was in the offing, it was clear that we would have to pursue it in every way we could," says Tim Capon, a director of the CSO and De Beers, who is closely involved in the Australian contract. "The developers, the Ashton Joint Venture, considered all their options, and when they got to talking contracts we produced a simple draft. Once we had agreed on principles everything had to be spelt out to the last detail, probably because they had bankers and two partners to satisfy, none of whom was familiar with the diamond industry. A major issue was the assertion that the anti-trust laws in the United States, where the leading partner had interests, prevented Ashton from selling us the entire cheap gem and industrial production exclusively. Until then we had insisted on exclusivity in all our contracts with producers. After they had satisfied us that this was in fact so, it became a question of what percentages and types of goods would be excluded, and by the time we finished, the contract had grown to fifteen times its original length."

"Harry Oppenheimer displayed great ingenuity and flexibility," recalls Crawford, who participated in the negotiations. "He accepted that there were legal impediments to their signing a contract for the whole production, and as they would be by far the biggest producer of the cheap gem and industrial qualities of diamonds, he felt that he could justify a contract that would allow them to market twenty-five per cent of their cheap gem and industrial production separately." Commercial production started in January 1983, and three months later the CSO completed its first purchase in Perth.

"The discovery of the Australian mines was important, but in the beginning the importance was exaggerated, because people looked to the weight of the diamonds and not the value," Harry Oppenheimer says on reflection. "In some extraordinary way, where God provides diamonds in abundance He provides them in very low qualities."

The boom in the diamond market persisted right up to 1981, and when it collapsed the CSO's annual sales dropped by more than half, from a peak of $2.7 billion in 1980 to $1.25 billion in 1982. To reduce the flow of unwanted diamonds to the CSO, De Beers had to be ruthless in cutting its own production, while the outside producers were required to limit deliveries to the level of their quotas, or maintain production and stockpile the excess on the mines at their own expense until the market recovered. As the mines in Botswana were producing categories of diamonds that could be sold, to cut back would have reduced the production of saleable as well as unsaleable stones. Debswana therefore continued in full production, placing in stock the categories that temporarily could not be sold, and in time built up an enormous stockpile, which the company had to finance. When the diamond market was firmly set on the road to recovery and people could give thought to the problems ahead, the disposal of that stockpile was one of the challenges that had to be faced.

Although Harry Oppenheimer resigned as chairman at the end of 1984, to be succeeded by Ogilvie Thompson, he continues to be an active member of the board. It was he who, prior to relinquishing the chairmanship, conceived the idea of utilizing the stockpile to enable Botswana, as the Western world's largest gem producer, to establish an even closer relationship with De Beers. It then fell to Ogilvie Thompson to lead the complex negotiations with the government over the stockpile and the renewal of the sales agreement. Eventually, in 1987, it was agreed that part of the stockpile would be exchanged for a five per cent shareholding in De Beers itself, with the government having the right to appoint two directors to the boards of De Beers and the DTC. "This was advantageous to both parties and important for the long-term stability of the industry," says Crawford. "It brought the Botswana government into the central structure of the industry and, as a participant in the survival of the whole business, confirmed its long-term commitment to sell through the CSO."

At the same time that Ogilvie Thompson was elected chairman, Nicky Oppenheimer, who earlier in 1984 had been sent to assist Sir Philip in London, became deputy chairman of De Beers. In April the next year he assumed overall responsibility for the London operations, and in February 1986 he was appointed chairman of the newly formed CSO executive committee.

Until then the CSO had been run effectively by a triumvirate headed by Sir Philip, with Charles responsible for the diamond side and Dawe in charge of the administrative side of its activities. "The system worked extremely well, so long as those three, with a century of diamond experience between them, were there," says Capon. "But the younger people moving up through the various departments into leading positions naturally hadn't been in the business as long, or gained as broad a view of the whole business, which would have been needed to continue running it in the same way."

"The way the organization had been run had been entirely in keeping with its size and the ethos of the time," Nicky Oppenheimer says, "but I hadn't had all their years of growing and creating to equip me for heading the office in the same way. Furthermore, the growth of the business necessitated that we bring the managers of the various departments more into the whole management process. So my appointment provided the opportunity to introduce a more devolved system. It was an important change, not in the philosophy but in the style of management, to one that is more in accord with the size of organization we have now."

The new management structure that Nicky Oppenheimer introduced replaced the triumvirate with an executive committee, chaired by himself, and diamond and administrative committees, headed respectively by Alex Barbour and Tim Capon.

"We had been worried for some time about the problem of giving younger people more opportunity, because there aren't as many high positions in the diamond business as there are in other businesses," says Sir Philip. "With Nicky's management structure, which gave expression to the policy of bringing forward the younger people, we've gone a long way towards solving the problem."

The restructuring provided a wider forum for discussion in the company, and the greater responsibility given to managers encouraged personal initiative and innovation. "Although the structure became more formal, the style of management has been freewheeling," says Capon. "Our offices are close together, we lunch together most days, and form an executive on a continuing basis, able to discuss problems as they come up, and eliminate a lot of bureaucratic processing." This has been possible, says Ralfe, because of the family character of the business: "Our size dictated that we adopt more formal structures, but the family content enabled us to avoid becoming rigidified into a bureaucracy in the way that more republican structures often are."

Nicky Oppenheimer had been appointed chairman of the CSO in the aftermath of the recession of the early eighties, which had highlighted the importance of being even closer than before to the marketplace, to try to ensure, among other things, that excess stocks do not accumulate in any section of the pipeline between the CSO and the ultimate consumer. This entailed having more people to gather, process and communicate information.

"Everything in the world is happening faster, and to fulfill our traditional role we have to have more and more information, so as to be able to foresee changes and react quickly to them," says Nicky Oppenheimer. "We had learnt the value of information during the recession, when, because of the retail promotions network my father initiated in the late thirties, we knew enough about what was going on at the retail end to detect the trend and make a good estimate of the final retail consumption. If there was one thing that kept De Beers, at the most senior level, encouraged that finally things would come right, in spite of the immense debt and our own sales plunging, it was that retail consumption of diamond jewellery continued at, not only a healthy, but a generally growing rate during those years. That gave us the incentive to discover more about what happens elsewhere in the pipeline, and led us to set up a research and information department and a marketing liaison department. We became more conscious of the fact that because of our pre-eminent position in the diamond business, everything that happens is of concern to us."

As the whole diamond industry ultimately rests on the demand for diamond jewellery, one may wonder whether the growth of demand can keep pace with increasing production indefinitely – whether there is a saturation point for diamond jewellery.

"If there is a limit to the long-term growth of demand for diamond jewellery worldwide it is certainly a very long way off," says Ogilvie Thompson. "Economic development around the world, with a greater number of people becoming more prosperous and having a larger proportion of their incomes available for discretionary spending, provides the potential for growth, in the traditional markets and particularly in the burgeoning prosperity of the newly industrialized economies of the Far East."

From the producer's point of view, the ability of the CSO to maintain market stability provides every incentive to prospect for diamonds and develop new mines. "With careful handling and a bit of luck, future supplies should meet increasing demand at steadily improving prices," says Ogilvie Thompson.

The most persistent criticism levelled at De Beers from *outside* the industry is that it is a "monopoly" and, for that reason, undesirable. Indeed, anti-trust legislation in the United States prevents it from doing business there. As De Beers' own production in South Africa and Namibia is at least equalled, in terms of value, by the productions of Botswana and the Soviet Union, and in terms of volume, by those of Zaire and Australia, it clearly cannot be claimed that it has a monopoly of production, but as it controls the marketing of some eighty per cent of rough gem diamonds, the CSO may be said to have brought about an oligopoly in distribution. The rationale for this is that gem diamonds are not an essential resource but a unique luxury product, which people may buy if they wish, according to the strength of their desire and how much of their income is available for luxury spending. Furthermore, it is argued, a centralized system of selling is vital to the stability, even the survival, of the whole industry, for only by regulating sales can stable prices be maintained, and if diamond prices were to fluctuate in the way that is normal with other commodities, nobody would want to buy diamonds.

"Given the inevitability of fluctuations in supply and changes in the stocks held by the trade, the need for the CSO system of sales is as great today as ever it was," says Ogilvie Thompson. "It has succeeded because it has been seen to serve the interests of everyone in the industry, from producer to end user, and at the bottom of their hearts they all hope that it will continue forever."

The position of De Beers as a major producer gave it direct control of a substantial part of the total production and a basis for persuading other producers to co-operate. Prudent management of its cash resources and investment outside the industry furnished it with the means to finance a surplus of diamonds when supplies exceeded the market's immediate demands. As the business grew, the CSO developed and refined the technical and sorting skills essential for handling the mammoth task of presenting to its clients, in a manner acceptable to them, some fifty million carats of gem diamonds a year. It cultivated close contact with the trade and created channels for receiving information from cutting centres and retail markets that enable it to react swiftly to changes. Having selling control over enough of the total production to warrant generic advertising, it could mount, on a scale that individual producers could not contemplate, an ongoing international promotional campaign to stimulate and broaden consumer demand for diamonds. And its success encouraged other producers to see advantage in selling through the CSO and in bad times accepting the quota system, upon which the whole edifice depends.

Independent rough diamond merchant Jack Lunzer with basins of boart that he has for sale in his London offices.

"The knowledge we have built up, the specialist skills we have perfected and continually update, collectively constitute a kind of moving patent that makes it unlikely that anyone else could take over our role," says Ogilvie Thompson. "Any major producer that chose to operate outside the system and challenge our position would run the risk of disrupting the whole industry and having to suffer for it along with the rest."

London rough diamond merchant Jack Lunzer, although in daily competition with De Beers, accepts that its influence works to the ultimate benefit of everyone in the industry. "We fight them tooth and nail over some things, but more often than not we find ourselves on the same side of the table where the industry as a whole is concerned," he says. "There isn't a financial institution in the world that would assume the responsibility for supporting the industry to the extent that they do, and for this we are all indebted to them."

"Certain basic things about the diamond business and De Beers' position in it are unchangeable, and any change could only be to the detriment of the whole business," says Bonas. "One feels about De Beers much as Voltaire felt about God: if it hadn't existed we would have had to invent it."

CHAPTER 7 THE PIPELINE

Small diamonds are fed through a pipe to a vibrating table which sorts them into sizes and shapes in the automatic sorting section at 2 Charterhouse Street.

To handle the enormous task of sorting some eighty per cent of the world's production of rough diamonds into five thousand categories, the CSO has had to develop a specialized technology to measure and sort diamonds automatically.

Accumulated knowledge, specialist skills and continuous innovation in sorting technology constitute a kind of moving patent that enables the CSO to react swiftly to changes in what the market is demanding.

Performing its traditional stabilizing role, the CSO maintains a fine balance between supply and demand, regulating the flow of diamonds through what is known in the trade as the "pipeline", which runs from Charterhouse Street successively to dealers and manufacturers, jewellery makers, wholesalers and retailers, and ultimately the consumers of diamond jewellery.

London sights week – in a private room at 17 Charterhouse Street a leading Antwerp sight-holder, Bram Laub, draws on his cigar, while Alex Barbour, head of the CSO's diamond division, examines a stone from his box. With them are Laub's broker, Ben Bonas, standing, and son Philippe Laub.

A rare gathering of rival DTC brokers and their assistants around a table heaped with sealed boxes. They are, from left, (seated) Gerald Rothschild and Willie Nagel, (standing) Christopher Hourmouzios, Jack Morgan, Brian Marr, Vivian Prins, Chris Dundas, Jack Abrahams, Mark Boston, Harry Stanfield and Ben Bonas.

Probably the most automated diamond factory in the world, the Lens Diamond Industries sawing factory at Berlaar, in the Kempen outside Antwerp, was established in the seventies to clear a blockage in the pipeline. Today six thousand computer-regulated saws produce enough sawn goods to keep ten thousand polishers in several countries busy at their wheels.

Sir Philip Oppenheimer

TEN TIMES A YEAR, at intervals of five weeks, some one hundred and fifty of the world's leading diamantaires from all the major cutting centres gather in London at 17 Charterhouse Street for "sights week", when The Diamond Trading Company presents its customers with the boxes of rough diamonds it has prepared for them. These are the diamond manufacturers and traders selected by the company to do business with it as "sight-holders". Once inside, behind heavy teak doors that frame diamond-shaped panes of thick, bevelled glass, they are conducted through broad, carpeted passages, between walls hung with an outstanding collection of contemporary art, to private rooms, where they are given their boxes and left to "sight" the contents at their leisure. This is where the "pipeline" – the conduit through which some eighty per cent of the world's gem diamonds pass from the CSO to cutter and polisher, wholesaler, jewellery manufacturer, retailer and finally consumer – begins.

The "Third Battalion", as the former guardsmen who make up the CSO's security corps describe themselves, parade in the reception hall at 17 Charterhouse Street (left), under the command of security manager Major P.A. Lewis, MBE. Teatime all the time – Winnie Crowley (right) has been serving tea and coffee on request to sight-holders for almost twenty years.

To an outsider the sights may seem to be something of a ritual, for neither the contents nor the price of the box is open to negotiation. The sight-holder must either accept his box as a whole at the asking price, or refuse it. He may complain and argue, but rejection is rare, not because there is any truth in the widely held belief that a client who refuses his box is not invited again, but because the relationship between the DTC and its clients is of a unique kind.

"When I try to explain this relationship to business friends outside the industry they think I'm making it up," says Vivian Prins, partner in the London diamond broking firm of I. Hennig. "No outsider is willing to believe that in difficult times a DTC client will actually apply for, come and see and pay a million dollars or more for goods on which he knows from the start that he will lose money, and that he does so as part of a long-term arrangement in which benefits eventually outweigh disadvantages."

"We will take the box, even if it is unsatisfactory, because the continuing relationship is more important to us than the individual purchase," says Belgian sight-holder Charles Trau. "We may be able to get a parcel more cheaply outside, but not regularly, not in the quantities we need – and we can't base our whole business on an occasional parcel."

"We may not always get what we want, because the DTC, in making its allocations, has to consider what it is doing from a world viewpoint and take many factors into account," says another Belgian sight-holder, Alfred Lachowsky. "But being a sight-holder assures us of a constant supply, and it is important to be sure of regularly getting a basic quantity, even if we have to shop around for the rest of our requirements."

And why, if they know they will accept their boxes regardless, do they bother to attend sights at all? "Partly to see what we will be receiving, so that we can prepare ourselves for handling it, partly for contact with fellow diamantaires and partly because it gives us an opportunity to discuss our problems and requirements with DTC people," says Trau. A further reason for attending, for those who buy large stones, is that the prices of diamonds over 10.8 carats are settled by negotiation.

Clearly there is also a certain cachet attached to being a sight-holder. As Prins says: "Nothing enhances a man's reputation in our business as much; just as some people would rather receive a knighthood than make more money, the diamond man wants to be a Syndicate client."

"Syndicate" clients are of two kinds. Most are manufacturers, who immediately turn the rough they buy into polished and sell it to polished wholesalers or jewellery manufacturers. A number, however, are dealers, who receive large boxes, which they split into smaller units and more specialized assortments for resale to manufacturers who do not qualify to buy from the DTC. As they may also extend credit to their customers, they assist in both distribution and finance.

"We hope that the clients we choose will participate in a genuine building up of the industry, rather than trying to create a sort of short-term speculative commodity market," says CSO diamond division head Alex Barbour.

The criteria for selection are stringent. "A sight-holder must be well established and have diamond expertise," says DTC director of sales Nigel Wisden. "It is also very important that he has substantial capital. If he is a manufacturer, he not only needs to pay cash for the sight, but must also finance the work in progress for several months. If he is a dealer, he may have to hold stocks because of market fluctuations and also extend credit to his clients. The market itself wants us to have strong clients who will be able to carry on the trade. We don't necessarily limit their number, but we want to be sure that they won't fall by the wayside when demand weakens."

"A sight-holder must have the determination to survive in difficult as well as easy conditions, the courage to lay it on the line, instead of running for cover, in recessionary times," says Prins.

For a would-be sight-holder there is no way to the DTC but through one of the broking firms accredited by the DTC – I. Hennig, Bonas and Co, W. Nagel, J. Morgan and H. Goldie – and it may take him many years to achieve. After he is accepted, he continues to work through the intermediacy of his broker in his dealings with the company. The brokers mediate, helping each to understand the other's point of view.

"If we feel that an individual is suitable, we will try to interest the DTC in him, so that it will watch his progress," says Prins. "Someone whose business is growing is more attractive to it than someone who may be bigger but has stopped growing. But because the DTC prefers to sell in large lots, the size of a man's operation is also taken into account. Given two companies of equal choice, the larger usually gets the green light."

"When we endorse a prospective client our own credibility is at stake," says Hennig's senior partner Gerald Rothschild. "We assure the DTC that he is the sort of person they insist on, putting his case to the best of our ability, but without exaggerating his claims, as he might be inclined to do himself. Our first duty is to our clients, but we also have a duty to keep the DTC informed in a balanced way about what is going on; it is in nobody's interest to mislead the DTC. We are in a sense brokers of trust, building trust between our clients and the DTC. We would have no role if the DTC didn't trust us."

As generally a broker will be representing several clients who are competing with one another as sight-holders or aspirant sight-holders, he must continually be aware of which cap he is wearing. "When presenting prospective clients to the DTC, I avoid entering into comparisons," says Willie Nagel. "I point out the advantages of each, and it is up to the DTC to find the drawbacks and decide between them. If the DTC points out drawbacks to me, I will try to minimize them, but I cannot deny them."

"It's the DTC's responsibility to decide how they cut the cake; we must simply try and convince them of the good qualities of each individual, without claiming that the person is better or stronger than he really is," says Ben Bonas.

Brokers receive no payment from the DTC. Sight-holders pay their brokers a commission on the value of their sights in line with market practice.

In deciding whether to give a candidate a sight an important consideration is the range of goods that he specializes in. When the DTC is receiving a surplus of small goods and not enough large goods to satisfy existing customers who specialize in large goods, it is more likely to grant a sight to a specialist in small goods. For this reason, a client is granted a sight in a particular range.

"That is what he was accepted for, and that is what he gets," says Wisden. "Being wholesalers, we make up boxes for a client that contain the type of diamonds that he requires. If he wants something extra, we may include it in his box. But the chances are that if he is asking for something new it is because the market wants it; other clients will, therefore, also be asking for it, and the supply will have been fully allocated. The only reason he would want to change his range completely would be if what he is getting has become unpopular and unprofitable, and we would then try to accommodate him in a different range."

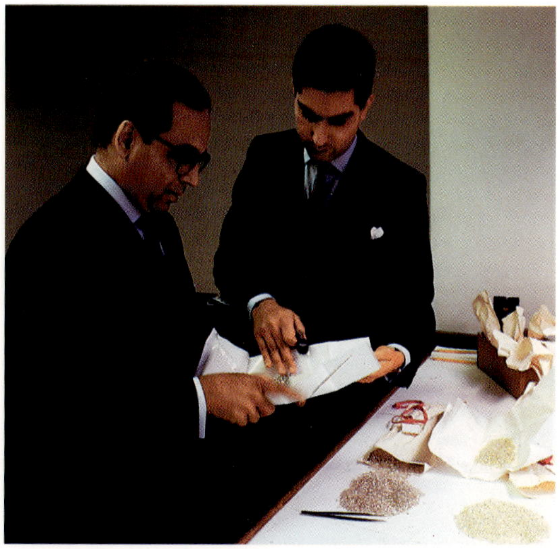

Sight-holder Madhu Mehta, wearing spectacles, discusses his box with Rajiv Bhandari, the CSO representative assigned to him during sights week.

A sight-holder's speciality is usually related to the cutting centre in which he operates, because the centres themselves have tended to concentrate on manufacturing particular size and quality ranges. Before World War II the principal cutting centres were Antwerp, New York and, to a declining extent, Amsterdam. For reasons that will receive fuller treatment in a later chapter, the industry in Amsterdam failed to survive the war, while European diamantaires who fled to Palestine for the duration of hostilities were so successful in establishing a cutting industry in and around Tel Aviv that after the war the DTC began awarding sights to manufacturers there. In India, a small cutting industry that employed about ten thousand people in 1947, grew rapidly to the stage where participants could be numbered in the hundred thousands, and in 1964 the DTC started giving regular sights to Indian manufacturers. Owing to higher labour costs, Antwerp and New York today specialize in manufacturing the larger, better quality stones, as the labour component of their manufactured value is relatively small. Israel has found its niche in manufacturing medium-sized stones of good quality, particularly fancy cuts, while India, with its abundance of cheaper labour, is able to manufacture enormous quantities of very small, poor quality stones.

"We have an interest in supporting all the established cutting centres and try to supply each with the type of goods it needs, without favouring one centre at the expense of another," says Nicky Oppenheimer.

Three or four weeks before a sight the sight-holders apply, through their brokers, for the goods they want. If the market is strong, and if the supplies are available, they may get everything they asked for. Alternatively, when, in the DTC's opinion, to supply everything applied for would put too many diamonds into the pipeline and weaken the market, they get less. They only know what they are getting when the sight is announced.

On his frequent business trips to India, Rajiv Bhandari, who works at the CSO's "Indian desk" in London, regularly sees his parents, Major-General and Mrs K.K. Bhandari, who live in Bombay.

"The DTC decides on the size of the sight and in which types of goods, and then divides the cake as it sees fit between the clients it has for those types of goods," says Prins. "In this it is entirely autocratic, for it is part of its skill that it makes the best possible allocation. Under-allocation may lead to speculation, and over-allocation to a weaker market. The DTC has to decide on the size of the sight six weeks ahead, and still get it right – and they are very good at it."

But the sight-holders are seldom completely satisfied. To their way of thinking, they receive either too little of what they want, or too much of what they don't want.

"When a client feels he is not getting enough, I must try to keep him happy with what he has and at the same time push the DTC to give him more," says Nagel. "In bad times I have to encourage my clients to take the longer view and accept their goods, even though they may be losing money, because when good times return they will need their connection with the DTC."

During sights week the brokers visit their clients in the rooms assigned to them at 17 Charterhouse Street and sort out any problems that may arise. If they feel a client has a legitimate complaint they will convey it tactfully to the DTC official immediately concerned, and take it higher if necessary. "The client's complaint is noted and could be taken into account when we make up his box for the next sight," says Wisden.

"It happens in negotiations that a client becomes overheated, and we have to patch up the wounds and try to bring the two sides together again in such a way that everybody saves face," says Prins. "Often the best way is for the broker to accept the responsibility for a silly mistake that was not his. It's diamond diplomacy."

Deputy chairman of the CSO and head of its diamond division Alex Barbour (left) with some of his "toys" – the large goods.
Senior sorting staff at 17 Charterhouse Street (right) blend productions from many lands to make the CSO's London selling mixture.

Technically the deal is concluded on a handshake, but often the formality is dispensed with. The box is returned, the weights are checked by the DTC and verified by the broker, the goods are invoiced, the client pays and the goods are shipped to him. Ten days later his "shopping list" for the next sight goes in.

The London sights are the culmination of an immense and complex operation that requires great expertise in the gathering and processing of intelligence about every aspect of the diamond business world-wide.

Although the size of the sights may be influenced by short-term changes in the levels of stocks held at different stages of the pipeline, in the long run it is the consumer demand for diamond jewellery at the one end that decides what the DTC puts in at the other. While this demand grows steadily with increasing affluence round the world, the demand for particular size and quality ranges fluctuates in accordance with what at different times and in different places people are able to spend on luxuries. "The CSO therefore has to conduct its trade in rough diamonds with the consumer in mind, and in such a way as to ensure stability and confidence in the price of diamond jewellery, so that the luxury article does have a lasting value," says Julian Ogilvie Thompson. "This, in turn, enables the trade at all levels to operate smoothly."

Tempting though it may be at times to take advantage of a strong market and increase prices, the CSO has to be wary of short-term gain and adhere to the policy of maintaining stable prices for rough diamonds, increasing its own selling prices at least to match inflation, but only to the extent that they can be maintained and that the resulting polished diamonds can be sold in jewellery at prices acceptable to the consumer. "We have to resist the easy option when times are good," says Nicky Oppenheimer. "We can make profits, but we have to be careful how we do it, so as not to spoil the market and harm ourselves in the process." In recessionary times CSO prices may be higher than rough prices on the market, and in boom times lower. What its clients lose on the swings they gain on the roundabouts.

The physical task of preparing several million carats of gem diamonds for every sight is an awesome undertaking that demands the skills of more than six hundred highly trained sorting staff as well as continual technological innovation in the sizing, sorting, weighing and parcelling of diamonds. "Diamonds of all kinds come in here from different producers and have to be sorted and presented in a form that a client can use: the right blend, the right sort of diamond for his purposes," says Barbour.

All the diamonds received in London from various sources are combined in the "London selling mixture", which consists of a full range of sizes, colours, qualities and shapes that can only be obtained by mixing all the productions together. "Each production has its own characteristics, which at different times may be more or less popular than those of other productions," explains Gary Ralfe. "Pooling them brings together the strengths of diamonds from different sources, which are then blended to particular types." Only certain qualities of Australian diamonds, which are so different in appearance that they cannot be blended with other productions, are sold separately.

Applying technology to solve problems in sorting, valuing, discerning flaws and working gem diamonds – Garry Stewart, technical director of the CSO and head of the research and development centre at Maidenhead, at his scanning electron microscope.

The sorting operation occupies ten floors of two buildings in London. "The diamonds are sorted against standard samples," says Jack Young, CSO director in charge of sorting. "These samples ensure that CSO sorting offices throughout the world are producing an identical assortment, and that our clients can rely on a consistent presentation. The entire assortment is made up of over five thousand categories, each grouping together diamonds of the same size, shape, colour and quality. Diamonds below .75 carats are sorted by sieve-size rather than weight because the sheer volume of stones produced in these sizes makes it impractical to weigh them individually. From the start of the sorting process, diamonds above 10.8 carats are handled separately."

DTC prices are based on the probable value that the rough stones will have after being polished. "But remember, we're sorting millions of carats into thousands of categories, and to value every stone individually is plainly impossible," says Young. "Only diamonds over 10.8 carats are valued individually; for all the others, we have to assume that over the particular range a manufacturer buys from us, he expects to get a certain overall return from the polished article. Working back from that estimated return, we calculate an average value for each category of rough."

"In any negotiations between our buyers and a producer, or between DTC sales staff and a sight-holder, both sides are looking for the best value that can be achieved by manufacturing," says Young. "They consider what the final colour will be and, in terms of the flaws in the stone, its likely value if the best of several approaches to manufacturing it is adopted. There are always alternatives, and so buyers approach a stone differently, although all with the idea of getting the most out of it."

The problem of having to sort very high volumes of small, low quality diamonds from Zaire – and later Australia – led in 1982 to the establishment at Maidenhead of a research and development centre to devise mechanized systems to measure and sort diamonds automatically. "Our brief is to be able to provide a technical solution to any problem associated with the sorting, valuing, discernment of flaws in and working of gem diamonds," says Garry Stewart, who heads the centre. "It is the CSO's job to even out the peaks and troughs in the market, and it is ours to give it the technical means to react quickly to them."

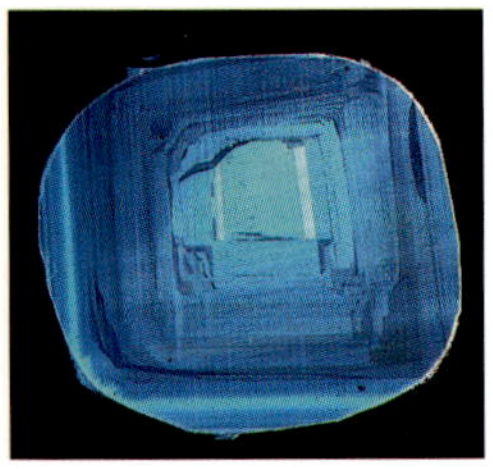

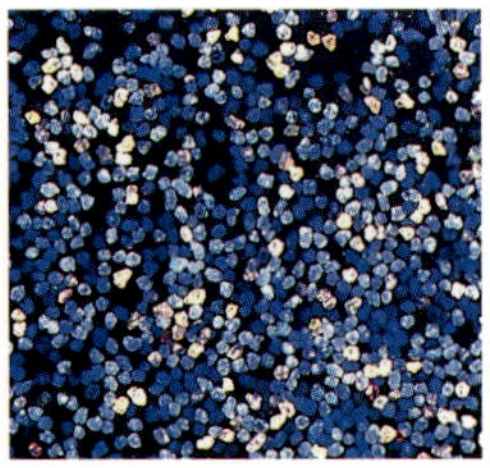

Seen in cross-section under a microscope a diamond displays what look like the annual growth rings of trees.

Fluorescent in ultraviolet light, diamonds behave differently in infra-red light or under X-ray.

The emphasis at Maidenhead is on perfecting tools to do the more tedious routine work of handling low-value articles in volume, and so to free skilled personnel for doing the more interesting work and doing it more thoroughly. The centre has developed, and continually improves on, machines capable of sorting diamonds in terms of their size, weight and, to some extent, their average colour and shape. "We are working on the easier things that mechanization can handle," says Stewart. "There are certain things, such as assessing the effect that cracks, piqués and different sawing options will have on value, that can still be done better by hand and eye, but eventually technology will be able to do them too."

All the machines developed at the centre are designed to be linked to computers, and details of the operations they perform are automatically recorded in the company's data base, giving the DTC accurate, up to date information to enable it to reduce its reaction time to market changes that require changes in sorting. "The control problem is vast," says Stewart. "Every stone is handled a dozen times or more during processing, and the DTC needs an organizational system that can handle it quickly and smoothly if it is to sell what everybody requires – which is different for every sight – and still keep control."

The cares of the DTC do not end when it sells its diamonds. After they enter the pipeline, which starts at Charterhouse Street, they pass through the hands of, and at different stages belong to, manufacturers, wholesalers of polished diamonds, jewellery manufacturers, retailers and jewellery catalogue houses all over the world. If an accumulation of stocks builds up and causes a blockage at any stage, the market further back up the pipeline is weakened. When the blockage is caused by speculative stockpiling, there may be shortages resulting in unstable, artificially high prices further down the pipeline. "We must see to it that the manufacturers neither over supply nor under supply the market," says Barbour. "At the same time we have to monitor the whole pipeline to ascertain whether blockages are occurring, identify the problems and see what we can do to ease the flow. We must ensure that not only our clients, but their clients and their clients' clients have the through-flow."

The complex structure of companies, subsidiaries, divisions and departments by means of which all this is achieved today has evolved over a long period. Parts of it bear the stamp of having been in the long-term plan from the start, others have come into being in response to new problems, and have been built into the plan along the way.

"The CSO knew very little about what was happening in the market when I started in the business," says Harry Oppenheimer. "We put what we thought were the right prices on the diamonds we sold and adjusted them when we saw that demand for particular qualities was rising, but our knowledge of what was occurring in the cutting industries in different countries was slight. Now we know a great deal, and our pricing of diamonds is a much more scientific business than it used to be."

Until Monty Charles became director of sorting and valuation in 1958, scant attention was given to what became of the diamonds in the pipeline. "The way in which we went about sorting, valuing and selling had to be completely re-organized in order to bring the business forward into the modern era," he recalls. "Needing to know more about what was happening outside, we sent our staff out to work in cutting factories, to learn about the qualities of diamonds from the manufacturer's point of view, and into the market-places of the world, to find out what was going on there."

"Where formerly the role of our sales staff had been largely administrative, they became experts, able to assess diamonds and discuss them in minute detail with sightholders," says Wisden. "Visiting clients' businesses between sights, to gather the information we need to determine the size of future sights and how much we should sell in different ranges, became a regular part of their work."

In the early sixties the CSO realized that Flemish diamond cutters in the Kempen, the countryside around Antwerp, were having difficulty in obtaining sufficient rough for their cottage industry in competition with the burgeoning manufacturing industry in Bombay and Surat, which could polish their type of goods more cheaply and so afford to pay more for it on the Antwerp market. Having no wish to see the skills and enterprise of this region lost to the industry, the CSO made more rough available to them through an Antwerp dealing company.

For an understanding of what was happening on the rough market one clearly needed knowledge of the polished market, but the two are worlds apart, and to know the polished world it was necessary to enter it to a limited extent. The CSO had no intention of going into competition with its clients, but it needed to have, as it were, a window on their world.

"It would be difficult to get an accurate idea of the value of polished on the market without some small participation in it," says Jeremy Richdale, who today heads the CSO's polished division. "Like paintings, diamonds aren't really comparable purely on the basis of measurement. No two are alike, and they are never presented in the same way. What the retailers say they sell is different to what the suppliers say they supply them with, and what they tell us they've been selling doesn't necessarily accord with the way that the CSO grades diamonds. There are even more grades in polished than there are in rough, and we need a more accurate translation from polished into rough. The valuation of rough depends on what polished will come out of it and what it will fetch on the market, and determining the relationship between rough and polished is our most important purpose. We manufacture boxes of rough, to find out what polished comes out of them, and then sell the polished on the market to find out what the price is."

In his Ramat-Gan office Henri Brunner, chairman of Diamdel in Tel Aviv (left), discusses a parcel he is offering for sale with a client.
Gabi Tolkowsky, manager of Diatrada in Antwerp (below left), in philosophical mood as he toys with the 599-carat Centenary Diamond.

"The polished division helps the sales department to anticipate strengths and weaknesses in the market and to advise the executive on what and how much we should be selling," says Wisden. "What the consumer wants is what the jewellery manufacturer wants, is what our client wants, and through the polished division this sort of information gets back to us much faster than formerly."

In 1967 an associated company, Diatrada, was set up in Antwerp to manufacture and trade in polished diamonds, and thereby to gather accurate market intelligence. It is managed by Gabi Tolkowsky, under whose direction part of the cutting operation is dedicated to developing new cuts, particularly for problematic Australian diamonds.

"When the Australian production, much of which has a brownish colour, started coming through in the eighties, we had a problem in determining values and how much the market could absorb," says Richdale. "The value would of course be what the market would pay for polished brown diamonds. So we polished a number to test the market, and developed new cuts, such as the Fire Rose and Marigold, to suit their qualities and enhance their attraction. The relatively high cost of working them was another factor affecting their value. Owing to their peculiar characteristics, they take thirty per cent longer to polish than stones from other sources, and the polishing wheels wear out more rapidly. So we did research into developing new wheels for polishing Australian diamonds. And for grading purposes we had to define degrees of brownness that had not previously been reflected in the selling assortment."

Most of the polished division's diamonds are manufactured in Portugal, at a factory that belongs to Sociedade Portuguesa de Lapidação de Diamantes. When after Independence the Angolan government nationalized Diamang's assets in Angola, the Portuguese government responded by nationalizing the company's assets in Lisbon, which included the factory. Cut off from its source of rough, the factory has been able to continue operating by polishing DTC rough under contract to the CSO's polished division, which sells the production in London, exclusively to DTC sight-holders, to avoid competing with them.

"There is no way we could, nor would we want to, polish all the diamonds we market, or even a part of them," says Ogilvie Thompson. "The manufacturing business is highly entrepreneurial, and we couldn't hope to get people to work for us for a salary with the same dedication that they have when working with a profit motive in their family businesses. Manufacturers also have between them a good few billion dollars of their own capital invested in the business, on which they borrow more. There is private investment at all stages of the pipeline, and the industry couldn't do without it."

Diamonds being placed in the dops (left) that will hold them while they are being "sawn" automatically with a laser cutter at the Lens sawing factory at Berlaar, outside Antwerp. A laser saw operator at Lens inserts a dop with a diamond into the saw feed (below left) while watching the closed-circuit television screen to ensure that the diamond already on the cutting line is held at the correct angle during sawing.

A study of clients undertaken in the seventies revealed that a number who had been faithful customers for many years were in fact not manufacturing their boxes but simply selling them on the market. After much agonizing, the DTC deprived them of their sights, so that the diamonds they were receiving could be allocated to others who would manufacture and keep moving them.

"It was revolutionary stuff," says Anthony Oppenheimer, "but it was essential that we prune our list of customers, and in the process the number of our sight-holders was halved. Those taken off our list couldn't have carried losses if there'd been a severe downturn in the market, and they wouldn't have been able to continue taking boxes, because they couldn't have sold them on. We needed to know that our goods were going to strong customers who would be able to stick with us in difficult times."

During the boom years of the early seventies a blockage occurred in the pipeline because there were too few sawyers to cope with all the "sawables" that needed to be sawn before they could be polished. DTC clients were unable to move their stocks quickly enough to finance future sights, and the DTC found itself sitting on large stocks of small sawables. To saw these stones before selling them would not only enable its clients to commence manufacturing and moving them without delay, but would place the DTC in a position where, should there be a sudden surge in demand, it could level the market more effectively by releasing stocks of "sawn" that would bypass the sawing bottleneck.

In collaboration with Jan Lens, a leading Antwerp manufacturer, Lens Diamond Industries was established, and in 1974 a sawing factory was built to his specifications at Berlaar, in the heart of the Kempen, where it could give work to under-employed craftsmen and draw on their traditional skills. Since then it has grown into probably the most automated diamond factory in the world. Of six hundred staff, two hundred are sawyers, who between them mind six thousand computer-regulated saws. According to Carlos De Meyere, who succeeded Lens as managing director, the factory produces enough sawn goods to keep ten thousand polishers in several countries busy at their wheels, and encourages more mechanization in manufacturing by providing quantities of the type of stone that can be polished automatically on Piermatic machines.

"We are in a period when science, in the form of computers and lasers, is coming more and more into a very traditional trade," says De Meyere. "So we also have a research function, in which we are trying to determine precisely what the diamond skills consist of, and to construct mathematical models of them. The difficulty is that the craft lies in all the senses of the craftsman. Ask a sawyer what he is doing, and he will say that the stone he is working on doesn't have a good feel, that it trembles a bit, that it's too hot, that the colour is wrong, or that it doesn't sound or smell right."

As sawn goods have to be re-sorted before they can be sold, the Belgian Sorting Company was formed in Antwerp in 1977 to sort the Lens production and send it on to London for inclusion in DTC sights.

In boom times, when the industry is making good profits, diamantaires may be inclined to question whether they need the CSO, but when the market weakens and prices are threatened they are thankful that it is there to withhold supplies and relieve the pressure on the cutting centres.

The ability and willingness of the CSO to support the market has never been more severely tested than during the "boom and bust cycle" of the late seventies and early eighties. At a time when hyper-inflation was causing a flight of money into tangibles, speculation in gold with money made in oil drove up the prices of gold and silver, and the runaway increase of the gold price, from an average of $304 a fine ounce in 1979 to a peak of $850 in January 1980, gave rise in certain quarters to the notion of an "investment diamond".

"The sudden injection of hundreds of millions of dollars into the market, without any comparable increase in production, stimulated greater speculation, which was fuelled by the eagerness of banks to advance money for buying diamonds," says George Burne, the DTC's diamond consultant in southern Africa, who was joint sales director in London at the time. "In Israel, where inflation was over a hundred per cent, the government was lending money at six per cent, thus enabling diamantaires to speculate, secure in the knowledge that what they bought in the morning would surely be worth more by afternoon. Almost everywhere, people who had neither the knowledge nor the expertise began speculating in diamonds, putting their trust in certificates of quality issued by various organizations, not all of them reliable."

"People saw diamonds as a one-way ticket to wealth," says London diamantaire Milos Vainer. "The CSO had preserved an orderly market for so long, that everybody believed that prices would continue to rise faster than either inflation or interest rates, and this gave excessive confidence to clients to borrow money, to the banks to lend money, and to everybody to buy diamonds."

"Because there had been no crisis in the diamond world since the war, even bankers tended to believe there would never be one," confirms Antwerp banker Paul De Groote. "There was a tendency to believe everybody and to follow everybody, and with the prime bank rate at one point reaching almost twenty-five per cent, the bankers were inclined to follow too, and so everybody became involved in the boom, to their cost."

Believing that the stability of the industry depended on the steady demand for diamonds by consumers who wanted to wear them for their beauty and enduring value, the CSO had never promoted diamonds for speculative investment. It warned the banks that the market was unsound, and advised them not to lend money to diamantaires on collateral of diamonds valued at the "casino" prices they were paying. But the warnings and advice went unheeded, and although the CSO did its best to discourage the investment market, it was powerless to respond in the traditional way and cool it down by increasing supplies; the types of diamond most sought after by investors had always been in short supply.

At the best of times only about fifteen per cent by value (two per cent by carats) of the CSO's sales were suitable for the investment market in terms of colour, quality and size, and the shortage of suitable stones was exacerbated by promoters who punted certain items, particularly the celebrated one-carat D-flawless, as the ultimate "investment diamond".

"Because there are relatively few of them about, the price rose steeply, and because people were paying more for them, they began demanding higher standards," says Wisden. "Where normally a diamond is classified flawless if no flaws are visible under the ten-times magnification of a jeweller's loup, they began examining them under microscopes. As even fewer diamonds could pass the microscope test, the effect was to further restrict the supply of the very stones that speculators were demanding, and the price of the magic one-carat D-flawless, which had been $1650 in 1971, went through the roof and rose exponentially from $16 000 in 1978 to $65 000 two years later, when gold peaked."

"This comparative rarity gained unreasonable importance as a market indicator for the prices of not only the so-called investment diamonds, but of polished diamonds in general, thereby affecting sentiment in the retail market for the more expensive type of jewellery," says Ogilvie Thompson. "In spite of everything we did, including pushing production from De Beers' own mines and drawing down CSO stocks to put all the goods we could muster onto the market, prices of polished stones rose to levels that bore no relation to either the CSO's selling prices or the prices they could command as items of jewellery in the retail trade."

From the collection of Johannesburg diamantaire and jeweller Rob Schwartz, a perfectly proportioned one-carat D-flawless, the ultimate so-called "investment diamond" of the late seventies that peaked at $65 000 in 1980, just before over-speculation caused prices of large polished diamonds to crash.

Early in 1981 the market for "investment" diamonds began to falter. With the return of realistic interest rates and indications that governments were at last set to tackle inflation, investors began converting back into money. The withdrawal of funds weakened the market, confidence ebbed and, in what Ogilvie Thompson describes as a "classic example of speculation feeding on itself, followed by over-reaction at the top of the cycle", the market crashed, and the one-carat D-flawless plummeted to below $20 000.

"Everyone in the chain, from the retail jeweller backwards, sought to reduce his stocks," he says. "Prices of polished in the cutting centres, having gone up too far and too fast, came down rapidly, with the result that the market in investment diamonds fell into disrepute, and the diamond business as a whole became the victim of adverse publicity it did not deserve."

"The outcome had been predictable from the start, but it happened very quickly," says Wisden. "Being human, many speculators had believed that they would be the last to cash in before the crash, and when it came they were left holding the goods they had accumulated, with no outlet for them. As values tumbled by more than fifty per cent, anyone working with fifty per cent borrowed capital was bankrupted." In the cutting centres, many large companies that had been in the business for generations were wiped out almost overnight. Particularly hard hit was Israel, where the speculation had started and had been greatest.

The CSO's difficulties were compounded by the fact that during the boom phase of the cycle the contract producers, well aware of the extravagant premiums being paid on the polished market, had pressed for higher returns for themselves. The CSO, knowing that the boom would not last forever, and not wanting to be left with an unduly high price structure after the market turned, decided on a compromise, and took the novel step of adding surcharges to its list prices of rough. The surcharges were not popular with the trade, or even among producers, and in time they were incorporated into a price increase. With hindsight, however, it would have been preferable to revert to them, instead of the price increases adopted toward the closing stages of the boom, for when the market turned the negative effect on demand was greater than it would have been otherwise.

"The situation had been unique, and the concept of the surcharge had been a good one," says De Beers' financial director Bertie Lincoln. "Our mistake was that, instead of retaining it as a device that could always be withdrawn, we decided to raise our prices and were hoisted with our own petard."

To relieve pressure on the cutting centres, the CSO slashed its sales by half in 1981, holding back particularly the larger top quality stones that by then nobody wanted, because the pipeline was already choked with them. During the five years that the recession lasted, CSO sales dropped by more than half, to a low point of $1.25 billion in 1982. At least half of the sales were in smaller and cheaper diamonds, which, as they had not been speculative items, had been relatively unscathed by the crash, and still found a ready market in the expanding Indian cutting industry, which likewise had not been seriously affected. At the same time the CSO introduced changes in its sorting and classification of diamonds to accommodate more precisely the individual needs of sight-holders under the changed market conditions.

"The effect of all this was that the stock of diamonds held and financed by the De Beers group increased very substantially," says Ogilvie Thompson. "And as the cash-flow wasn't enough to finance the interest, we had to commit the large cash resources we had built up over the years and borrow more than $1 billion against our investments outside the business. Although interest rates rose to an unprecedented level and remained there far longer than we had thought they would, we considered it part of our function to carry large stocks for as long as it took to reduce the stocks already in the pipeline."

Not wanting to add to the stockpile it was obliged to finance, and needing to reduce expenditure drastically, De Beers cut back production, closing two mines and a number of plants on other mines, reducing the labour force by a quarter and dividends by half. In addition, to reduce the flow of unwanted diamonds from contract producers to the CSO, the quota system was implemented. At the same time, Dicorp buying offices increased their purchases of rough on the free market to support the price. At the other end of the pipeline, the emphasis of consumer marketing was altered to promote internationally the types of diamonds that were not then in much demand.

"Instead of running for cover, De Beers put its money into backing the business and setting it on its feet again," says Prins. "Probably the key thing it did was to demonstrate its commitment by announcing that it would support the industry and had the resources to do so. It continued to buy diamonds from producers, and gave effective price support by buying large parcels of goods that desperate people would otherwise have allowed to go very cheaply. By creating a floor price in this way it helped restore confidence. In the end it was its financial strength that counted: the power not to allow the market to have more diamonds than are good for it."

The CSO realized that, in spite of all its efforts to keep in touch with the industry – with the manufacturers and dealers through the sales department, the polished market through the polished division and the retail jewellery trade through the consumer and advertising division – there had been grey areas in its information about the pipeline. To colour them in, it established, as mentioned in the previous chapter, a new department under Michael Grantham, formerly head of sales, assisted by Harry Garnett, also from sales, to undertake the function of marketing liaison, an important task which Nicky Oppenheimer felt had been overlooked for too long. By developing and working closely with new contacts in the cutting centres, the jewellery manufacturing centres and the consumer markets, the new department supplements and extends knowledge of what is happening in the various sections of the industry, particularly in regard to stock levels, movements of goods, the trading patterns and jewellery manufacturing requirements.

"The problem was obviously not in the consumer market for diamond jewellery, where sales increased appreciably every year of the recession but one," says Wisden. "The real problem was the stocks that had accumulated outside our control, and it took time to get them moved through the pipeline and to re-establish confidence in diamonds and the CSO. As a lot of money had been lost, a lot had gone out of the business, and we had to work at bringing it back into the business again."

Between 1980 and 1984 the value of stocks held by the De Beers group more than doubled to $1.95 billion, while those in the pipeline were reduced by some $5 billion. In 1985, however, the group was able to reduce its stocks by $52 million, and stocks in the cutting centres were lowered to the point where CSO sales could again be more directly related to retail demand. And when in 1986 it became evident that the cutting centres were again in a position to finance expansion, without having to borrow more from the banks, it was possible for the group to divest itself of another $51 million worth of stocks.

Where CSO sales of $1.6 billion in 1984 were up only one per cent on the previous year, they increased thirteen per cent in 1985. While the CSO offered for sale only the types of diamonds for which there was an immediate demand and continued withholding the larger and better quality stones, demand progressively broadened into these sizes and categories. When in 1986 normal, profitable trading returned to all sectors of the industry, CSO sales rose forty per cent to $2.56 billion and it was again able to sell all sizes and qualities. The balance between the demand for diamonds from the CSO and the current production available from its many sources around the world had been restored.

Having triumphantly weathered the storm, the CSO was able to announce that its sales during 1987 had increased by another twenty per cent to a record of over $3 billion, and De Beers could declare its highest dividend ever in its Centenary year, when sales established a new threshold of over $4 billion.

"Diamantaires who complain about De Beers and the CSO often make the mistake of expecting them to be some sort of philanthropic society," says Abraham Fischler, chairman of the Beurs voor Diamanthandel in Antwerp. "They are there to defend their own business, and to defend it well. The better they defend it the better it is, in the long run, for all of us."

DTC sight-holders' boxes arrive at the import/export room in the Diamond Exchange Building at Ramat-Gan. A diamond security officer and officials from the Diamond Controller's office unpack the consignment, looking for the box addressed to the eager sight-holder on the right.

CHAPTER 8 DIAMOND CAPITAL

Antwerp, an important diamond cutting centre since the fifteenth century, took over from Amsterdam as the capital of the polished diamond world after World War II.

Although the diamond manufacturing industry in Antwerp has declined since the mid-sixties, owing to competition from countries that can manufacture more cheaply, it has sustained itself by specializing in larger and more difficult stones, and remains the principal trading centre.

Independent producers and traders go there to sell their rough, manufacturers to replenish their supplies of rough and sell their productions of polished, dealers and jewellery manufacturers to buy polished.

The availability of a complete range of goods derived from many sources, the tradition of excellence, the success of the government in creating a free trading climate, all contribute to preserving Antwerp's position as Diamond Capital.

The trading floor of the Beurs voor Diamanthandel, second largest, in terms of trading turnover, of Antwerp's four diamond bourses. Although today most of the trading is done in private offices, the bourses are important meeting places, where diamantaires exchange gossip and keep in touch with everything happening in the market.

It is flowers that make money in parts of the Kempen today, and the polishing wheels have become decorations. Jeff Diels is one of the two self-employed cutters left in Vorselaar, where previously there were more than a hundred. The workshop in which he once employed forty polishers is now a hot-house for his plants.

International stars and groups take part in the Diamond Awards Festival of pop music held annually at the Sport-paleis in Antwerp and sponsored by the city's diamond community, who contribute stones used in the diamond-studded trophies that participants receive for their contributions to contemporary music.
The event attracts live audiences of twenty-five thousand and is televised to millions world-wide.

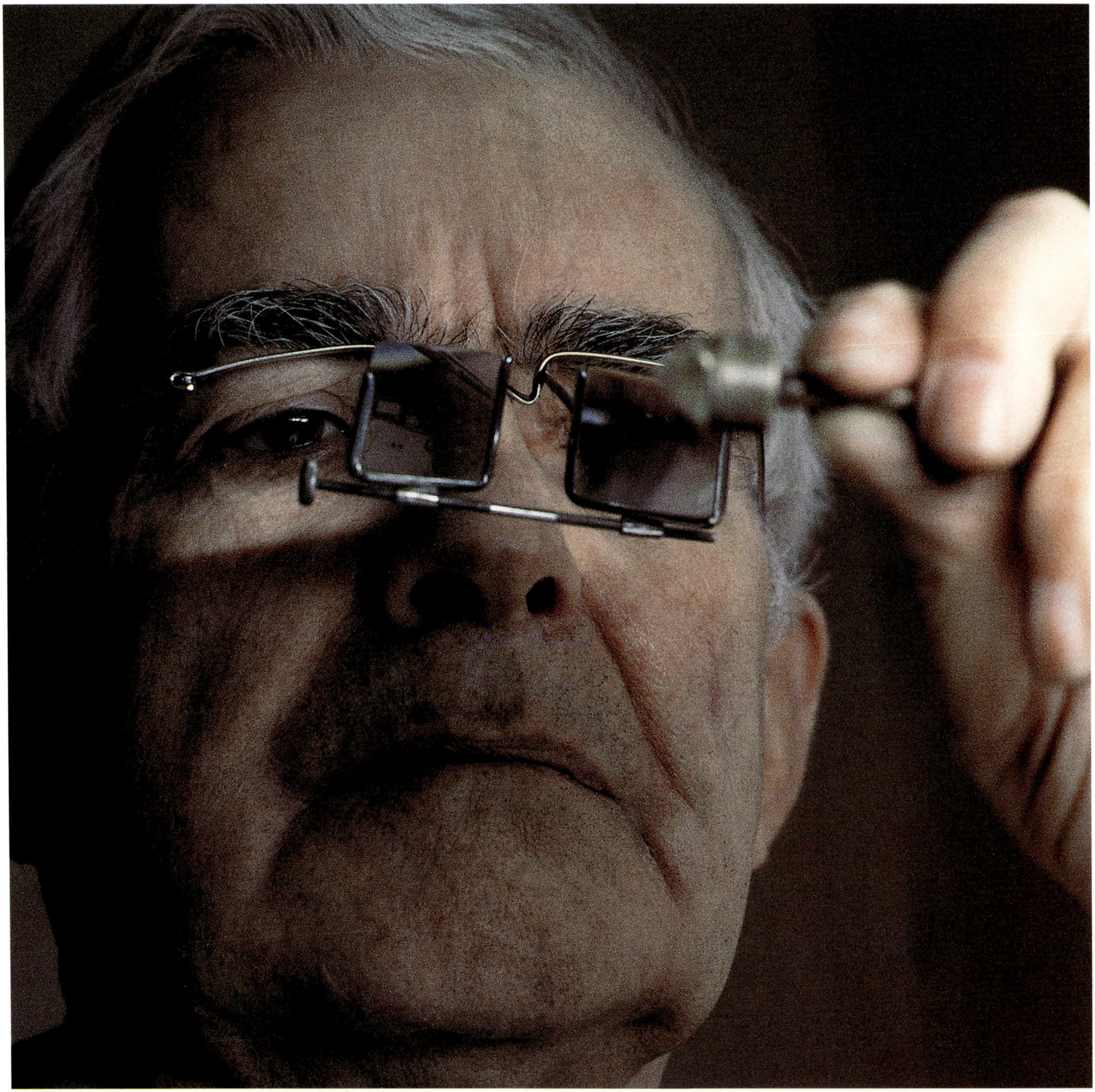

Diamond manufacturers in Antwerp remain competitive today because of their expertise in cutting large and difficult stones. Here diamond sawyer Theo Jansen examines the position of a large diamond in its holder before sawing it.

DIAMONDS HAVE BEEN CUT AND TRADED in Flanders for more than six hundred years, ever since the great ages of Venetian and Portuguese exploration in the East, when Flemish ports – first Bruges and later Antwerp – handled some forty per cent of all European trade with the rest of the world. Venetian merchants, who monopolized the import of diamonds to Europe from India during the thirteenth century, sent them northward down the Rhine valley to Bruges in the rough, for it would have courted greater attention from footpads to transport cut diamonds by that route. A cutting industry consequently grew up in Bruges, which remained pre-eminent until the fifteenth century, when the silting of the Zwin River stranded the port inland, and the trade passed to Antwerp.

Church records in Antwerp reveal that a *diamant snijder,* a diamond cutter, was married there in the fourteenth century, but it was only towards the middle of the next century, after traders and cutters began moving there from Bruges, that the diamond industry became important to the city. Vasco Da Gama's opening of the Cape sea route to India in 1493 caused the diamond monopoly to shift from Venice to Lisbon, Antwerp became the principal distribution centre for Lisbon's Indian imports, and several prominent Portuguese diamond traders established themselves there.

When in 1582 a Diamond and Ruby Cutters' Guild was formed, its recognition by the aldermen of Antwerp was opposed by the guild of dealers in used clothing, who saw it as clashing with the profitable trade in the jewelled buttons and buckles removed from the cast-off garments of the gentry. The cutters prevailed, however, for thereafter church records note that they attended a special mass on the name days of the patron saints of diamond cutters, Peter and Paul, and that members who stayed away were fined by the guild.

Religious intolerance in the sixteenth century caused the centre of the diamond industry to move to Amsterdam. Protestant diamond cutters who fled there from Antwerp during the Spanish occupation of the Catholic Lowlands provided a manufacturing base. The Sephardi Jewish community of wealthy traders and shipowners in Portugal, exposed to the full weight of the Inquisition after Portugal came under the Spanish Crown in 1580, also found sanctuary in Amsterdam and became prominent in diamond trading there. Dutch seizure of the mouth of the Schelde River and control of access to the port of Antwerp in 1648 gave Amsterdam a near monopoly of both the diamond industry and the trade in diamonds. Its ascendency was completed during the first half of the eighteenth century, when diamonds from Brazil, in quantities never seen before, began pouring into Europe through Portugal, because the presence of a large Portuguese-speaking Jewish diamond community in Amsterdam ensured that most of the diamonds from the new source went there.

An English-born Antwerp merchant, James Dormer, attempted valiantly but in vain to reverse the position, proposing to the Portuguese Crown, which held the monopoly of Brazilian diamonds, that he be appointed commissioner to purchase the entire production. After his death in 1757 Antwerp continued in Amsterdam's shadow for the next century and a half.

Amsterdam reached its zenith after the South African diamond discoveries towards the end of the last century. Hans Wins, a fourth-generation diamantaire of Dutch Sephardi extraction, recalls that his father and grandfather used to speak of diamond cutters making so much money at that time that they spent Mondays recovering from the weekends, and arrived at work on Tuesdays wearing silk hats and riding in horse-drawn traps. "Ironically, it was the affluence of this period that initiated the decline of Amsterdam," he says. "The unions grew so strong that they pushed wages and prices through the roof, and costs were further increased by an inflexible official attitude to red tape, taxes and import and export duties. The combination of strong unions and a rigid fiscal climate thrust the Dutch diamond trade into decline."

The Antwerp cutters in the meantime had honed their skills in trying to make the best of the inferior goods to which the Amsterdam merchants had for so long restricted them. They were able to reassert themselves when the South African rough, which initially had brought new heights of prosperity to the Amsterdam industry, also found its way to Antwerp. There it gave work to thousands of craftsmen and provided a basis for the rapid revival of manufacturing and a resurgence of trading in an economic climate characterized by fiscal policies that were liberal and unions, precursors of today's Algemene Diamantbewerkersbond van Belgie and the Christelijke Vervoerarbeiders en Diamantbewerkers, which were flexible and prepared to negotiate in the long-term interests of the industry as a whole.

A quieter day than usual on the trading floor at the Antwerpsche Diamantkring (left), where diamantaires deal mainly in rough diamonds.

The discovery of Premier mine in 1902 and the Namibian alluvial deposits a few years later, neither of them under the De Beers umbrella at the time, released to the market large quantities of smaller stones, which, though not profitable enough for the major polishing firms, were perfectly suited to the needs of a cottage industry. This gave birth to a parallel manufacturing industry in the Kempen, the countryside around Antwerp, where poor soils made it desirable for the farmers to have another source of income, and by 1908 there were already over a thousand polishing wheels and fifteen hundred workers operating there.

Jeff Diels, the son of a Kempen farmer, was apprenticed to a local manufacturer in 1926. "There was no apprenticeship contract," he recalls. "You started by making the tea and sweeping the factory, and then went on to crushing boart to make grinding powder for the wheels. The first essential thing you learnt to do was setting diamonds in a lead matrix to hold them firmly during polishing. Eventually you went on to polishing, first the table and four basic facets of the crown and the pavilion, then the smaller and still smaller facets. As apprentices were not paid and the cash guarantees their parents had deposited with the manufacturer when they started had to be returned when they finished their time, manufacturers tried to prolong the apprenticeship for as long as they could. Often you had to forfeit the guarantee and go to work for someone else."

Diamond trading in Antwerp had begun in the Pelikaanstraat cafés next to the central station, but the lack of privacy and security had led a group of major dealers to establish the city's first diamond exchange, the Diamantclub van Antwerpen, in 1893, and five years later a group of smaller dealers had founded the Diamant-Casino, which was reconstituted as the Beurs voor Diamanthandel in 1904. An exchange to provide for the needs of the Kempen manufacturers, the forerunner of the Vrije Diamanthandel, was launched in 1911, and in 1929 the last of the surviving Antwerp exchanges, the Antwerpsche Diamantkring, opened its doors.

Amsterdam diamantaires who, like Hans Wins's father, moved their businesses to Antwerp in the early 1930s, fared better in the Holocaust than their colleagues who remained behind. The rapid recovery of the diamond industry in Antwerp after the war, and its inability to revive in Amsterdam, can to some extent be attributed to the contrasting histories of the Jewish communities of the two cities.

and members remain in good standing, to give them a better chance of recouping losses and honouring commitments.

Members most frequently found on the exchange floors of the bourses are the city's four hundred brokers, who need to have a day-to-day knowledge of which articles are available and which are in demand. "They are a very active element in our trade," says Zucker. "They act as go-betweens, introducing our goods in offices that we haven't time to visit ourselves, smoothing out negotiations and saving us any embarrassment we might feel if we had to give in to a poor offer in direct negotiation."

"A buyer knows that somewhere there are goods that he can use, but if he starts asking around for them he places himself in a weak position and the seller in a strong position," says Kiek. "He will probably end up paying two or three per cent more, whereas if the broker asks, the seller doesn't know who the client is." Dealers and manufacturers with businesses to manage need someone they trust who has time to run around and sell for them; diamonds worth millions of dollars are handed over daily to brokers without any guarantee save the broker's good name.

A manufacturer with a parcel to sell calls a broker who specializes in his type of goods, and, if interested, the broker takes it on consignment and shows it to people he knows are looking for that type of goods and tells them the asking price per carat. An intending buyer seals the envelope, or *cachet,* containing the goods, by folding it in a specific way, writes his offer, to which he is committed for thirty-six hours, on the outside, signs it and hands it back to the broker. From then until the deal is concluded or negotiations are broken off, only the bidder may open the *cachet.* The broker takes the offer to the seller, who may reject it or offer a compromise price. If the bidder rejects the compromise, the broker can show the goods to someone else. If he accepts, the deal is sealed with a handshake and the Hebrew words *mazel en broche*, meaning "good luck and blessing". The goods are then weighed officially at the weighing station in the bourse, and payment is calculated and made on that weight. Deals are normally for cash, and it is the broker's responsibility to see that payment is made by the end of the week. He receives a commission of one per cent, paid by the seller if the terms of the sale are net, or by the buyer if not.

"Diamonds are there to be sold, and the importance of brokers is that they help push deals through," says Fischler. "There is a Hebrew saying, 'sell and regret, but sell', and that is as true today as two thousand years ago. The diamantaires who survived the crisis of the early eighties were those who sold instead of holding out for a better price. Stop selling and you are no longer in business."

Two major banks specialize in financing diamond business, the Antwerpse Diamantbank, and the Algemene Bank Nederland. Without them the diamond market in Antwerp would collapse, says Paul de Groote, director, general manager and chairman of the executive committee of Antwerpse Diamantbank. "We finance the purchases of DTC sight-holders, to carry them over until they can sell, and we finance the manufacturing process. With traders we finance receivables only, as we believe it is in the interests of the business that they finance their stocks with their own capital. This bank alone is financing the diamond market in Antwerp to the tune of between ten and eleven billion Belgian francs, without contracts, and we have authorized facilities for twice as much."

Diamond trading differs from trading in other commodities because diamonds cannot be traded on sample, he says. Another difference is that one is not dealing with the executives of multi-nationals but directly with the owners of the stones, which makes the diamond business far more personal. "We have to develop personal relationships with clients at all levels and adapt to dealing with people of diverse cultures who are accustomed to different patterns and procedures. Heavily involved financially, we need to know not only details of deals we are financing, but also about the diamantaires themselves, what they are doing from day to day, the volume of their trade, their capital reserves and who they are doing business with. Only with a good overall picture of a man can we consider giving him credit. We finance them in the short term – preferably not beyond 120 days – and not beyond the amount of their own equity."

Trust and confidence in individuals is as important in diamond banking as in other aspects of the diamond business. "A sight-holder may telephone us from London to say that he has a sight of one or ten million dollars – whatever it is – and ask us to pay. If the amount is outside our agreed credit lines, we must be able to decide, within minutes, whether to give him more. Because we know him well we can immediately confirm with a London bank that the amount will be paid; the London bank informs the CSO, and the man gets his parcel."

While satisfied with the way the trade has picked up again since the slump of the early eighties, diamond dealers in Antwerp are concerned about the future of their manufacturing industry in the face of competition from low-wage areas. "Thousands of foreign customers come to Antwerp because they can get a complete range here," says Fischler. "If we can't supply an item, they will go elsewhere for it and perhaps buy their other requirements in the same place. We need the local product to attract the buyers, and when we get the buyers the other manufacturing centres will send their goods to be sold here. The two work together. Without the manufacturing we cannot keep the business."

"The industry in Antwerp encourages the modernization of manufacturing and the introduction of new techniques," says Wins. "But it is costly to invest in new techniques, and impossible to recoup the costs in a limited number of hours a day. Manufacturers feel that they can recover the costs of investment only by working three full shifts and running their machines twenty-four hours a day, but the unions won't allow it. The situation is reminiscent of what happened to manufacturing in Amsterdam seventy or so years ago."

At a creche for children of diamond workers, nurse Katia Tolkowsky, right, daughter of Gabi Tolkowsky, and nurse Nathalie Trau initiate activities to occupy their charges: Zeevi, Baruch, Patrick and Dovi.

Albert Slap was one of the first major manufacturers to embrace the new technology. "Automation is essential to the Belgian industry; it is the only way we can beat high labour costs and increase production to reduce overheads," he says. "A saving of just one per cent of costs is substantial in this industry, and by progressively introducing automatic girdling machines and automatic grain seekers in our workshops we can increase our production, with the same number of men, by about ten per cent a year."

De Groote regards conservativism in the industry as posssibly the greatest danger to its survival. "Too many diamantaires in Antwerp are still working today as they did forty years ago, and their sons join the business while still in their teens," he says. "They learn from their fathers, but acquire no academic background, and so contribute nothing new. This is no help to the business in facing future challenges. What Antwerp needs most of all is a new generation of broadly educated diamantaires capable of developing new initiatives."

Once I THOUGHT
I Was Wrong
But I Was
MISTAKEN!
To Err
Is Human,
TO FORGIVE
IS NOT MY POLICY!

CHAPTER 9 WHEELING AND DEALING

Midday sunlight in Manhattan produces brilliance the colour of molten gold in the sixty-five facets of the aptly named Golden Giant, displayed here for his three sons by New York diamantaire Marvin Samuels.

In partnership with fellow New Yorker Louis Glick, Samuels had this distinctively triangular 407.43-carat gem cut from a 890-carat rough stone – the fourth largest of gem quality ever found.

The sparkle of stones such as this kindles a light in the eyes of diamantaires everywhere: the manufacturers who polish them on their wheels and the dealers who trade in their seductive charms.

Deals in progress at one of the tables on the exchange floor of the New York Diamond Dealers Club in West 47th Street – hub of the industry for the club's two thousand members. Among those at the table are Shlomo Friedman, Samuel Rimpler, Henry Lindenbaum, Samuel Hershkovitz, David Roth and Sal Flaks.

His characteristic corona in one hand, some of the large fancy-cut stones for which he is famous displayed on the back of the other, ebullient New York diamond manufacturer and dealer Bill Goldberg reminisces in his West 47th Street office about the thrills of the diamond business.

Excluded by anti-semitism from the trades and professions, many Jewish families in Eastern Europe turned to money-lending and diamonds as the only avenues for advancement open to them, and when they emigrated to more favourable environments they transplanted their skills. Consequently, in many parts of the world today the diamond business is largely a Jewish business, and Judaism – symbolized here by the Wailing Wall in Jerusalem – is a potent force in preserving the integrity of the industry.

Untrammelled by a long tradition, the relatively youthful Israeli diamond industry has the flexibility to adapt and innovate and so remain competitive. At all levels in the Israeli industry there are more young people – like Shlomo Arusa working on a ten-carat stone at Ramat-Gan – than in the older cutting centres.

Ferryboats await the bustle of the new day in the lee of the Gateway to India as a pale dawn permeates the mist over the Bombay waterfront. Here the forefathers of many of today's leaders in the Indian diamond industry traded originally in natural pearls, and switched to diamonds after the advent of cultured pearls spoilt the market for the natural product.

Being set out to cool (left) are polishing wheels cast in the foundry at Samir Diamonds' cutting factory outside Surat. The foundry is one of several spinoff enterprises that were started to supply the factory's own needs and have become commercial undertakings in their own right.
There is the aura of the sweatshop (right) about the old-style polishing operations in the back streets of Surat, where the polishers work long hours and sleep beside their wheels at night, but working conditions are improving with the establishment of modern factories that can provide proper facilities for their workforce.

MOORE

BILL GOLDBERG WAS ON THE TELEPHONE when Billy Nelkin bounded into his West 47th Street office, took a biscuit from the coffee tray and placed a folded paper *cachet* on the desk in front of him. He waited while Goldberg turned back the corners with his free hand, lingering just long enough to see the expression on his face when he caught sight of the matched pair of large, pear-shaped pink stones inside, then he took another biscuit and made for the door. "I've got to have these," Goldberg, hand over the mouthpiece, called after him. Cutting short the telephone conversation, he studied the stones – well over a million dollars' worth – for a few minutes, and then summoned one of his daughters to lock them in the safe. "Billy knows he won't be seeing those again," he said. "He's a reasonable man; he'll bill me for a fair price, and I'll pay him. That's how we do business."

Bill Goldberg at work in his office behind a façade of old New York in the heart of the diamond district, where for over thirty-five years he has occupied premises on the south side of West 47th Street – the side that gets the indirect northern light in which diamantaires prefer to examine their goods.

Outside, autumn rain lashed midtown Manhattan, sending bearded Hasidic Jews in frock-coats and black Homburgs scurrying for shelter in doorways. From his glass cubicle just inside the entrance to the retail jewellery store below Goldberg's office, Nelkin, steaming polystyrene mug of coffee before him and purloined biscuit in hand, surveyed the scene in the street that a sign at the Fifth Avenue intersection designated "Diamond and Jewelery Way". Now in his eighties, he had dealt in diamonds for almost seventy years, and had been "on the street" ever since the diamond industry began moving uptown in the late thirties.

In 1921, as a boy of twelve, Nelkin started in the business selling his mother's sandwiches to diamond cutters in the Wall Street area – Maiden Lane, Canal Street, John Street and Nassau Street – where the industry in New York had been concentrated since the 1880s. He worked as a diamond setter in a cutting factory for a few years, but after the stockmarket crash of 1929, when manufacturing was in the doldrums, he began dealing in diamonds.

"I went to pawnbrokers' auctions in the Bowery and picked up bargains at the Dead Men's Sales organized by the police department to sell the personal effects of the heirless intestate," he recalls. "A lot of beautiful pieces, with big stones cut at the turn of the century, used to come up at the auctions. I bought and sold, and little by little, starting with the smaller pieces and going into partnership with friends for more expensive items, I developed a business. In 1932 an insurance payout of $3800 for an automobile accident placed me in the big league. I put it all on a single purchase, sold for five per cent profit, and I was the happiest guy in the world."

Sidney Landau, a DTC sight-holder since 1935, recalls that in 1920, as a boy of fourteen, when people of that age could hold a driving licence in New York, he used to drive down to Maiden Lane after school to pick up his father and fellow diamond dealers. While preparing for an academic career in the Liberal Arts, he was drawn into the diamond business five years later by a land boom in Florida.

"For my summer vacation my father sent me off with a parcel of diamonds to sell in Florida, on the understanding that whatever I got for them over his price I could keep," he says. "The discovery that a girl who interested me was a bootlegger's moll quelled any amorous intentions I might have had, but she introduced me to her boyfriend and his circle, and in six weeks I made $10 000. It was an enormous sum in those days, and so, instead of returning to college in the fall, I continued selling diamonds."

He put all his profits into real estate, and when land values collapsed he lost most of what he had made, and found himself back in New York, peddling diamonds in the suburbs for his father. It was a small business; the goods his father bought in Antwerp the one week, he sold in New York the next. But ever since hearing his father's Maiden Lane cronies talking in awed tones about "The Syndicate", he had hankered after becoming a Syndicate client himself. He started his own manufacturing business in New York, and after reading in a 1934 issue of *Fortune* magazine about the newly formed

Diamond Trading Company he applied to London for a sight, which, with the help of his father's friends in Antwerp, he received the following year.

"Their minimum purchase then was $250 000, almost an impossible sum for a beginner to raise in those days, but a friend who was trying to revive a small bank he had taken over staked me," he says. "That was my start with the Syndicate, and I've been making and losing money ever since."

Another New York diamantaire and DTC sight-holder, whose modest start in the old diamond district led to a suite in midtown Fifth Avenue, is Louis Glick, son of a Lower East Side grocer. He arrived in New York from Rumania as a boy of five in 1928. When his father died ten years later, an uncle in Antwerp began sending him diamond powder, which he sold to diamond manufacturers for use on their polishing wheels, charging them the cost of the powder plus the price of a new hat or some other article of clothing for his brothers and sisters.

"I came in at the tail-end of the industry in the Wall Street area," he says. "By then most of the people I was dealing with had moved uptown, to be closer to the fine jewellers and the big hotels at which out-of-town buyers stayed. Traffic and public transport snarl-ups made business between the two parts of the city difficult, and after the New York Diamond Dealers Club, the larger of the two diamond bourses, moved from Nassau Street to 47th Street in 1941, most of the industry became established between 47th and 57th Streets."

When the war closed Antwerp, creating a shortage of tapered baguettes, Glick started a small factory in John Street with borrowed funds. "As soon as I'd manufactured ten carats of baguettes I'd rush uptown to sell them," he recalls. "But one thing led to another, and eventually I moved uptown in the sixties and became a DTC sight-holder." Today he still polishes his own rough, has a wholesale export business selling loose diamonds of a carat and up, and supplies most of the major retailers in New York.

"I have had to create my own range of jewellery as an aid to selling my goods," he says. "Pieces for $300 000 and $400 000 are not unusual for me. I have made necklaces for $5 million and do diamond layouts running to several millions, in which the diamonds are set out in a design to show buyers what can be done with them. In this way we can work together with our clients to come up with, not only a beautiful layout of diamonds, but also one that fits the needs of the ever-changing market."

The diamond business in New York operates on many different levels, from the small manufacturers who turn over their own productions on 47th Street, to the great wholesale houses on Fifth Avenue that buy from and sell to the world. Many individuals and firms operate on several levels at the same time, and branch out into related trades, such as jewellery manufacturing, in order to improve their profit margins.

For the more than two thousand dealers and manufacturers who do business in the Diamond Dealers Club, West 47th Street is the hub of the American diamond business. "The major stones are turned over by big shops, but that's only ten per cent of the business," says Nelkin. "The major part is in small goods, from half a carat down, and that business is done right here." Others agree that, although it is the big stones that get the publicity, the bulk of the business in the United States is in small stones. But, they say, the really serious business is no longer done in the club; it is done where the inventory is, in the offices of a few big wholesalers.

"Forty-seventh Street isn't at the centre of the business," says Philip Hahn, president of the wholesaler Fabrikant and Sons. "Four firms handle an important part of the business, and none of us has much to do with 47th Street. The Fifth Avenue folk who deal in really big stones are a different ballgame; medium to cheap goods is where the business is."

Hahn's grandfather, Max Fabrikant, began selling jewellery house-to-house in 1895, established a loose diamond business downtown in the 1910s and moved it to midtown Fifth Avenue in 1932.

"The business has changed totally since his day," says Hahn's cousin Chuck Fortgang, chairman of the company. "To make money today you have to be either very small, with low overheads, and do everything yourself, or you have to run a major operation, competing with and selling to other major firms. For that you need a big inventory and a big staff, and you have to run it, not as a traditional diamond business, but as a modern business."

Fabrikant is today perhaps the largest diamond wholesaler in the United States, dealing partly in the loose diamond business and partly in the jewellery business, selling loose and mounted goods to every segment of the jewellery industry: manufacturers, wholesalers, and retailers. By the mid-eighties the firm was probably the largest importer of diamonds in the United States. The manufacture and mounting of polished are done by outside contractors around the world. The firm employs some 350 people, fifteen of whom comb the international markets for suitable polished, and has offices in Toronto, Antwerp, Tel Aviv, Bombay, Bangkok and Hong Kong.

"We are a sales oriented company," says Fortgang. "We do our own merchandising, and like to have an active, fast-moving business, with lots of commotion and lots of people working close together. We can no longer make profits from illusion in the way that the smaller operators always have. The people we do business with know everything that we know about the foreign markets and the goods we are dealing in. The only way people like ourselves can stay alive is to be more active, work harder and turn over more goods."

"The bulk of our business is in diamonds under two carats," says Hahn. "To sell a lot of goods we need to have large supplies. Where diamond manufacturers can limit themselves to certain categories, we require large stocks in many sizes and colours."

In the manufacture of the sort of fine jewellery sold by such renowned New York retailers as Tiffany's, Van Cleef and Harry Winston the demand for top quality diamonds, of all sizes, is constant. In the grassroots retail market, however, although diamonds, as objects of perennial desire, are in a sense above fashion, changes in affluence and taste do alter the fashion for different sizes and qualities of diamonds.

"Ten or fifteen years ago the demand was for larger stones of fair to better quality," says Harry Schukar, president of the wholesale diamond division at Harry Winston, "but in our wholesale business today we seem to have two tiers of customers. Most jewellers now want smaller, lower-quality stones set in high-fashioned, well made jewellery. When the prices of gold and diamonds were high at the start of the eighties, jewellers found they couldn't economize by lowering the gold content, so they started using less expensive stones, and discovered that these would sell. This, in turn, has spawned a flash-for-cash market for big stones of inferior quality and colour. It is the same sort of thing that happened in other industries, as in the substitution of plastics for genuine leather upholstery in expensive cars."

Between the fine jewellers and the mass distributors in the multi-layered American diamond industry there are niches for all manner of specialists, and important business emanates from the offices of manufacturers and dealers in 47th Street.

Walter David, who today heads the manufacturing business started in 1940 by his father, an immigrant from Czechoslovakia, learnt to saw diamonds in 47th Street, but today – as is typical in New York – the sawing and cleaving of the goods he receives from the DTC and other sources are done by a contractor. Everything between two and ten carats is manufactured by his seventeen polishers at W. David and Company in 47th Street. The smaller stones he has manufactured in Israel on contract. He presents himself as "the sight-holder to the American jeweler", and through a subsidiary, the American Diamond Syndicate, he supplies over five hundred regular customers across the country, from the smallest independent jeweller to the largest jewellery chain. He is also a major exporter to Japan.

Chairman of the American Diamond Industry Association, Lloyd Jaffe, his hand slightly raised to emphasise a point, talks to the president of the New York Diamond Dealers Club, grey-haired Ralph Barr, beside a fruit vendor's stand on the corner of Fifth Avenue and 47th Street.

Mercurial Martin Rapaport, publisher of controversial price lists for polished diamonds that some diamantaires swear by and others swear at.

"Selling to everybody except the retail customer, we have to carry a large inventory to come anywhere near supplying them with what they want," he says. "As they depend on us for everything, from the smallest to the largest stones, we have to supplement our own production by buying polished from our close associates outside the United States."

"There is a classical conflict between being a manufacturer and polished dealer," says Richard Werdiger, who entered his father's industrial diamond distributing business in 1970 and diversified into gem diamond manufacturing. "As a manufacturer, you must sell what you make; as a dealer in polished diamonds, you have to supply your customers with what they want. As a manufacturer you can never produce enough of what you need, and your customers often do not want what you have to sell. Resolving that conflict is really what the business is about."

Examining rough gem diamonds at his desk, with a container of industrial diamonds on a side table, DTC sight-holder Richard Werdiger is one of a new breed of university educated New York diamantaires.

A DTC sight-holder, he manufactures better quality goods over two carats and special stones over 10.8 carats in New York, and smaller goods in Antwerp and Israel. His customers are wholesalers, jewellery manufacturers and large retail jewellery chains in the United States and the Far East.

"The only way to know how to price your goods is by trading," he says. "You may be an expert, but if you stop trading for six months you can't simply pick up where you left off and start pricing goods effectively again. There are times when the rough is worth more than its polished yield, because it's trading on a forward price, and times when there is a fair margin in converting the rough into polished, because the rough market is depressed. As a dealer in polished, you have to be close to all the markets and sell where the demand is strongest."

There is also an irrational factor, spoken of in the business as "illusion". One may have the "illusion" that it is favourable or unfavourable to deal with a specific firm, or manufacture a certain type of goods, or sell in a particular market. One may have faith in something one sees in a stone that no one else sees.

"Coming into the business as a young man with a degree in Economics, I found the concept of 'illusion' very difficult to accept," says Werdiger. "But it plays a big part in the industry, although not so much at the level of the big dealers, who are in most senses beyond the point of illusion, except perhaps in their buying from the DTC."

Native New Yorker Bill Goldberg, now in his sixties, started as an apprentice cutter at eighteen, and later specialized with a partner in manufacturing matched pairs of baguettes, which required limited capital. The firm prospered, took on more cutters, started manufacturing other fancy shapes, and moved to the south side of 47th Street, where at various addresses it has been for over thirty-five years.

A DTC sight-holder since 1973, he keeps sixteen people fully occupied cutting large stones in his workshop and puts out smaller goods to contractors. "Everything we produce is for inventory, not for specific customers," he says, "but there are several fine jewellers who depend on us for certain types of goods. They may, for instance, need thirty or forty stones of one to two carats and a nice oval or marquise for a necklace. We may produce until we have enough and then offer them to the jeweller, or supply stones to fit a customer's design."

Although he sees himself as principally a manufacturer, Goldberg trades extensively in polished goods and has a reputation for dealing in fancy cuts and colours and particularly big, high-quality stones. The most notable of those that have passed through his hands is the celebrated 137.02-carat Premier Rose, which he sold in 1979 for about $10 million, but he will never forget buying his first really big stone two years earlier.

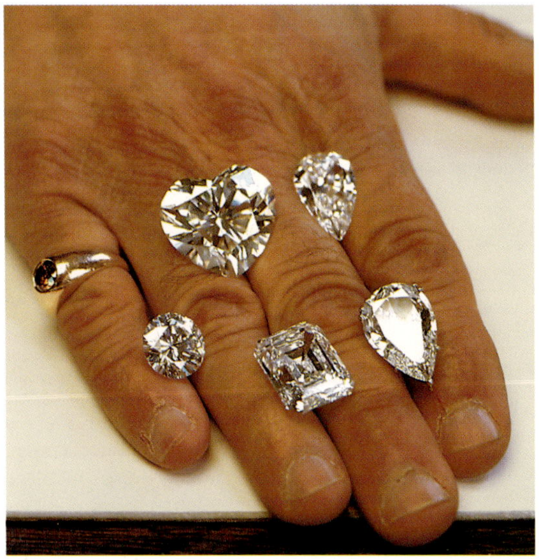

One brilliant and four fancy cuts display the beauty of top-colour diamonds offset by skin tones.

"We had been on a wild-goose chase after a parcel of rough in Geneva," he says. "Instead of watching the ducks on the lake while waiting for our flight home, we went to look at a big stone that we'd heard was in Lausanne, although we only half believed that it existed. It turned out to be the historic cushion-shaped 136.25-carat Queen of Holland, which had been in the family of the Maharajah of Nawanagar for many years. I bought it, had it recut to 135.92 carats, and sold it for $7 million. That launched me on a career in important stones, and I often wonder whether I'd be where I am today if we had found the rough we went for in the first place, or if we had decided to watch the ducks."

Frequently Goldberg will recut a stone, even though this slightly reduces its size, if he feels he can improve it. "It may not add to its cash value, but we have the satisfaction of having maximized its brilliance and beauty, and living up to our signature: The Magic is in the Make," he says. "I may get the lowest yield in town and not get a better carat price, but it improves our turnover, because up against another stone ours will sell almost every time."

New York, Amsterdam and Antwerp were the only major cutting centres before World War II. Today, labour is too expensive for manufacturers in America to make anything but the larger, more costly stones, and new cutting centres have arisen to fill the gaps and supply, among others, the American jewellery industry with the enormous quantities of smaller and less-perfect stones it requires. Of these new centres, the first to emerge was Tel Aviv.

Whenever he looks at the Diamond Exchange buildings dominating the Tel Aviv skyline at Ramat-Gan, Asher Dascal thinks of how it all started with a diamond he cut at Petah Tikva in 1937. While children carrying flowers in the street outside celebrated the harvest, he polished his first stone. Pleased with his handiwork, he put it in an envelope and kept it, until some fifty years later he donated it to the Harry Oppenheimer Diamond Museum in Ramat-Gan, where it is on permanent display.

Asher Dascal, along with Zvi Rosenberg and Oved Ben-Ami, was a founder of the Israeli diamond industry. Although he and Rosenberg both came from Transylvania and learnt the trade in Antwerp, they first met in Palestine, and worked together for a while in a cowshed at Rosenberg's home in Petah Tikva. Palestine-born Ben-Ami, who had founded the city of Netanya, was eager to attract industry to the new Jewish settlement there. Learning from a friend in the customs department that diamonds were being imported, he obtained the names of the importers and persuaded the two men, with offers of free industrial and residential sites, to move to Netanya and train apprentices.

In 1938, when war seemed inevitable and the fledgling industry in Netanya faced being cut off from its Belgian sources of rough diamonds, Ben-Ami urged Antwerp manufacturers to set up factories in Palestine in partnership with local finance, and went to London to ask the CSO for supplies. Feeling that he had a commitment to Antwerp, Sir Ernest Oppenheimer was at first reluctant to agree. Assisted by the London broker George Prins, Ben-Ami was able to sway him, however, with the argument that, if there was nobody to manufacture the small stones, the CSO would have difficulty selling its larger stones in the United States, because jewellery could not be made with large stones alone. The CSO agreed to an allocation, and the forerunner of the Israeli Diamond Manufacturers Association was formed to split it and distribute it to manufacturers.

After war suspended operations in Antwerp and Amsterdam, Palestine became for a time the major supplier of polished diamonds to the free world. "The goods arrived from London every six weeks via the Belgian Congo, Sudan and Egypt, and we sent the polished to New York by way of Egypt, Sudan, Angola, Belgian Congo and Brazil," says prominent Israeli dealer Joseph Nadel, who was among the Antwerp-trained cutters who began manufacturing in Palestine in the late thirties.

From his penthouse overlooking Netanya, Oved Ben-Ami surveys the city he founded, and where, at his instigation, the Israeli diamond industry was first established.

Because the diamond industry required little in the way of water, energy and transportation, it was ideally suited to a country in which the infrastructure was not highly developed. Men with money went into business with men who knew the trade, and whereas in 1939 there had been only four factories, employing two hundred workers, more sprang up in Netanya, Tel Aviv and Jerusalem, and by early 1941 there were some forty factories employing three thousand workers. By the end of the war there were four thousand workers operating legally, and another two thousand working without permits.

"The industry prospered in wartime; prices were high and wages were good," says Yehezkiel Goldman, a leading Israeli diamantaire who used to do the subdivision of the CSO parcel for the Manufacturers Association. "And this continued after the war until 1947, when a crisis developed."

"As the Belgian industry revived, the demand for our production fell away," explains Menachem Fruchter, another pioneer of the industry in Netanya. "Prices dropped dramatically, and many of the financial partners in businesses that had stocks in hand lost much of what they had made. Believing that pressure from the Belgian industry would soon prevail upon the CSO to abandon the industry here, they withdrew. More than eighty per cent of the factories closed, and the number of active cutters fell to a few hundred."

Following the creation of the State of Israel in 1948, the regeneration of the industry was undertaken by the diamond workers themselves, who formed small groups to manufacture, with reduced overheads, at lower prices. One of them was Moshe Schnitzer, who would later preside over the Israel Diamond Exchange for more than twenty years. He had arrived from Rumania in 1933, when he was thirteen, and was studying Philosophy in Jerusalem when his father, finding out that he had been detained several times by the British authorities for his political activities, cut short his studies and placed him in a cutting factory, where he could keep an eye on him. After commanding a cavalry regiment in the War of Independence, Schnitzer began building up his own business.

"Being diamond workers, we knew better than the financiers how to get the best out of the rough," says Schnitzer. "We also didn't have the money to speculate, and were able to work on smaller profit margins. We had to cut, and sell immediately, treating diamonds like any other commodity."

"Under its agreement to purchase the Belgian Congo production, the CSO was obliged to resume supplying Antwerp, while it was under no obligation to the new manufacturers in Israel, who were not the same people as those who had been its regular customers," says Fruchter. "But Belgium and Holland were receiving allocations of melee, which they had not worked before, and we, who had become skilled in its manufacture, could buy it from them, at a premium. The industry survived through those years only because the manufacturers themselves worked at the wheel."

Independence had brought thousands of immigrants – survivors of the Holocaust as well as refugees from the Arab countries and North Africa – who had little education, and

In a timeless scene beside the road to Jericho (left) a Bedouin tends his flock in a spring field dotted with poppies beneath the walls of the Holy City.
The Diamond Exchange floor at Ramat-Gan (right) is buzzing with activity all day every working day.

Celebrating Pesach Seder with family and friends at his home in Herzlia, Charles Hollander (left), wearing a white open-necked shirt, ritually dips his little finger in his wine.
David Shalom Yakobovitz (right) examines a 100-carat rough black diamond which he bought at a considerable risk – as it might not have been pure black – but the gamble paid off, because it polished to a perfect 62-carat gem.
The first facet polished (far right) revealed its jet black perfection.

it was necessary to develop industries that required little investment in buildings, equipment and services, and for which people could be trained quickly. "The diamond industry answered positively to all these requirements," says Jona Hatsor, a former government Diamond Controller and representative in Israel of the London brokers I. Hennig. "And since it is largely a Jewish industry everywhere, we believed we had a good chance of selling our production through Jewish people all over the world."

Moshe Schnitzer, a founder of the Israel Diamond Exchange and its president for over twenty years, in the chair at a meeting of the board.

In order to train workers quickly and enable them to start earning within two or three months, the Israelis developed the chain-of-six system, in which each worker is trained to specialize in one of six phases in production. Renewed representations to the CSO secured a supply of rough for small manufacturers who formed themselves into groups to satisfy its criteria.

Towards the middle of the fifties Israel began receiving from Lebanese dealers in West Africa a greater variety of goods than the CSO supplied. Fruchter went to Monrovia and persuaded a few of the Lebanese who had been sending goods to Antwerp to sell at least some directly to Israel and save the broker's fee in Antwerp. The first shipment was in 1959, the idea caught on quickly, and in 1960 Fruchter was importing as much from West Africa as the CSO was supplying from London.

"Until then no dealers, only manufacturers, had received sights in Israel," says Hatsor. "The Syndicate supplied much less than half our needs, and we were buying a lot of original boxes (unopened DTC boxes) from Belgium. As Diamond Controller at the time, I was able to demonstrate to the DTC that the Israelis, not the Belgians it was supplying, were the real clients for these goods. As a result of the talks that followed, the DTC agreed to supply us with five-sixths of its total melee intake. A joint committee of the DTC, the Israeli industry and the Israeli government was set up, and two dealers – Menachem Fruchter and Joseph Goldfinger – were given sights to supply DTC rough to young manufacturers who hadn't the capital to warrant sights of their own."

In Israel today some eight hundred manufacturing plants, employing some twelve thousand workers, cut and polish, by value, about fifty per cent of the world's rough, almost entirely for export. The industry provides a living for an estimated twenty-three thousand families. It is Israel's major industry, with exports valued at over $2 billion a year – a quarter of all industrial exports – representing a substantial net gain in foreign exchange.

Traditionally, owing to the nature of the CSO allocation, Israel manufactures melee, between ten and fifteen stones to the carat. As a relatively expensive rough that requires little expertise, melee is the least attractive article from the point of view of the national economy, because the value added in manufacture is low. The Israeli industry has therefore expanded into other types of goods. Where formerly it could afford to work stones as small as a hundred to the carat, the smallest today is about thirty to the carat. It also manufactures much larger stones, and the categories it does not make itself it imports as polished from elsewhere, so as to have the full range to attract buyers. Although in value terms Israel has far surpassed Antwerp as a manufacturing centre, Antwerp remains the chief trading centre.

During the war years the industry had no use for a diamond exchange, for the British authorities, fearing that the diamonds might fall into enemy hands, forbad internal trading, and the entire production went directly to customers in the United States. "Needing a place to trade after the war we opened a club with nineteen members in a Tel Aviv coffee shop in 1948, and in 1952 the manufacturers combined with the dealers to form the Israel Diamond Exchange," recalls Schnitzer, who was elected president in 1966. Today the exchange has well over two thousand members and occupies a multi-towered building complex at Ramat-Gan, which has some nine hundred private offices and the biggest trading floor of any diamond bourse in the world.

Parcels of clients' diamonds may be stored for safe-keeping in the vaults of the Union Bank.

As the founders of the industry were artisans, who were unable to finance the purchase of rough, the banks have always played a vital role in the industry. In 1940 the forerunner of the Union Bank of Israel developed a system of "trust drafts" in terms of which manufacturers undertook to polish the rough financed by the bank and only to sell the polished against repaying the debt to the bank. The system was adopted later by other banks and the industry developed rapidly. "By also financing exports the banks helped increase the volume of trade, and enabled the manufacturers, who had been largely confined to melee production, to diversify," says Jacob Raif, manager of the Union Bank's diamond branch.

"Although an industry that needs relatively little fixed capital, diamond manufacturing requires proportionally more working capital than other industries, to buy rough and finance client credit," says Gideon Lahav, managing director of Israel Discount Bank. "Because the value added is small, working capital cannot accumulate fast enough for the manufacturers to be self-sufficient."

The sums involved are large, and banks that do diamond business have specialized branches, situated in the Diamond Exchange building, which employ diamond experts and supply services tailored to the needs of the industry. Union Bank handles about half the business, and Israel Discount Bank a third.

"In the recession of the early eighties we found that loss was built into our system of financing the diamonds that diamantaires deposited with us as collateral," says Raif. "When prices fell they couldn't sell and pay back the loans, and everybody lost heavily. The losses – more than the capital of the banks themselves and equal to the value of the entire diamond export for a year – could not be covered from previous gains, because banks were limited by law to a two per cent margin on their credit facilities, and at that rate it would have taken fifty years to cover the loss. So we switched from financing stocks, which we feel the diamantaires should finance themselves, to financing the credit that the diamantaires extend to their customers; from diamond collaterals to first-degree collaterals, such as real estate, savings and bank guarantees."

Over a period of four years these measures reduced bank financing by two-thirds, while financing with the diamantaires' own capital more than doubled. But the reluctance of exporters to ask American and European importers for collateral is restricting trade, says Raif. "In other businesses the exporter is covered by a letter of credit from the importer's bank, but in the diamond business the letter of credit is viewed as inimical to the principle of mutual trust. Israeli banks consequently have to limit the credit that exporters extend to importers in Europe and America, while export to Japan, which is on a COD basis, is booming."

Facing competition from the low-cost areas of India and South-East Asia, the Israeli industry, like the Belgian, has to explore the potential of new products, new methods of production and new technologies.

"On the one hand we have had to break into a better range of goods, in which the wage factor is less important," says Henri Brunner, chairman of Diamdel in Tel Aviv. "In smalls the labour component is forty per cent, whereas in melee it is ten per cent and in large only two per cent. Assuming that Indian manufacturers want to make at least ten per cent profit, we can, by moving into a range in which labour is less than ten per cent, break even at the price that they could get for the same goods, and then add a few per cent for a better cut. On the other hand we have to work towards greater efficiency to improve our profit margin."

Uri Schwartz, a strong advocate of technological innovation in the industry, discusses the angles of the "princess cut" among the Piermatic automatic polishing machines in his factory at Ramat-Gan.

When the pressure of Indian competition was first felt in the sixties, the Ministry of Trade and Industry established the Israel Diamond Institute, financed by the industry and representative of all its components, the trade unions and the ministry, to seek technological solutions to the problems of reducing labour costs and increasing productivity. "The only way we can compete with cheap labour is by using our brains," says Schnitzer, chairman of the institute.

"The trouble is that many of our diamantaires don't believe in machines and argue that any machines we develop will simply be copied by our competitors," says Efraim Raviv, managing director of the institute. "We have to convince them that, even if they are copied, they will give us the advantage of a few years in which to make better machines, and so to continue advancing ahead of the competition."

"Not only will we be a few years ahead in technology, but if our competitors have to adopt our methods they will lose the advantage of cheaper labour and have to compete on equal terms," adds Zvi Shur, general manager of the Israel Diamond Manufacturers Association.

Not having a long tradition in the diamond business, Israel has the advantage of not being bound too tightly by it. Fathers have stepped aside, and young men, who have had the education their elders did not, have come into the industry with new ideas and the will to carry on business in their own way.

"We saw what happened to Belgium and are afraid that the same will happen to us," says Uri Schwartz, who runs the manufacturing side of the business his father established after the war. "Our manufacturers and dealers tend to differ about the solution, with the former favouring technical innovation and the latter wanting more spent on public relations to attract customers. Advertising may attract clients, but only by offering them better goods at slightly lower prices will we be able to hold them."

Daniel Legziel, who developed the polishing factory that he established after the War of Independence into an international business, welcomes the changes his sons have made since entering the business. "Being at the centre of Europe, Antwerp could survive on the trade alone, but we have to produce, and produce at a slightly lower price, to get buyers to come here," he says. "Our newest factory is automated."

Lev Leviev came to Israel from Tashkent as a teenager in 1971. The small factory he established in 1976 has grown to several factories, with an annual turnover of well over $100 million. "We have put a lot into developing our technology, not simply to replace the worker, but to improve the quality of production and increase the rate of turnover; to reduce manufacturing costs without adding to overheads," he says.

International broker and dealer in polished diamonds, Charles Hollander, who launched his firm in Israel in the seventies, has carried the spirit of innovation over to the dealing side of the business. "A large part of my business is with Japanese importers," he says. "Very early on I realized that there is a communications gap between people of different cultures and philosophies that is not merely a question of language. To bridge that gap I set about learning all that I could about them and their style of doing business.

One thing I discovered was that they will go anywhere to learn. Westerners laughed at them, thinking the Japanese were trying to copy them, when actually they were learning from the West, and nobody laughs at them now. So I travel, I learn and I adapt."

Elliot Tannenbaum, who since 1983 has managed the Israeli manufacturing interests of his father-in-law, leading New York manufacturer Leo Schachter, departed from the traditional, partner-dependent structure of diamond firms and created a middle management level in the business. "Because we can put together structures here that would be impossible in New York or Antwerp, the opportunities are limitless," he says. "To get out of the financial mess of the early eighties, the new Israeli diamantaires had to discard the classic premises of the business, such as the adage that you make your profit from your inventory, not your operations. Having no interest in accumulating unusable inventory and unusable profit, they adapted to manufacturing quickly for immediate profit, incurring little or no debt. They are the young lions, adapting a nineteenth century business to the twenty-first century."

Keen competition between Israeli and Indian manufacturers does not inhibit trade in diamonds between the two countries, however, and Indian dealers buy rough and sell polished on the trading floor of the Israel Diamond Exchange, where several have permanent offices.

Octogenarian Kirtilal Mehta, who settled in Israel in 1965, because he liked the people and the quality of the Israeli cutting, is so much a part of the scene that he is widely known as the "Indian Israeli". The son of a Bombay diamond merchant, he was running the Rangoon branch of the family business at the age of fourteen, and at twenty he took charge of the main business in Bombay. When in 1948, a year after Independence, the Indian government prohibited the importation of polished diamonds and restricted the importation of rough, he established offices in Antwerp, Hong Kong, New York, Bangkok, Tokyo and, finally, Tel Aviv. He has a factory employing eighty workers manufacturing larger stones in Israel, and some four thousand workers polish traditional "Indian goods" at his factories in Bombay and Surat. A patriarch, with seven children, fifteen grandchildren and three or four great-grandchildren at last count, he has no shortage of reliable managers for the various branches of the family business.

In Indian business, as in Jewish, the family is central, and the surname "Mehta" is confusingly common in the industry. Although many who bear it would have to go back several generations to establish any degree of consanguinity, they are all linked historically to the town of Palanpur, in Gujarat. The Mehtas are said to have migrated in the thirteenth century from Rajasthan to Palanpur, where they adopted the Jain faith. In accordance with the Indian tradition that various communities follow defined occupations, the Palanpur Jains served for centuries as administrators and accountants for the ruling nawabs, and in more recent times became specialists in money management.

Towards the end of the last century a number of Mehtas, among them the great-grandfathers of those who lead the Indian diamond industry today, moved to Bombay, where they engaged in the pearl trade, acting as intermediaries between the pearl merchants in Surat and the markets in Europe. When in the 1940s the advent of cultured pearls knocked the bottom out of the market for natural pearls, many returned to their native villages. Those who remained in Bombay began dealing in polished diamonds and repolishing old-cut stones, there and in Surat. After imports of polished diamonds were prohibited, they began importing rough from Antwerp and polishing it themselves.

"My great-grandfather was one of the first to go into the pearl business in Bombay, my grandfather started in pearls and ended re-cutting old diamonds, and my father was a pioneer in polishing rough," says Arun Mehta, who began dealing in polished in 1957 at the age of seventeen, and founded the Arunkumar company in 1960 with his uncle Bhanuchandra Bhansali. Combining his experience in polished dealing and the polishing skills of his uncle, who had imported cutters from Brazil to teach Indians the art,

At early-morning practice at the Bombay Cricket Club grounds, Arun Mehta, with folded arms, considers the selection of his firm's cricket team to tour Jaipur.

Ma-niketan, a home for some five hundred homeless children from all communities and religions outside Bombay, is sponsored by retired diamantaire Mafatlal Mehta, who now devotes himself to charitable works in India, and run by the Sisters of the Society of the Helpers of Mary. Here Mehta and Sister Fatima, seated, and Sister Mercy are surrounded by some of the beneficiaries of their generosity and devotion.

they began buying rough from a local dealer and polishing for the domestic market. When in 1963 war with China caused the domestic market to slump, they began buying rough in Antwerp and selling their polished in Hong Kong.

"The devaluation of the rupee in 1966 made Indian labour more competitive, and we were able to take full advantage of the international boom in diamond sales that followed, receiving a DTC sight in 1969 and growing every year until 1973, when the oil crisis caused demand to slacken," says Arun Mehta.

His youngest brother, Dilip, had meanwhile formed the Rosy Blue company in Antwerp, to buy rough and promote the sale of Indian polished. Dilip Mehta went on to promote sales in Hong Kong, the United States and, later, Japan. He also became a major manufacturer in Belgium, and in 1981 he bought a large share in the Blue Diamond factory in Sri Lanka, which was polishing sawn diamonds on semi-automatic machines. In 1984 they began using semi-automatic machines to polish in India.

"With the knowledge we gained of polishing makeables – whole stones – in Belgium and sawn goods in Sri Lanka, we were able to improve our yield and our make," says Arun Mehta. "We employ seven hundred workers at our Bombay factory and another twenty-five thousand work for us on contract in different parts of the country. We export about $100 million worth of polished a year, with a net foreign exchange gain to the country of about $25 million."

At five in the afternoon, Varachha Road in Surat, the second largest city in Gujarat, is in a frenzy of activity. Swarms of motor scooters, bicycles, motorized three-wheeler rickshaws and wooden-wheeled bullock carts weave through the dense throng of people. On the eve of the national kite-flying holiday, stalls lining the street are festive with multi-coloured kites and spools of vivid kite strings for sale. In small kiosks open to the alleys and side streets, in adjoining buildings and on the saddles of Vespa scooters in the street itself, diamonds are being traded. This is the so-called Varachha Road "switching market".

"It used to be purely a switching market, where small cutting contractors would exchange their clients' stones for the slightly smaller or poorer quality stones of other cutters' clients, and pocket the difference in value," says Nanu Mehta. "But today seventy per cent of the business done there is honest trade. Everything that is switched must first be manufactured and eventually be traded. A lot of the small manufacturers trade their own stones there and take payment partly in cash and partly in rough. With rough diamond imports increasing thirty per cent a year, there is likely to be much less switching than actual trading. Without all those thousands of people trading in the streets of Surat there would be no industry, because there is no way the big manufacturers on their own could polish all the cheap goods that are being produced."

Over the years, migrant diamond workers trained in Surat have returned to their villages and set up small units of their own throughout Gujarat, and many of the diamonds traded in Surat today are manufactured by thousands of cutters operating in surrounding towns. In the early sixties there were about a hundred manufacturing units employing some five hundred workers in Surat, by 1981 there were five thousand units employing forty thousand workers, and today there are probably 150 000 diamond cutters in Surat itself, and more than half a million in the whole state, trading their productions in Surat, Palanpur, Bhavnagar, Ahmedabad and Navsari.

Nanu Mehta's grandfather dealt in polished diamonds in Bombay at the beginning of the century, and his father, Mafatlal Mehta, started one of the first cutting factories there after Independence. Following the banning of all diamond imports, his father in 1960 established the Jayam company in Antwerp, where he now lives in retirement and devotes his time to charitable work in India.

In 1962 the government relaxed its ban on rough diamond imports, on condition that the value added in manufacture was exported, and in 1966 Nanu Mehta and his brothers formed Samir Diamonds. At first their manufacturing was done entirely by contractors in

Surat, whom the company helped to develop small factories. In 1980, when they felt confident of being able to handle larger units, they bought seventy acres of land ten kilometres from Surat and, in partnership with the heads of small units they had worked with before, established a factory that could employ two thousand workers.

"The idea behind creating a bigger unit in an organized way was that it would enable us to modernize when the time came to do so, and we bought a big piece of land so that we would have room for development," says Nanu Mehta.

The factory has become something of a showpiece and an example of what the manufacturing industry in Surat, still confined largely to small primitive workshops, could do to improve the standard of production and the working and living conditions of those it employs. About half of the twelve hundred workers employed there are housed on the estate, the unmarried in dormitories and the families in self-contained apartments. The farm provides the workers with fresh vegetables and milk from the buffalo herd at subsidized prices, and partners in the factory have established subsidiary businesses – a foundry to manufacture polishing wheels and a sawing works to cut marble tops for polishing tables that are made for sale – on the property.

Half the factory is still working with old equipment, but semi-automatic machines have been introduced in the other half, and eventually the entire operation will be modernized and expanded to the full complement of two thousand workers. "At present the factory provides only twenty per cent of our production," says Nanu Mehta. "We cannot do without all those thousands of people outside who polish our small goods for us."

Bombay diamond manufacturer Jatin Mehta and his son Vishal (left), whom he frequently takes with him to work and on business trips to familiarize him with the business.
One of the modern apartment blocks (below) for married workers on the Samir Diamonds factory estate glimpsed through holes in the ventilation panel on the stairway of the block across the road.

Another descendant of the Palanpuri Jains is Jatin Mehta, who at an early age was dispatched during his school holidays each year to work in his uncle's office in Antwerp, where, as he says, "all I had to do really was sit around, play with diamonds and listen to the conversation". A wheel was installed at his home so that he could learn to polish in the afternoons after school. At sixteen he became actively involved in his father's business, and at eighteen he began managing it.

"Because we manage the business ourselves, instead of employing people to do it for us, it is important that we experience the industry when young," he says. "Between fifteen and twenty, when you are getting the industry into your blood, is the best time for adapting your style of thinking to the business. The great strength of our industry is the commitment of the young people to the business and the joint family system, in which

The transition between old and new technologies at the Samir Diamonds factory outside Surat, where Nanu Mehta has introduced an up-to-date bruting workshop (right), but still has to modernize the cleaving workshop (below), where cleavers heat the wax for holding the diamonds over candles that are housed in what look like miniature galvanized iron huts.

three generations live together and are associated with the business. Almost everybody who is really active in the industry today is under forty, but by the time you are forty you can have had twenty-four years' experience."

His company has three factories in Bombay and one in Jodhpur employing a total of about two thousand workers, while company offices in various parts of the country give out work on contract to between twenty-five thousand and thirty thousand workers. Administration and the assortment of polished are done at offices in the Opera House district of Bombay, where all the leading diamantaires are based. The company has offices to sell the production in Antwerp, New York and Tel Aviv. Another office in Opera House buys polished and deals in rough supplied by buying offices in Antwerp and Tel Aviv.

"The industry has consolidated its position, is competing on world markets and is now looking for new ways to maintain itself against possible competition from other countries in South-East Asia," says Jatin Mehta, who is chairman of the Gem and Jewellery Export Promotion Council.

During the eighties the Indian diamond industry has benefited from the government's reappraisal of its value to the national economy as a foreign exchange earner and employer of labour. "For a long time diamonds were looked upon as a sort of black market commodity, but in recent years the government has recognized their importance and is trying to find ways of making it easier for us to compete."

Company tax, once ninety-seven per cent on the diamond business, has been reduced to almost nothing. The Gold Control Act has been relaxed to allow the importation of gold for re-export in jewellery, and a free trade zone for gems and jewellery has been established in Bombay.

Jatin Mehta was one of the first to establish a factory in the free trade area, half of it for polishing diamonds and the other half for making jewellery. "Quite a few diamond people are going into manufacturing jewellery for export, and there is a jewellery boom around the corner that could create another million jobs," he says. "By bringing the polisher and the jewellery manufacturer closer together, it will be possible to create jewellery lines to absorb sizes and qualities of diamonds that at any time may not be selling well, and so make the industry more stable.

"We are aiming at the mass American market," he adds. "We will make jewellery to our customers' designs, and can save them the trouble of having to look around for diamonds. Many major manufacturing jewellers in America have for some time had their lines made up in Hong Kong and Thailand, and we can compete with both those centres. What we did in diamonds we can do in jewellery."

"It is easier to go into jewellery than to go into fancy cuts and larger stones," says Nanu Mehta. "The purpose of moving into jewellery is to promote the whole production. Because India manufactures mainly cheaper roughs, and mines around the world are producing ever larger quantities of so-called Indian rough, we need to make and market our own jewellery in order to dispose of it. We will sell our jewellery all over the world."

Diamonds are cut today in thirty-odd countries around the world. In Thailand the art of polishing coloured stones – notably ruby and sapphire – has been a cottage industry for centuries. Encouraged by the Thai government, a diamond cutting industry, specializing in a better make of small goods, has grown rapidly since the early eighties. In 1987 there were seven factories; a year later there were thirteen.

Vichit Durongkapitaya's gem business was started by his father some eighty years ago. From a small jewellery store in the Chinatown district of Bangkok the business grew to have retail, wholesale, coloured stone and jewellery manufacturing divisions. Durongkapitaya was a partner in the country's first diamond cutting venture, General Diamond Cutting, but separated a few years ago to form his own company, Premier Diamond Cutting. Today he is a DTC sight-holder, with a cutting factory employing over five hundred workers.

"We could have expanded far quicker, but we didn't want to relax our cutting standards," he says. "Labour here is more expensive than in India, so we have to work with a much better quality rough and cut to a higher standard."

His former partner, Boonyong Assarasakorn, who is also a DTC sight-holder, now has two factories, General Diamond Cutting and Thai Diamond Cutting, each employing about eight hundred workers, cutting between them some nine thousand stones a day. "There are other countries that can produce a medium make more cheaply than we can, so we have to produce a good make to be competitive," he says.

Many workers from the People's Republic of China are trained and employed on contract at Helix Diamond Company's polishing factory in Hong Kong, where Andy Wan gives the final polish to a diamond on his wheel.

Although Indian manufacturers, having the advantage of lower production costs, are in little danger of losing their traditional business to Thailand, there is much speculation about what would happen to the Indian industry if the People's Republic of China, with its even cheaper labour resources, were to go in for diamond manufacturing on a larger scale than its current production of some 200 000 carats a year. Most Indian diamantaires believe, however, that the danger is still a long way off.

"We do not need to move our businesses to China to maintain our competitive edge," says Arun Mehta. "We have hardly touched the labour potential of this country. There are many states in which it is not yet as expensive to manufacture as in Bombay, and by having the work done in those areas we can remain competitive. We are training managers to become entrepreneurs and extend the business to their home towns and create centres of employment throughout the country."

The Indian industry has its "young lions" too. Like the Belgians and the Israelis they are adapting to the new technology, like the Americans they are diversifying into jewellery, and they have half the world's production of diamonds to do it with.

"It is said that we have democratized diamonds," says Arun Mehta. "Perhaps therein lies our strength."

One of the founders of the diamond manufacturing industry in Thailand and chairman of General Diamond Cutting, Boonyong Assarasakorn relaxes with his family in the gardens of his luxury apartment building, Le Cullinan, in Bangkok.

CHAPTER 10 VARIOUS SETTINGS

The Diamonds-International Awards, the premier diamond jewellery design contest sponsored by De Beers, is held every second year, alternating with the Diamonds Today national and regional contests.

In preparation for the 1988 Awards in Paris, which attracted over two thousand entries from twenty countries, a Parisian model who is to wear an award-winning piece on the night has her hair styled for the occasion by the celebrated Alexandre of Paris.

The piece, which she is wearing, a brooch that may also be worn as an ornamental hairpin, was created by the Japanese designer Miho Inoue, sponsored by Sakamato Kikinzoku, and made of traditional material – silk thread, paper and lacquered wood – combined with 280 diamonds weighing over seventeen carats.

The contest helps stimulate new design talent and ensure that jewellery manufacturers and retailers have fresh concepts to put before consumers; spin-offs of these aspirational products in due course find their way into the wider market.

Waiting to serve her guests at the home of a friend under whom she has studied the ancient art of the tea drinking ceremony is jewellery designer Makiko Takahashi, who has thrice brought Diamonds-International awards to Tokyo.

On the gala night of the 1988 Diamonds-International Awards at the Chambre de Commerce et d'Industrie in Paris, a model displays several of the twenty-nine winning entries, prominent among them Swiss designer Gilbert Albert's necklace of platinum and yellow gold set with 399 round diamonds weighing forty-three carats, and accented with fanciful Chinese butterflies and cultured pearls.

Sam and Alisa Moussaieff of Hilton Jewellers, in the foyer of the London Hilton, are widely known for their collections based on fancy coloured diamonds.
The stones cupped in her husband's hands (right) will eventually be set in the designs of Alisa Moussaieff, here wearing a butterfly brooch of her own creation.

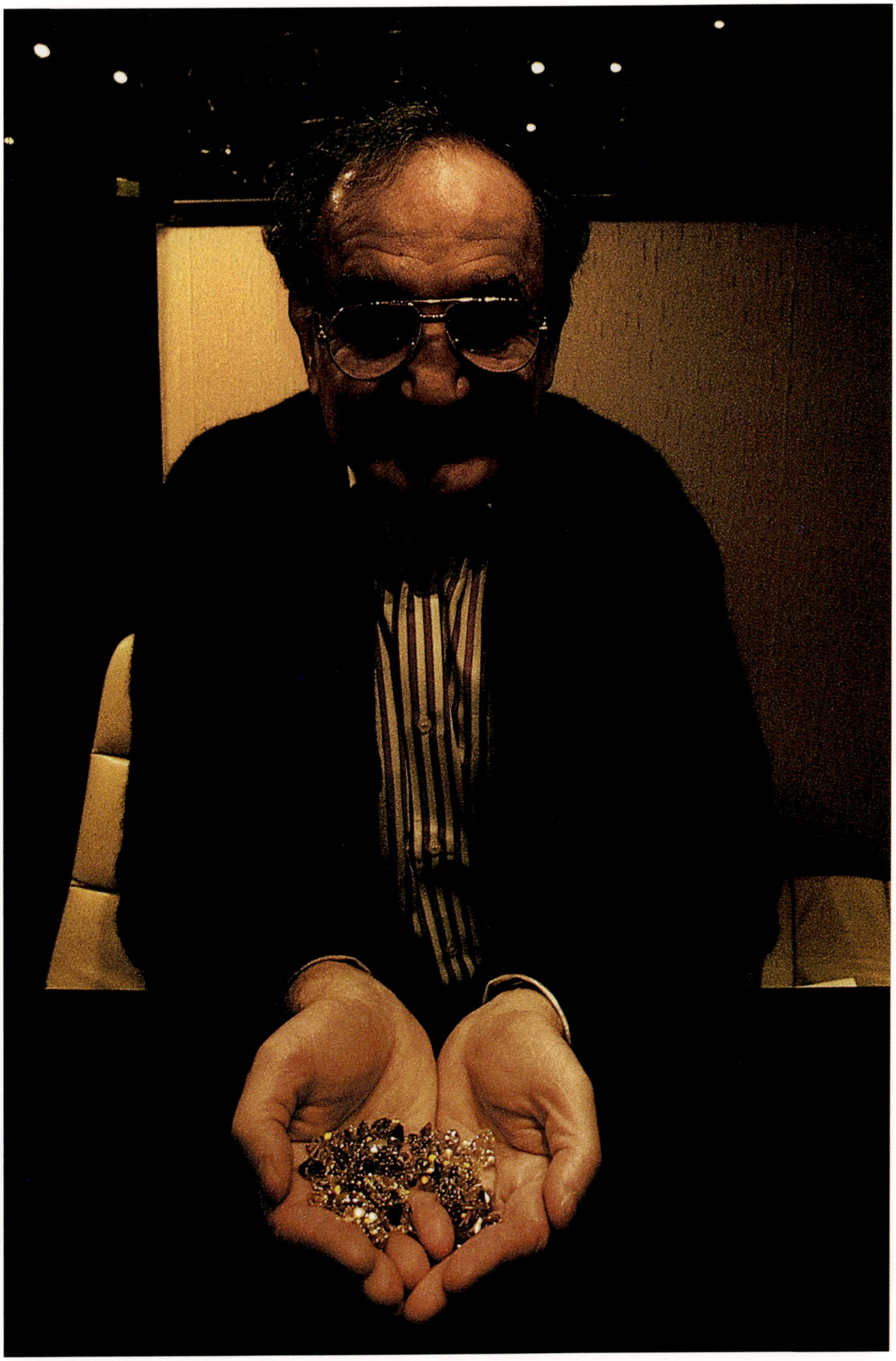

With a view of where Fifth Avenue meets Central Park from the window of his office above probably the world's best-known jewellery store, Tiffany's director of design, John Loring (right) holds a copy of the book he wrote for the 150th anniversary of the company, which he considers to be the custodian of American good taste.
Held by many to be the leading jewellery designer in America today, Ambaji Shinde (left), who began designing jewelled sword scabbards for maharajahs in India and has been the designer at Harry Winston, in New York, for over forty years, discusses the technical features of one of his characteristic creations, a choker worth several hundred thousand dollars (below left) that can be separated into single strings of diamonds.

TIFFANY TASTE

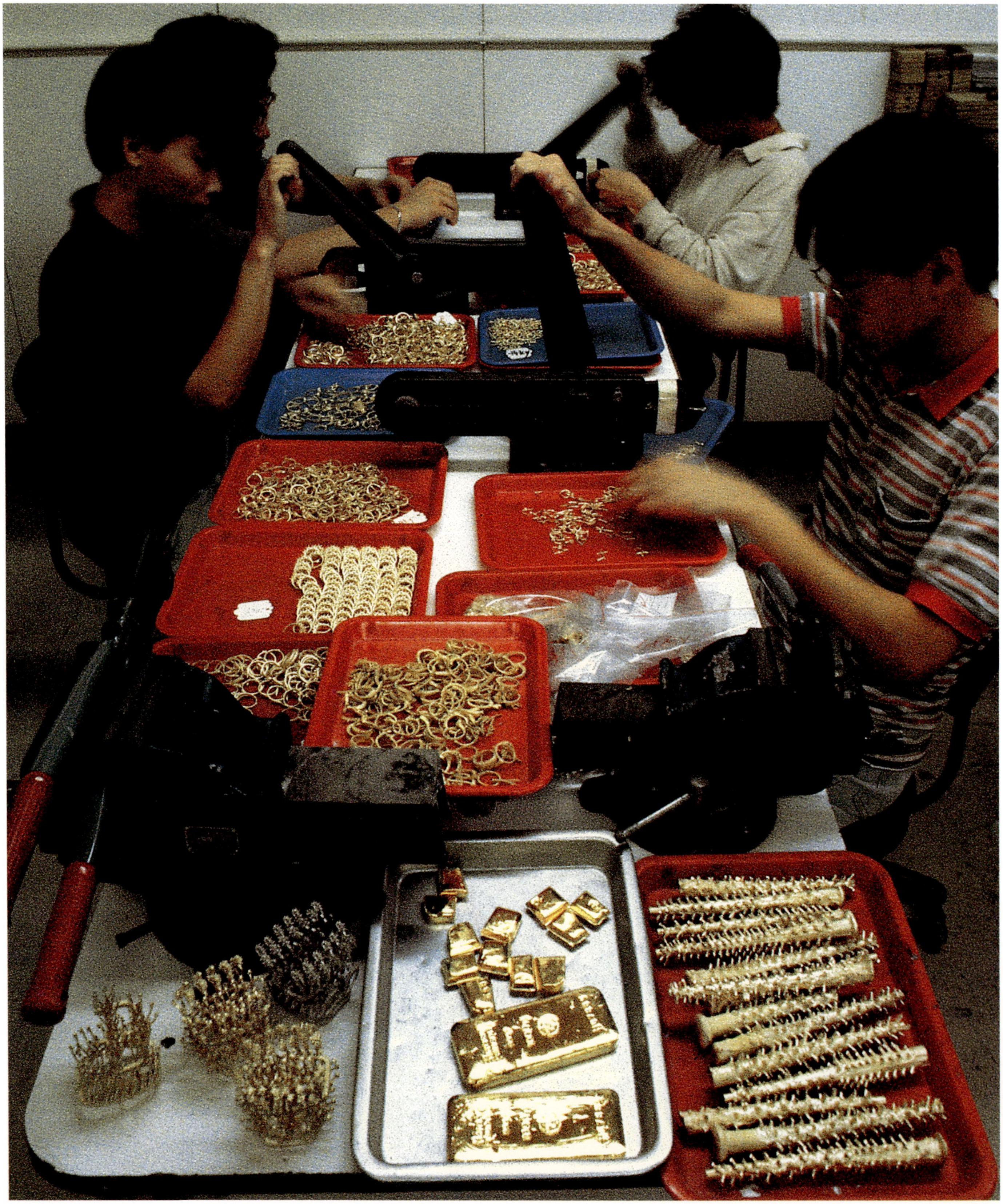

Workers at Charles and Shirley Chan's Continental Jewellery factory in Hong Kong (left) separate and trim the rough gold castings of rings and other items of production jewellery that will eventually be set with diamonds and other precious stones. At the same factory Sara Sum (above) selects the right diamond for a setting.

Avant-garde New York jewellery designer Whitney Boin at his Lower Manhattan studio with a selection of his creations. He derives much of his inspiration from the industrial design he observes in the everyday objects of an urban culture.

ARRIVING HOME FROM WORK LATE one wet night in Hong Kong, Alan Tam Yiu Cho became fascinated with the road as it unfolded in the beams of his headlights before him, disappeared beneath his car and then reappeared in his rearview mirror. The rain-slicked highway became a ribbon of black silver, divided into lanes by continuous white lines of diamonds, winding through turnpikes, arching over bridges, dipping into underpasses. At home he committed his impressions to paper, and his sketch developed into the design for a pair of diamond and black silver cufflinks. On another occasion, walking through the city's Central district, he caught a flash of sunlight reflected off a glass panel that workers high above the street were fitting into a new building. The view he glimpsed of tall, glass-sided structures reaching up on all sides to an irregular patch of sky framing the noonday sun became an award-winning brooch of white gold and tapered diamonds converging on, but not quite reaching, a single brilliant-cut diamond set at the focus of perspective.

Tam derives the ideas for his creations from his surroundings, and Hong Kong, with its hilly topography and confined level spaces, provides a cornucopia of engineering structures to inspire his designs. "Jewellery design is inspiration through observation," he says, "and I find inspiration in everything I see and touch."

He began learning the trade some twenty-five years ago as a fourteen-year-old apprentice jewellery setter in a small Hong Kong factory. Twelve years later, a visit to an exhibition of works by Henry Moore started him thinking about expressing through jewellery the sort of feelings that Moore expressed in his sculpture, and set him on the way to becoming one of Hong Kong's leading designers.

Whether the design of a piece is traditional, contemporary or futuristic, he believes that its form should develop a strong new image. "Designers need to experiment continually with the unique characteristics of different materials to find new ways of expressing design themes and creating fresh visual effects," says Tam, who has himself developed a method of setting diamonds in titanium, to utilize the iridescence produced by the oxidation of this space-age material. "I like to convey the feeling that my designs are for modern people."

Perhaps the most basic requirement of jewellery is that it be wearable. Body decoration, the precursor of other forms of decorative art, has traditions that reach back at least a hundred thousand years to the specularite miners of southern Africa mentioned in an earlier chapter. In the hands of designers like Tam the various traditions of adornment have been shorn of their regional associations and blended to the tastes of a burgeoning international urban culture, with the diamond as its emblem-in-chief.

In a renovated former tent factory in an emerging artistic neighbourhood in downtown Manhattan, Whitney Boin, winner of several Diamonds Today awards, a Diamonds-International award and a host of other distinctions, creates a highly individual line of jewellery for a select clientele. Like Tam, he draws inspiration from the architecture and industrial design about him. The cooling fins of motorcycle engines provided the inspiration for one of his most popular collections, while the names he gives to some of his pieces, among them the Suspension ring and the Cantilever ring, acknowledge a debt to civil engineering.

Breaking with the convention of making the stone the centrepiece and the metal merely the setting for displaying it, Boin treats the diamond purely as an element of design. "I use a diamond as a source of light within what may be essentially a gold creation," he says. "It is there not to be shown off by the field but to create a point of light in the field. Only a diamond has the brilliance that gives me a bright enough point around which to build a piece. Different cuts emit different types of light: round stones sparkle and break up light into twinkling patterns, whereas the broad facets of an emerald cut give off large flashes of dynamic light."

Although gold and diamonds are the principal materials he works in, Boin often combines others with them to produce special effects. "I may, for instance, use platinum with diamonds," he says; "not polished platinum, in which the stone tends to be lost, but platinum with a matt finish, where the diamond is the hard crystal structure and bright light, surrounded by a softer grey glow."

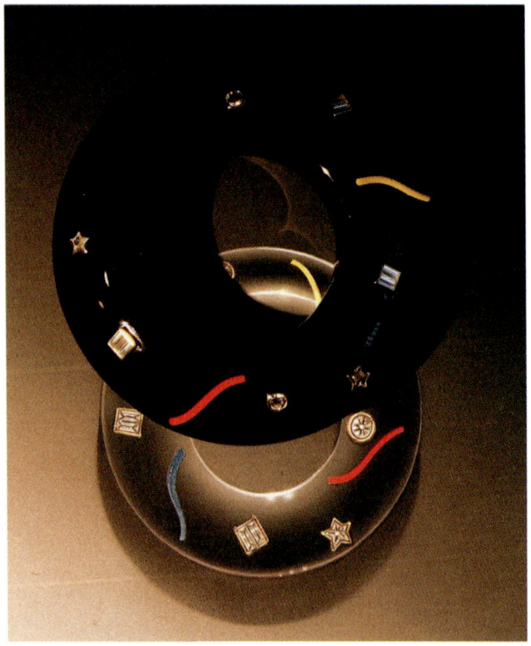

Whitney Boin, sponsored by Nova Stylings, received his first Diamonds-International award in 1988 for this doughnut-shaped onyx bangle studded with bezel-set diamonds of different shapes and colours.

The piece that won him his first Diamonds-International award was a thick doughnut-shaped onyx bangle, studded with twenty carats of diamonds, with rods of silver coated in coloured rubber that form little neon-bright squiggles on the black surface. "The concept was simply to have a startling, very dense geometrical shape to offset the diamonds," he says. "It had to be big and dark to have the effect of a galaxy in the firmament, and as the diamonds were of different sizes, cuts and colours, each became a unique element in the galaxy."

Boin learnt the basic skills of working with metals from his father in the basement of their New Jersey home. After completing a degree with high honours in jewellery design at the Rochester Institute of Technology, he went to work as a benchman – soldering, casting, filing – for a jewellery manufacturer on Canal Street who was turning out thousands of engagement and wedding rings every day.

"At Rochester the emphasis had been on the artistic side of design," he recalls. "On Canal Street I learnt to respect the people who produce things quickly in a commercially efficient way. I learnt to work fast, to be a craftsman rather than an artist, and my love for the craftsmanship grew up from the materials. But I reached a point where I felt that my future lay in combining my creative ability with my craft skills, and so I went out to work for the smaller independents, who were, as I am now, designing and producing their own lines to sell to retailers."

In 1983 a collection of diamond and gold earrings won him the New Designer of the Year award at the Jewelers of America international trade show in New York. Since then he has introduced a new collection every year. "I don't make up complete sets, but debut a thought with a suite of five or six pieces, which I add to as time goes by," he says. "So an idea that starts out as rings broadens into earrings, bracelets and necklaces."

Although both Boin and Tam are clearly artists in their field, neither is so preoccupied with being an artist that he fails to appreciate that his creations must also be wearable, affordable, desirable and, in a word, commercial. Design competitions and private commissions give them opportunities to express themselves freely and develop new concepts, which they can then modify and adapt to the commercial collections they produce.

"Jewellery is an art, but not a pure art in which the intrinsic value of the materials is irrelevant and the work itself has no practical application," says Hong Kong designer Charles Baldinger. "It isn't enough for jewellery to be aesthetically pleasing; it must be made of noble materials; it must have value. If I can produce the same effect with white gold that I can with steel, I'd rather use the gold. And because jewellery is for wearing, it shouldn't have sharp projections which, no matter how pleasing to the eye, may inconvenience the wearer. Above all, jewellery designs should be new and different, but without running to extremes."

While the avant-garde may well be charting future directions in jewellery design, they cater primarily to the more sophisticated and adventurous wearers who, although growing in number, are still only a part of the market for designer jewellery, and a very small part of the total jewellery market. Of all the jewellery sold world-wide every year, by far the greater part is more traditional in concept, more conservative in design.

"Because I was inexperienced, I tried to be too innovative when I started designing in the sixties," says Madison Avenue designer and manufacturer José Hess. "I had to tone it down and start making jewellery that would still be different, but acceptable. I had to allow the taste level of my customers to determine to some extent the direction I was going in. I have to work within the tradition, but try to extend it a little with every piece I create."

New York designer José Hess, winner of several Diamonds-International awards, adjusts one of his diamond necklaces, which is worn by Philadelphia model Jennifer Amicone at a photographic shoot for a countrywide wedding fashion promotion.

A fugitive from Germany during World War II, Hess began learning goldsmithing in Colombia in 1948, when he was fourteen. At sixteen he went to the United States and worked for goldsmiths in New York, where he attended art classes at night school and went on to complete a three-year course in design. Eventually he set up on his own and hired craftsmen to execute his designs. As the business grew he moved to larger and larger premises. In the Madison Avenue suite he has occupied for over a decade his staff of forty do everything from making the original models of his designs to the final production of some five thousand pieces of jewellery a year.

"Almost anything I see can spark an idea for a design," he says. "I may get ideas from nature, but I don't try to reproduce nature. As I work on an idea, whatever it started out as develops into something else, because what I am doing is playing with shapes. There is no end to shapes; the challenge is to find the right ones. I make the diamonds the heroes in my pieces, but I use them to create the design and make the whole piece interesting. I start with a shape and then, as an artist might apply paints of different colours, I fill it in, using the gold, the platinum and the diamonds as contrasting colours."

Although less than twenty per cent of his time is spent actually designing, thinking about his designs, he says, is a full-time occupation. If anything he sees suggests a design, he immediately scribbles a sketch in a pocket notebook and later files the page. "Every few months, when I have a fat folder of scribbles, I go off by myself to an island for a week or so, to work through them," he says. "I toss out the dud ideas, develop the rest, and come back with designs for a new collection, which I have an assistant draw and paint precisely. Then I ask my craftsmen, sales people and a few clients to vote on which we should make. Often ideas that seemed great in the beginning get thrown out in the end."

Twice a year Hess brings out a new collection of about two hundred pieces, and invites the retail stores he deals with to place their orders. Within a collection there are usually several sets of companion pieces, each set having a different "look", as well as a number of individual pieces that help extend the appeal of the collection to a wider range of tastes. Most of the pieces retail for between \$2000 and \$100 000, none for less and only a few, usually special commissions by customers of client stores, for more.

"The sort of woman I have in mind when I design is very modern, casual and secure, who likes to wear her jewellery during the day and prefers it to be understated," says Hess.

New York designer Henry Dunay, winner of thirty-eight international design distinctions, including three Diamonds-International awards, believes in designing jewellery for women from a man's point of view, "the way men like to see them and therefore the way women want to be seen." When he started designing back in 1965 he imagined an archetypal woman, his "Suntan Lady", for whom he would create jewellery. "She wasn't necessarily beautiful, but she worked at being beautiful," he says. "Afterwards I created other imaginary ladies, with different types of faces, and designed different styles to suit them."

Dunay began as an errand boy for a jewellery firm on the Bowery, worked seven years for a manufacturing jeweller, and has been in business for himself for over thirty years. Describing himself as "conservatively modern", he likes to think that he moves ahead of the times and sets the pace.

He envisages every piece he designs as an item in a collection, partly because this provides him with a creative framework for developing a concept, and partly as an aid to selling. "If I show a client a pair of earrings on its own it is simply an odd pair of earrings, but if I show her a collection, I can sell her the concept," he says. "Then she may start with the earrings, and later come back for the ring, the bracelet, the necklace, the whole set."

Dunay considers the adjustment of learning to think more like a business man and less like a designer as the most difficult in his life, and there is still, he says, "a continual internal battle between the designer who wants to conceive and the business man who must harness his creativity."

He compares his sales strategy to the saltwater fish he keeps in a tank at his Manhattan showroom. "Drop a piece of bread into the tank and as it sinks to the bottom different kinds of fish attack it at different depths and then draw back as it passes to another level," he says. "I target a new look at the ladies who are the trendsetters at the very top of the socio-economic scale. But those they influence may not be able to pay as much, so I follow up with slightly smaller pieces using the same concepts, and then more modest compositions, which I adapt to different facial types to broaden the market. It takes three years for a concept to filter through. People buy at the level which, whether they know it or not, is the level that is most comfortable for them."

He designs exclusive pieces, as well as limited editions, for which he makes two or three of a piece, and production items in slightly larger runs. His workshop staff of seventeen turns out pieces that retail through major stores in the United States, Europe and Japan at prices ranging from $2000 for gold earrings to half a million dollars for a diamond necklace.

Although Dunay keeps an eye on couture fashions, they have no great influence on his work. "It takes me a year to complete a collection, by which time couture fashions will have changed," he says. "My jewellery has to be above fashion, because the lady who's paying ten or twenty thousand dollars for a 'Dunay' doesn't want it to be here today and gone tomorrow. Working in diamonds, gold and pearls, I have something classical, to which I can give a beautiful shape and a feeling that it will always be a masterpiece."

As Baldinger says: "Jewellery is too expensive to be governed by fashion; because the materials endure, the piece must endure in all respects. A well-designed piece in good materials should last several lifetimes and never see the melting pot again, because it is good regardless of fashion. There may be more demand for bangles when short-sleeved dresses are in vogue, and when it is fashionable for women to wear their hair up they will want to wear big earrings, but good quality bangles and big earrings made for their grandmothers should be as perfect for the occasion as any made today."

Madison Avenue manufacturer of fine jewellery Kurt Wayne rejects the idea of creating for an ideal woman. "That would be far too limiting," he says. "When designing a piece we visualize how it will look on a woman, but with the view that it should look equally good, although in different ways, on all women."

Wayne went to America from Austria in 1939 and worked eight years for manufacturing jewellers in New York before establishing his own firm. Today his four sons handle various aspects of the business, but he still initiates all the design ideas and oversees their execution by in-house designers.

"I don't design to try to please the public," says Wayne. "It would be disastrous to let other people tell you what to design, because few really know what they want until they see it. As an originator, I make what I think is nice, and then let the public decide whether they want it or not."

"Techniques may change and trends come and go, but father's styling is so classical that what we make today would have been saleable ten years ago and will still be saleable ten years from now," says his son Gary. "Naturally there is continual renewal and development in our designs, but they are not Contemporary, or Modern or Art Deco, which have had their day. Our pieces can be worn at all times, not only on special occasions."

Surrounded by his contemporary art collection in the workplace, Los Angeles jewellery stylist and manufacturer, Martin Gruber, whose Nova Stylings has sponsored a string of Diamonds-International Awards winners.

The company makes a limited edition of each design it produces and sells them through stores at retail prices of anything from two thousand to several hundred thousand dollars. "The big stores are an important part of our business, but they don't account for a great percentage of our sales," says Gary Wayne. "We rely a lot on the small stores that have a dozen good clients and look to us to help them make an important sale at Christmas time. Often you find the wealthiest customers in out of the way places."

One of the most vexing problems that fine jewellers face is imitation, which is certainly not the sincerest form of flattery, according to company president Ronald Wayne. "We welcome fair competition from anywhere in the world," he says, "but we object to having to compete with other people's copies of our own designs. The industry and the consumer would greatly benefit if these manufacturers would put their energies into creating *original* designs."

Finding there were manufacturers who waited for him to set a trend and then made less expensive copies of his designs for the mass market, Martin Gruber of Nova Stylings, in Los Angeles, decided to join them, and formed a separate company to make more affordable versions of his own Nova designs. Since he began designing jewellery in 1973 Nova has won more than a dozen Diamonds Today and two Diamonds-International awards.

"Where design has to fit within the marketing parameters in most other industries, concept and design precede marketing in the jewellery industry," he says. "We start with a concept. For example, I saw a painting by Picasso in London and felt there was something in it for me, although I didn't know what. On the way back on the plane I made a rough sketch of a layout that became our Picasso collection, although it has nothing to do with Picasso, apart from the initial inspiration."

The concept may also grow out of the technique. "In the piece that won us a Diamonds Today award in 1985 we set baguettes on end, alternately facing in opposite directions, which produced the effect of a stained-glass window made entirely of diamonds. Here the concept grew out of our attempts to find a new way of setting diamonds, and we then adapted it in designing other pieces."

Gruber likes to indulge the luxury of being able to ignore cost and concentrate on concept and design. With a staff of over two hundred he produces several new collections a year, which he markets through major retail stores at the top end of the market in the United States and Europe. "Often we'll buy an important stone – which for us means ten or fifteen carats – and build a set around it," he says.

In the workplace he surrounds himself and his staff with original contemporary artworks, which he believes provide the right mood for creative activity. "We're not just selling diamonds, platinum and gold," he says. "Jewellery is our art, the form in which we express our creativity through the medium of diamonds and noble metals."

Rumanian-born Gregory Stewart works alone designing and making custom jewellery in a small sixth-floor studio in West 45th Street. His great-grandfather made jewellery for the Tsar of Russia and his grandfather was jeweller in Bucharest to King Michael of

Rumania. His father began teaching him jewellery making when he was nine, and he worked as a jeweller in Rumania until he was in his late twenties. In 1960 he emigrated, by way of Israel, to New York, where he worked for other jewellery manufacturers for four years before starting his own business. "Since then I have done everything myself, from the design to making the final piece," he says. "Nothing leaves my hands before it is complete."

Stewart too is an artist, without affectation; he enjoys being a craftsman, and there is a touch of alchemy in his craft. Distrustful of refiners, he refines his gold and platinum himself. Secretive about his designs, he works alone, changing his metaphorical hat as he moves between his setting bench, his polishing bench, his jewellery bench and his model-making bench, developing his own techniques.

His designs grow directly out of the materials. "When I get a parcel of loose diamonds I lay them out, rearrange them, think about what I can do with them, try to see the finished piece in my mind and visualize the procedure I will follow right through to the final product," he says. "Afterwards I may change a few small details along the way, but I never change course."

When making earrings, he first pairs the diamonds according to their colour, shape and size. With one of each pair, he then builds a model in wax, placing one stone at a time, trimming the wax around it, adjusting the levels within the three-dimensional design, until all the stones are in exactly the positions they will occupy in the finished piece. Next he removes one diamond at a time, makes a platinum wire setting for it, and replaces it in the model, cutting away a little wax to accommodate the setting. As an earring must be the mirror image of its partner, he makes a plaster cast on which to base the second of the pair. He then completes the mount by soldering all the individual settings in place on a foundation of platinum rings.

Stewart works almost exclusively in diamonds and finds his inspiration in new cuts developed by diamond manufacturers. "The metal has to be there, but not obtrusively," he says. "I prefer making all-white pieces."

In Europe, jewellery design is far from being homogeneous. Although many leading designers cater to cosmopolitan tastes, much of the jewellery produced reflects different regional lifestyles and traditional preferences.

Taste in southern Europe is for the more flamboyant designs in eighteen-carat gold. Because people who aspire to high-quality gold jewellery generally also aspire to better quality diamond pieces, Italy, which is renowned for its yellow gold jewellery, has become the key producer of diamond jewellery for the more expensive end of the market. Also within the yellow gold tradition, the growing Spanish industry manufactures jewellery chiefly for the internal market, and designs often reflect Moorish influences that are part of the Iberian ethos.

Typical of the southern tradition is the Barcelona-based designer, Victor Caparros, who has twelve outlets in Spain for his Catalan style of yellow gold and diamond jewellery. Another is Gianni Bulgari, who has established the house style, of yellow gold encrusted in diamonds and other precious stones, for the international business that his brother Paolo runs from Rome. Fourth generation Athenian jeweller, Ilias Lalaounis, is famous internationally for his gold collections. His designs, executed by some two hundred artisans in his workshop at the foot of the Acropolis, are inspired by the artistic creations of ancient civilizations and the discoveries of modern science, interpreted in a way that makes them eternally contemporary.

Designs with clean, strong lines appeal more to a sophisticated, quality conscious market in northern Europe. "There is a strong trend, particularly in Germany, where the tradition is for eight-carat and nine-carat gold, towards mixed metal jewellery, in which gold and platinum are combined in the same piece and diamonds are used to accentuate the design," says Susan Farmer, co-ordinator of the CSO's Diamond Information Centres. "There young women in business have greater spending power, and because they often go straight from work to their social engagements, they want good simple diamond jewellery that looks equally at home in boardroom and discotheque."

A leading exponent of the northern ideal, although he works in eighteen-carat gold, is Andrew Grima, who at his studio in Lugano, Switzerland, designs pieces for private clients, including members of the British Royal Family. He is regarded as having in the 1960s set new standards for modern jewellery, and designs pieces that have a random, free look, with great emphasis on texture, many of them based on *objets trouvés* – leaves, twigs, pieces of bark – cast in gold and set with gems.

Georg Hornemann, of Dusseldorf, is reckoned by many to be the most distinguished designer in Europe today. Winner of three Diamonds-International awards and many other distinctions, he and his staff of goldsmiths work in the finest traditions of the ancient guilds, turning out inspired, unconventional pieces. He eschews the uniform and the mass produced, and cultivates individuality and uniqueness. "A piece of jewellery," he says, "is a work of art used as a means of communication, reflecting the personality of its wearer, or giver."

Designs with clean, strong lines are not the prerogative of northern European designers, however. Milanese designers Sara and Fulvio Scavia, winners of a special award marking the twenty-fifth anniversary of the Diamonds-International Awards, create unique pieces that they retail themselves. Every piece, they say, has its story, its cultural reference, its aesthetic charm: "We believe that a piece of jewellery bears witness to a time and to customs; that it is a cultural message sent through time, and so must retain its value in time. Our jewellery cannot, and should not, be merely traditional. We use gold, platinum, diamonds and other precious stones, but also such materials as leather, rope and silk, to soften the tone and avoid ostentation."

"A relatively new development in Europe has been that young designers, whose concepts are probably closer to the tastes of young people with money to spend, have formed groups to produce excitingly different designs," says James Courage, one of the CSO's consumer and advertising division market controllers for Europe. "Because the outlay for diamond jewellery is high and young designers have difficulty finding the consumer, they can achieve as a group what they cannot as individuals, and as more young people become interested in acquiring individual pieces, the groups are finding greater demand for their talents."

In Europe, as in the United States, the market for expensive, designer jewellery is only the upper end of the diamond jewellery market, which has at its lower end a volume market supplying less expensive diamond pieces to people who, although they may never be able to buy fine diamonds, want to own diamond jewellery. Even the most exclusive designers and jewellers who cater to the top of the market acknowledge a debt to the mass market, on the principle that those who buy the less expensive pieces today are potential customers for the more costly items tomorrow.

London designer, manufacturer and retailer of fine jewellery Lawrence Graff, who scours the world for large, important diamonds of the best quality and creates exclusive pieces of jewellery, principally in the $50 000 to $100 000 price range, recalls that he started out in the business making jewellery with semi-precious stones that sold for two or three pounds. "Walk down any High Street in England today and you'll find people selling trinkets, fashion jewellery, copper bangles and silver rings," he says. "For as long as that trade continues there will be a diamond business, and for as long as there is a diamond business there will be somebody wanting to buy the important stones."

Germany is the major producer in Europe of cheaper diamond jewellery, and German jewellery manufacturers, making extensive use of modern technology, produce more of Europe's mass market diamond jewellery than is imported from South-East Asia. They offer a better finish at a better price than their Asian competitors, but compromises are made in the design of cheaper items to give them a more expensive appearance, and

With infinite care and precision, a setter (far left) mounts a diamond in a ring at Yamamori Chokin Kogei in Tokyo, where thirty employees make jewellery incorporating well over a million carats of diamonds a year.
Noble metals are alloyed in modern electric furnaces (left) for casting jewellery mountings at Yamamori Chokin.
In the Hong Kong workshop (right) of Continental Jewellery, a large-scale manufacturer.

Francois Machet (far left) begins piecing together a layout for a necklace at Henri Marteau's Georland Jewellers, in Paris, manufacturers of large, expensive pieces in the more classical European style for exclusive jewellery retailers world-wide.
Ivan Dias (left) assembles a necklace for a client in the Rio de Janeiro workshop of leading Brazilian designer and jeweller Kimelblat Natan.
The belief that diamonds are symbols of power is reflected in the strong designs of Koon Kow Lee (right), director and chief designer of Hong Kong-based J's Concepts, which is named after Jade Princess, the jade jewellery store his family started in Shanghai in the 1920s.

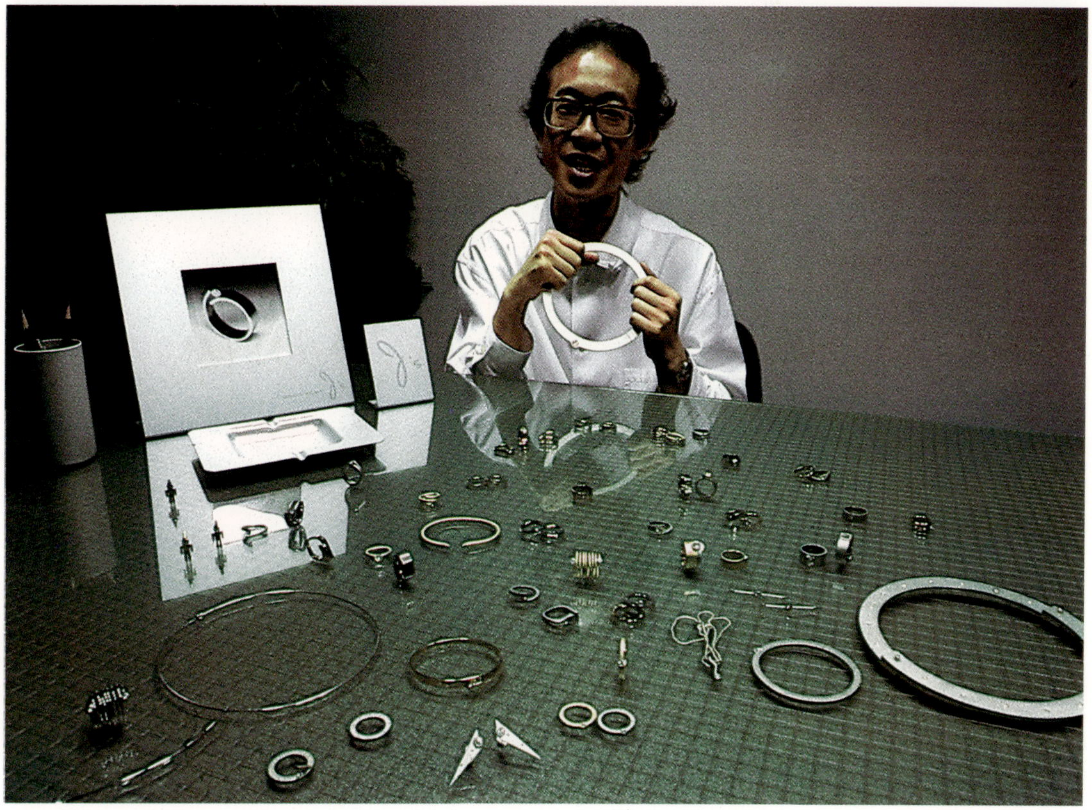

"illusion" settings, which make the stones seem larger and create an illusion of value, at a low price, are frequently used.

The recent histories of diamond cutting and production-line jewellery manufacturing are in some respects similar. Just as the manufacturing of smaller diamonds in poorer qualities was driven out of Europe and the United States by high labour costs and taken over by new cutting centres that could manufacture them more economically, so too has the manufacturing of cheaper jewellery been taken over to a large extent by new centres in South-East Asia, where labour is less expensive.

When diamond jewellery manufacturer and exporter Anton Weder arrived in Hong Kong from the Philippines in 1965 the only jewellery being made there was for local consumption. "What changed that was that Hong Kong – a free port, with no duties, sales tax or currency restrictions – developed into a regional trading centre, to which the Japanese, who didn't at that time travel much beyond Singapore, came to buy their diamonds, jade and emeralds," he says. "And in the mid-seventies this stimulated tremendous expansion into producing jewellery for export."

Initially Hong Kong jewellery manufacturers had the advantage of lower labour costs, but as the industry expanded it outgrew the available labour supply. With the steady improvement in the general level of education in Hong Kong, the supply of suitable labour shrank; new high-tech industries, requiring a better educated workforce, grew up and absorbed school-leavers who previously might have gone to work in the jewellery factories. Labour consequently became too expensive for jewellery manufacturers to continue in the old way, and a number established factories in the People's Republic of China, where inexpensive labour is plentiful, to manufacture their cheaper lines and part-make the more expensive pieces. In Hong Kong itself they were able to remain competitive by investing in modern technology and making better qualities of jewellery.

Frank Tang launched his manufacturing business, Myer Jewelry, in 1977 with five workers. Today he exports almost half a million pieces a year and employs over five hundred workers in three factories in China, where he manufactures jewellery for the lower end of the market, and two hundred in his Hong Kong factory.

"No matter how big you become as a manufacturer, you can never produce enough designs," he says. "It takes many manufacturers to make a range wide enough to satisfy everybody, and even then there is always room for more creativity in the market. We have to continually develop new ideas."

"Hong Kong is no longer a producer of cheap jewellery," says Stanley Chan, general manager of Larry Jewelry, a manufacturing and retailing business with factories in Hong Kong, Singapore and Canton. "Now that Hong Kong has a few good designers and has improved its workmanship, it is producing good quality jewellery that finds a ready market in Japan, Europe and America. As the industry grows, we face keener competition from other centres and have to give greater attention to designing better pieces."

"Design is ultimately what sells, and the success of any jewellery manufacturer depends on his designs," says Weder. "We are no longer competing with countries manufacturing for the lower end of the market, but with the European and American manufacturers, and for that Hong Kong has to be able to produce well designed jewellery at competitive prices."

As Hong Kong moved into the markets for better quality jewellery, Bangkok emerged to produce the cheaper ranges that had previously been made in the British colony.

"Although Thailand has for centuries produced jewellery for local consumption, there was for many years no export market for Thai jewellery, because our designs were unsuitable and our workmanship generally poor," says Frank Kingchatchaval, who today has a factory turning out about thirty pieces of jewellery a day, of which the cheapest retails for $2000. "But now the standard of our work is almost as good as the European, and we can manufacture very much more cheaply."

When Soonthon Pornprakit's grandfather started the family business in Bangkok over fifty years ago his jewellery was made to his own designs by traditional craftsmen working in their homes. The firm grew with the city, and today it has a diamond cutting factory employing two hundred workers and a factory manufacturing jewellery for both local consumption and export.

"Our designs for the local market are different to those we produce for export," says Pornprakit. "The Thai sense of beauty, which is reflected in our temple architecture, favours gently curved, graceful lines and a lot of fine detail. There is great satisfaction in doing this type of work properly, but it is not popular with Europeans, who prefer designs that are dominated by hard, straight lines."

"Thai women like wearing showy pieces of good quality and high value, and traditionally our jewellery is made in softer gold with carved motifs, silver inlays and rose-cut diamonds," says jewellery manufacturer and retailer Montri Ma, whose father started the business with a small lapidary shop in the early forties. "Most of the designs that we retail ourselves cater to traditional taste, but we also make pieces for export that are neither Eastern nor typically contemporary European, because our Japanese clients prefer simple, evergreen styles."

Jewellery is today second only to textiles as a foreign exchange earner for Thailand. A fiscally enlightened government levies no duties on diamonds imported for re-export as jewellery, while Japan and European countries that have trade agreements favouring Thailand as an under-developed country allow the importation of Thai jewellery duty free.

But already Thai manufacturers are looking over their shoulders at the export jewellery industry emerging in India and wondering how it will affect them.

"It will take the Indians quite a few years to catch up with us, and for the moment we still have the advantage of relatively cheap labour, but it is becoming more expensive, and in the long run the only way for us to remain competitive will be to move up-market, as Hong Kong has done," says Kingchatchaval.

"Most of Thailand's jewellery exports are still in the medium range, but we have begun producing more important pieces for the international market," says Ma. "We have to move into the higher grades of jewellery, produce quality, improve our designing capability and introduce improved technology to remain competitive. There is no reason why we shouldn't become the Fifth Tiger – after Hong Kong, Singapore, Taiwan and South Korea – of the newly industrialized countries in South-East Asia."

Running repairs – a Parisian model wearing designer diamond earrings takes a few minutes off from a dinner party to titivate.

CHAPTER 11

THE GIFT OF LOVE

The centuries-old symbolic association between "indestructible" diamonds and the ideal of everlasting love has made diamond jewellery the ultimate gift of love.

A gift in the form of a diamond engagement ring is an earnest of a young couple's intention to marry, and further gifts of diamonds throughout their life together are seen as a reaffirmation of their love, an enduring reminder of the occasions for which they were given.

Getting ready for what is a great moment in any woman's life, airline stewardess Kathryn Parsons tries on her wedding gown at Iris Dennis's Bridal Boutique in Sydney, assisted at the fitting by the proprietor's daughter, Bernice Dennis.

In the words of the timeless slogan that N.W. Ayer copywriter, Frances Gerety, wrote more than forty years ago: A Diamond is Forever.

The jewellery showroom on the ground floor of Tiffany's emporium in New York, tastefully dressed in its Christmas finery.

Diamonds are a frequent topic of conversation (top) when Hong Kong ladies meet for tea, as at this small party in the Regent Hotel, where Ina Chow serves for close friends Yvonne Ku and Nancy Wong.
Wearing the Natan diamond necklace and bracelet given her by her banker husband on their twentieth wedding anniversary, Isa Bozano (above) in the drawing-room of their home in Rio de Janeiro.
New York Diamond Information Centre staffer Carole Holmes (opposite) and her screen and television actress mother Arlene Dahl, looking like a million dollars in diamond and crystal jewellery created by David Webb of New York.

神栄石野証券
中華料理
銀座アスター
メイ・ウシヤマの
ハリウッド化粧品
銀座一丁目
読売広告社
GINZA-2
MELSA
GINZA ITO-YA
MATSUYA GINZA
MITSUKOSHI
スコッチウイスキー
バランタイン
中央宣興

Bejewelled at night with neon lights, the Ginza (left), in Tokyo, displays the exuberance of a highly sophisticated consumer society, in which diamonds have become an integral part of the new urban culture.

Ryo Yamaguchi, on the left of the group (above), managing director of Mikimoto, one of the best-known jewellery houses in Japan, discusses a forthcoming spring diamond jewellery promotion with senior sales staff at the entrance to the Mikimoto building on the Ginza.

Customers discuss the merchandise with sales assistants in a Hyderabad jewellery store (above). An item of jewellery more popular in the East than the West, a diamond nose pin (opposite), worn here in combination with a seven-diamond earring, for luck, by Sapna Bhatia, of Bombay.

Increasingly, the pledges whispered by young Hong Kong lovers (above) under the lights on the promenade outside the Regent Hotel are sealed with a diamond engagement ring.

Jewellery stores (opposite) alternate with restaurants and toy shops in crowded Nathan Road, Kowloon, one of several Hong Kong streets in which the density of jewellery stores looks to be the highest in the world.

KRUPS
康樂牌家庭電器
CHEONG HING
STORE LTD.
昌興
化粧
香水
HUMPHREYS AVENUE
BY
PHOEBE
TOYS
Kodak
彩雀
DRAGON LAKE SEAFOOD RESTAURANT
ORIENTAL ARTS & JEWELLERY CO.
WHOLESALE & RETAIL
FOOCHOW LACQUER CO.
JEWELLERY & ANTIQUES
ENTRANCE: Around Corner On Cameron Road
Roys Jeweller
OF SWITZERLAND
CHEONG HI
STORE LTD.
昌興士多有限公
McDonald's
HOYA

Retired now in the Pennsylvanian countryside, Paul Darrow and Charlie Coiner, who created the artwork for De Beers' first diamond advertising campaigns in the United States during the late thirties and early forties, reminisce over a glass of wine from a local vineyard for which they design labels.

AS A MARKETING SLOGAN, "A Diamond is Forever" has been as enduring as the precious stone it describes. Since it was penned in Philadelphia in the small hours of the morning some forty-odd years ago by Frances Gerety, a copywriter working on the De Beers account at N.W. Ayer, it has become part of the language, an aphorism that in popular imagination links the symbolism of the "indestructible" diamond to the ideal of eternal love. In the minds of young women, the symbolism of the stone made the diamond engagement ring an indispensable assurance of everlasting marital bliss and proclaimed that any subsequent gifts of diamonds they received from their husbands would be gifts of love, of reaffirmation.

Also living in retirement in Pennsylvania is Frances Gerety, author of the famous line: A Diamond is Forever.

The symbolic association of diamonds with everlasting love is an ancient one. De Beers did little more than reinforce, popularize and adapt it, and was not the first to do so. A century before De Beers began marketing diamonds in America, Charles Lewis Tiffany, who founded the world's most famous jewellery store in 1837 and ran it until his death in 1902, grasped the marketing potential of the association.

The first man to be named King of Diamonds in New York, Tiffany in 1877 bought a 128.51-carat canary-yellow brilliant, which he named The Tiffany Diamond and put on permanent display in his showroom as the emblem of his store. When the French Ministry of Finance auctioned the deposed Empress Eugénie's jewels, he bought twenty-four lots, and sold them amid great publicity to the "empresses" of industrial America. But perhaps his greatest service to the popularity of diamonds was his six-pronged setting – now the standard setting for engagement rings – which was designed to allow the most light into a solitaire. Not surprisingly, it became every American girl's dream to have a diamond engagement ring from the store that displayed the most famous diamond in the country and sold the jewels of Napoleon III's empress to the aristocracy of America's gilded age.

"Mr Tiffany's genius was in realizing that, in a new country with a relatively simple social life, design need not be conditioned by European traditions of ornamentation for elaborate court occasions and state ceremonies," says Tiffany's design director John Loring. "He identified the wedding as the all-American ceremony, the engagement ring as the most saleable form of diamond jewellery, and concentrated on a setting that would show off the diamond better than ever before. He positioned this company for the market that is always there – the bridal market – and today we continue this commitment to the mystique of the American wedding."

Although Tiffany's makes and retails many other more costly pieces of jewellery, "the firm's business is based on the one-carat diamond engagement ring and the standard things that every girl starting her jewellery collection wants," says Loring. "We work on the principle that young people who are pleased with the rings we sell them will come back to us when they want to add to their collections."

Today Tiffany's is not merely a jewellery emporium on the corner of Fifth Avenue and 57th Street; it is an American institution. "We have been custodians of American taste throughout our history," says Loring. "There was little indigenous taste to speak of when we started out, and as it evolved we helped shape it. We have always designed our jewellery to add glamour, pleasure and excitement to daily life and everyday American ceremonies."

In addition to its retail branches in Boston, Chicago, San Francisco, Beverley Hills, Houston, Dallas and Atlanta, Tiffany's has stores in London and Munich and fifteen stores in Japan. It sells the same designs on overseas markets that it sells at home. "We export our own taste, making clear statements that we feel are American statements," says Loring, "and the world has welcomed the American taste for simple, tailored pieces."

Where Charles Tiffany had taken diamonds from the courts of Europe and introduced them to the newly affluent of industrial America, a small-town Texan, Morris Zale, gave diamonds to the masses on the eve of the Great Depression. Starting with his uncle's jewellery store in Wichita Falls, he founded the Zale Corporation in 1924, and opened new stores in Tulsa, Oklahoma City and Amarillo to sell diamonds to workers in the booming oilfields of Texas and Oklahoma. Recovering quickly after the Crash, Zale added store after store to what grew during his sixty years as president of the firm into an international chain of 1700 jewellery stores, employing 13 500 people and turning over more than $1 billion a year.

Warner Shelly, retired chairman of N.W. Ayer, who was involved from the outset in launching and running De Beers' diamond advertising campaigns in the United States.

Credit, creative merchandising and an expansionist policy were the foundations on which Zale built his retail empire. "We started as a credit jeweller offering goods for a dollar down and a dollar a week," he recalls. "Jewellery stores until then had been forbidding places that catered only to the well-to-do; we identified the working people as a market that other jewellers had ignored. They had the income to spend with us if we made up lines that attracted them. We gave them credit and tried to make our jewellery as competitive as we could."

Zale sold his way through recessions by creating a demand for items that nobody had made previously. If he found that he had surplus stocks of stones of a colour or quality that few people wanted, he developed new lines to utilize them, and not only used up his surplus but had to buy more to meet the demand he had created. He made items he could sell for $100 or $200, and sold hundreds of thousands of them.

The jewellery that Zale sold in his stores he made in his own factories. His production line circled the earth. The diamonds he received in his DTC sight were polished by contractors in New York, Puerto Rico and India. His factories in Hong Kong and Puerto Rico made the mountings in which his New York workshops set the stones. "We used everything we got from the DTC in our jewellery; nothing was discarded," he says. "There's a market for every diamond, provided you can reach the people who would be interested if you made it attractive to them. We gave our customers what we believed they wanted."

Zale found that the merchandising concepts that worked in the United States worked equally well in his stores in England, Germany, Switzerland and Japan. "We were introducing new products, and whether the people we exposed them to were American, European or Japanese, they responded in the same way." Zale, now deep into his eighties, has retired from business, but the retail empire he built continues in other hands.

There are many similarities between the approach that Charles Tiffany took to marketing diamond jewellery and that taken by De Beers, first in America in the late thirties through N.W. Ayer, and since the early sixties by its own London-based consumer and advertising division, which works with N.W Ayer in the United States, and J. Walter Thompson, Ted Bates and other advertising agencies elsewhere. Like Tiffany, De Beers regards love and marriage as the foundation of the diamond jewellery market; it believes that diamonds should be gifts of love linked to special occasions, and views the engagement ring as the most suitable item for introducing consumers to diamonds.

De Beers is perhaps unique among producers and wholesalers of raw materials in that it spends well over $120 million a year on publicizing the finished products that other firms make and sell. Back in the fifties the company realized that, because world diamond production was continually increasing, it was not enough to balance supply and demand simply by regulating the quantities it fed into the pipeline; it also had to stimulate the demand for diamond jewellery, in order to pull greater quantities of diamonds through the pipeline. As the jewellery industry was too fragmented and lacking in players big enough to undertake the sort of "image" promotion that diamonds needed, De Beers was compelled, in its own interests, to do so.

Under Jeremy Pudney, the consumer and advertising division, which he started in 1962, has grown into an international marketing network with a head office staff of over fifty and three hundred employed full-time by the agencies. The division is active in every branch of the jewellery industry, seeking out points at which it can influence sales, expanding existing markets and creating new ones for the quantities of diamonds, in various sizes and qualities, that De Beers believes, from mine production forecasts, will be available.

Drawing on the services of social scientists, the division develops marketing programmes, based on extensive research into current buying habits and future potential, to fit the needs of different countries. It studies the traditional gift-giving occasions in different cultures and the lifestyles and attitudes of consumers, to identify occasions that can be associated with gifts of diamonds.

Advertising on television and in print around the world is, of course, the principal instrument, and the division mounts both image campaigns and more product-orientated campaigns in partnership with leading manufacturing and retailing jewellers.

Staffed by agency offices in twenty-nine countries, the division's Diamond Promotion Service interacts closely with the jewellery trade, partly to motivate designers and manufacturers to produce pieces that utilize the balanced mix of diamonds that De Beers needs to sell.

The Diamond Promotion Service, whose slogan is "We help you sell diamonds", also furnishes retailers with consultants, publications, and training and display materials to help them market and sell the products more efficiently, and encourages them to benefit from the money De Beers spends on advertising and promotion by participating in specific marketing campaigns. Leading manufacturing jewellers and retailers in each market are invited to join Carat Clubs, which serve as forums for the exchange of ideas between De Beers and the trade.

Operating from the same offices, the division's Diamond Information Centres excite consumer interest through media publicity, ensuring that every development in the industry, every piece of information that can enhance the desirability of diamonds, receives maximum editorial coverage from the press and television. They create newsworthy events, such as design symposia and contests that create an interest in new design and give a boost to both established and budding designers.

Of the design contests sponsored by De Beers, the premier is the Diamonds-International Awards, an international competition held every two years. In 1988 it attracted over two thousand entries from twenty countries, including the People's Republic of China and the Soviet Union. National contests, held under the name Diamonds Today in most countries, are run in the alternate years.

"The contests provide opportunities for our PR network, the Diamond Information Centres, to get editorial coverage for new trends in design. They also help stimulate new design talent and eventually ensure that jewellery manufacturers and retailers have fresh concepts to put before the consumer," says Pudney. "The participants may be producing one-off designs, but, as in the fashion industry, it is necessary to have the aspirational products, and then to help spin-offs of those products to get into the wider market. When there is a variety of design out there, women are persuaded to add to their collections, simply because they desire particular designs."

Pudney thinks of people who buy and wear diamond jewellery as members of an informal "diamond club", which they join when they acquire their first piece of diamond

DIANA ROSENBERG
CORNELIA KOEGEL
JAN CHENG
IRMA BALLESTEROS
RICHARD KUJAWSKI
BILL LEAR
SUSAN FARMER
YASMIN CRISOSTOMO
HUBERT DAGNALL
STEPHEN LUSSIER
NICHOLAS GRAHAM SMITH
DAVID KEITES
ALBERTO MONCADA
RAGI DHOLAKIA
FIONA SPENCE
NANCY KHOO
PETER MADDICK
KAREN LEVI
JONATHAN MANSON
PATTI SHUM
CHARLES PHILLPOT
EVYLOU DE VLEESCHOUWER
NICOLE TIXIER
ELENA BONAPACE
PETER BURKE
JONATHAN HARPER
MADELON SCHAAP
YANI BUDIWAN
MARY HAWLEY
LIZ FARRELL
TERESA SICUPIRA
DON ZIMMERMAN
KYEO SIMSON
CECILIA LOF
MIMI CZERNIN
JOAN PARKER
CRI CRI SOLAK EASTIN
JEREMY PUDNEY
JILL BACE
CAROLYN BODIE
LINLY KATE CHOU
JOHN EVASON
JOHN MACLAUGHLIN
DUANGCHAI TANTIVEJKUL
NORIKO OHE
SHELLEY BIRD
LOUSJE BRUGMAN
DEREK PALMER
TARQUIN DE LA FORCE

Jeremy Pudney, head of the CSO's consumer and advertising division, at a symposium (left) with his Diamond Promotion Service and Diamond Information Centre teams from advertising and public relations agencies around the world.
Andy Lamont of the CSO's corporate communications department is interviewed over lunch (right) by Neil Behrmann, correspondent of the *Wall Street Journal* and financial papers in other parts of the world.

On the set for the soap opera Growing Pains (left) at Burbank Studios, West Coast Diamond Information Service supervisor, Cri Cri Solak-Eastin, discusses the loan of a diamond necklace required for future episodes in the series with the property master and the product placement agent.
Leading Japanese photographer Masaaki Imai composes a picture (right) for a magazine advertisement with diamond model Masako Torikas on the balcony of a smart country restaurant outside Tokyo.

Glowing with pleasure after winning her first major race – the Dresden Diamond Stakes for lady riders, on Diamond Day at Ascot in 1987 – the Princess Royal (left) is congratulated by her father, the Duke of Edinburgh, who is evidently as pleased as she is. Special guests at Ascot (above), red-coated Chelsea Pensioners, having placed their bets, await the outcome of the Diamond Stakes.

The world's most expensive swimsuit, in black leather and 62.35 carats of diamonds – the largest weighing six carats – designed by Kiyoko Ishiguro and sponsored by manufacturing jeweller Sakaguchi. It is worn here at the Tokyo Diamond Fair by Yu Satomi, who also models a diamond necklace shaped like Walkman earphones by designer Kumiko Inagaki, also sponsored by Sakaguchi, and made by Soga Kobo.

Apprentice sumo wrestlers, in black, watch their masters practising at a training centre in Tokyo (above right).

Sumo master Yasokichi Konishiki (right), the first foreign sumo wrestler to be promoted to the rank of Ozeki, was honoured by the Diamond Information Centre as Diamond Personality of 1987 for achievement "as brilliant as diamonds".

jewellery, and in which they maintain their membership by periodically adding further pieces to their collections.

"We use every available form of communication, first to get people to join, and afterwards to place before them an array of new products to keep them in the club," he says. "The classical first purchase is an engagement ring. Thereafter the idea is present in the minds of both husband and wife that he expresses his love for her with gifts of diamond jewellery. As the husband improves his position, he buys his wife increasingly expensive gifts, and as her collection grows, she becomes the one who motivates new purchases for special occasions. Eventually purchases may no longer be linked to occasions, although they are still regarded as reaffirmations of love."

While De Beers naturally wants to sell as many diamonds as it can, it must at the same time preserve the image of the diamond as something special. "Our job," says Pudney, "is to foster, maintain and reinforce the mystique that has grown up in people's minds over generations – without it there would be no diamond industry."

In the value of diamond content, the United States, where each year consumers pay over eleven billion dollars for some nineteen million pieces, remains the biggest market for diamond jewellery, accounting for about one third of the total sold in the world each year. Seventy-five per cent of new brides receive diamond engagement rings, and nearly seventy per cent of American women have a piece of diamond jewellery other than an engagement ring. Annually more than eleven per cent of married women acquire a new piece of diamond jewellery.

"The United States is an enormous market for us," says Bill Lear, one of the division's directors. "Apart from gifts from husbands to wives, with the advent of career women and dual family incomes, a terrific number of American women are now buying diamond jewellery for themselves. The acquisition rate is in fact higher among single women than married women. Each year about one in seven single women acquire diamond pieces, and although the majority are gifts, a significant number are self-purchases. One of the reasons for the health of the market is the favourable attitude American women of all ages and income levels have towards diamonds and diamond jewellery."

In Europe the tradition of diamond jewellery is not as well established as in the United States, and the value of the diamond content of jewellery sold in Europe is a little less than fifteen per cent of world sales. "Jewellery – particularly gold jewellery – has long been part of the European tradition, but the diamond was not seen as a separate item of the culture, as it has been in the United States," says James Courage, one of the division's market controllers for Europe. "While in the United Kingdom some seventy per cent of women have diamond jewellery, less than half in the continental countries own a piece."

Largely an Anglo-Saxon tradition in Europe, the diamond engagement ring is as popular in the United Kingdom as in the United States. In Germany and the Nordic countries only a tiny proportion of brides acquire diamond engagement rings, compared with some twenty-five per cent in France and Spain and fifty per cent in Italy. Diamonds are nevertheless regarded as a gift of love, and there is a tendency to see the diamond solitaire as expressing a commitment to a steady, loving relationship, rather than a formal engagement or marriage.

"The diamond had to be contemporized in Europe," says Courage. "Where there was no engagement ring tradition people were inclined to see diamonds, not as something for their late teens and early twenties, but for their late twenties and their thirties – for when one had money and had achieved some success. It had to become something that expressed young, as well as mature, love."

Particularly in the United Kingdom, where there was a proliferation of non-specialist jewellery stores, the diamond engagement ring broadened from being a middle-class tradition into something that was available to all. The mystique of the diamond, combined with the wider availability of affordable diamond pieces, fostered a relationship for people who wanted to enjoy owning a piece of diamond jewellery, even with a very small stone.

Unable to compete with the chains, in either market position or price, independent jewellers have had to move higher up in the market and provide a more personal service and carry a wider range to cater for young people looking for "good value" jewellery.

"In northern Europe – particularly Germany – people did not want to be seen to be rich, and would even shop for expensive jewellery in another town," says Courage. "They didn't want flamboyant jewellery, and didn't need to display their wealth to others, as everybody in their peer group knew their position. The yuppie phenomenon has, however, produced a renewal of the need to display status, and Europeans have become prepared to wear more showy, slightly larger, more expensive jewellery than before."

Southern Europeans, on the other hand, are natural jewellery lovers who enjoy adornment, he says. "Having a more open approach to clothes and accessories, they go for larger, more flamboyant designs. Here the individual retailer, who has his own ideas about taste and design, has retained his importance, and works closely with the customer to develop designs."

The Japanese market, which is second only to the American, is a new market. During World War II Japanese women had to surrender their diamonds to the government for use in industry, and it was not until the mid-sixties that diamonds again became legally available. There is consequently little inherited diamond jewellery in the country, and only about forty per cent of Japanese women have a diamond piece other than an engagement ring, but the percentage of new brides who receive diamond engagement rings is as high as in America, and ownership of second and third diamond pieces is growing rapidly.

The re-introduction of diamonds to Japan is one of the all-time great marketing success stories. Working through J. Walter Thompson, De Beers positioned diamonds as the appropriate gift for specific people on prescribed occasions, and generated enough publicity to make gifts of diamonds on those occasions socially obligatory.

"Our studies of Japanese life revealed several points favouring diamonds," recalls Pudney. "There were a number of traditional ceremonial occasions marking important life events – notches on the bamboo of life – when it was customary to give expensive gifts. While pearls were symbolically associated with death and worn at funerals, diamonds were seen as ideal for celebrations. In fact, diamonds fitted in very well with the symbolism of Shintoism, the philosophy that most Japanese live by, which emphasizes the virtues of beauty, purity, clarity and brilliance. There was also a positive desire on the part of Japanese people at that time to adopt some of the more attractive features of the Western lifestyle."

Of all the notches on the bamboo of life, the wedding was considered the most suitable occasion for re-introducing the diamond. Then, as sometimes today, most Japanese marriages were arranged by the mothers of the young couple, and were marked traditionally by a formal exchange of gifts. As "face" – the way one appears in the eyes of others – is all-important in the Far East, it was essential to the bride's mother that the gift received by her daughter should indicate to her contemporaries that her daughter had married well. A diamond ring, which the bride could display on her left hand, was ideal for the purpose, and it became the established norm that the price of the ring should be three times the groom's monthly salary. In a country where the average cost of a wedding is over $60 000, and the groom may take many years to pay it off, the price of the ring was not thought excessive. Indeed, it was regarded as an index of the groom's worth and the value he placed on his marriage.

"In Japan marriage is seen as a partnership, though traditionally the wife is the homemaker, while the husband spends most of his time at work or travelling between home and the office," says David Keites, the division's regional director, who has been responsible for De Beers' marketing programmes in Japan throughout the eighties. "Some women boast about how late their husbands return from work, and there is even a feeling that a man who does not get home quite late fairly often cannot be very important. Because of this and because Japanese men are often not spontaneously demonstrative, wives can receive little attention from their husbands on a daily basis. As a result they expect, on key anniversaries, to receive important gifts that they can show off to their friends. The gifts of jewellery that a man gives his wife are the way in which he expresses his gratitude for the support she gives him and the success of their marriage, and perhaps also a public statement that he is a success in life."

Many diamond jewellery purchases in Japan are related to occasions, either as gifts received on the celebration of an anniversary or rite of passage, or as items of adornment worn at such festivities. Unlike American women, who have numerous occasions for wearing their jewellery, home-bound Japanese women wear theirs rarely. When they do, it is a statement of "face", and many of them acquire new pieces in anticipation of an important family event, at which they know they will again have to make that sort of statement.

"The gift of love element is increasingly an important part of all this," says Keites. "A Japanese woman wants her friends and relatives to know, not just that her diamonds are beautiful and that her husband is successful, but also that there is still sentiment and romance in her marriage."

Japanese women are well acquainted with the Four Cs, and discuss their diamonds in the same way that their husbands might discuss their cars. They lay great emphasis on quality, and demand the best diamonds in terms of Clarity, Colour and Cut, but to the number of Carats they attach less importance. The women are also designer and brand conscious, and would rather be able to say that they purchased their jewellery from a leading jeweller than admit that they bought it elsewhere at a bargain price.

Because diamonds were re-introduced to Japan through the promotion of the diamond engagement ring, the standard of quality was established initially by the solitaire setting, for which only the better qualities were acceptable. The colour of the stone was held to be paramount, and it had to appear flawless. But as the Japanese have grown more familiar with a greater variety of diamond jewellery, they have come to accord greater significance to design and, to keep within a reasonable price range, have begun to accept lower colours and qualities in jewellery containing many diamonds, where the quality of the individual stones is of less concern than the total design.

The limits to private living space that island geography imposes on a large population have also benefited diamond jewellery sales. Although the Japanese have the highest per capita and disposable incomes in the world, there are relatively few expensive items that they can spend their money on. They generally cannot buy a second home, and a second car entails the outlay of another $500 a month to park it in the street outside. Because the interiors of even the most affluent homes are tiny by Western standards, there are tight limits to the number of household appliances and pieces of furniture that can be fitted into them. In the competition for consumers' disposable income, overseas travel is the diamond's closest rival.

In different parts of the world a variety of local factors may influence consumer perceptions and preferences. In South Africa, for instance, there is a strong preference for flawless diamonds, and colour is less of a consideration. Years ago the country's largest retail jewellery chain stressed in its promotions that it sold only flawless diamonds, and such was the weight of its advertising that consumers insisted on "flawless". As they could not afford flawless gems in the top colours, they bought flawless, but yellow, Cape stones, which are less popular elsewhere. During a tennis tournament in Florida some years ago Chris Evert dropped her bracelet, a single string of diamonds that had been a stock item in jewellery stores for many years. The commentator exclaimed that she had dropped her "tennis bracelet". A jeweller in Miami latched onto the idea and started marketing "tennis bracelets", other jewellers followed suit, and a "tennis bracelet" craze swept America. The eternity ring, a modestly popular item in Britain, could gain no foothold in America, where the connotation of "eternity" had more to do with the hereafter than the reaffirmation of enduring temporal ties. When De Beers renamed the product the anniversary ring, however, and marketed it as "the band of diamonds that says you'd marry her all over again", the ring rapidly became a favourite second-purchase item with young American couples. In Brazil there is a high-volume market for pieces of low value. The number of people who can afford expensive pieces is relatively small, and street security has become a problem of such proportions that the people who can afford them are afraid to wear them.

While in Brazil security discourages the purchase of expensive pieces of jewellery, throughout South-East Asia security is the principal motivation for buying them. In a region that has not been particularly blessed with political stability, diamonds, like gold, are prized primarily as a compact, easily portable store of value – insurance against a rainy day.

"Diamond sales are a good indication of the political and economic situation in South-East Asian countries," says Hong Kong diamond wholesaler Maximilian Ma. "Before Vietnam fell in 1975 it was one of the biggest markets in Asia, and we could always tell which diamonds were going there, because the Vietnamese required a specific size and colour. After the fall of Vietnam there was a reverse flow, and for the next five years we were buying back many of these stones. Then in 1985 there was renewed demand for diamonds of this type, as Vietnamese refugees who had become established elsewhere began buying again."

"The reason why so much diamond jewellery is bought in the region is not that people have more money, but that they place jewellery higher among their priorities and make more money available for it than Europeans," says Hong Kong jeweller Charles Baldinger. "Because of political instability, even people with relatively small incomes will invest in jewellery as security."

According to Hong Kong jewellery manufacturer Frank Tang, this perception of jewellery dates back to the unsettled times of the ancient Chinese warlords, when gold and precious stones were the only investments that offered any security. "Even when a Chinese man makes a present of diamonds as a gift of love, the thought is always in the background that it will provide some security for the future," he says. "The gift of a mink coat might represent love, but not security."

In certain South-East Asian countries, where diamond imports are either prohibited or heavily taxed, much of the trade is conducted on the "black market". Despite official discouragement, consumption is enormous, and it has become usual in these countries, when asked where one acquired a diamond, to reply "like that" – with a gesture towards the top jacket pocket to indicate how it was carried through customs. Often there is more cachet to claiming that one acquired something "like that" than to admitting to having paid duty on it.

"Probably because of the ancient association of jewellery with survival in unsettled times, Asian buyers are fascinated by anything mildly illicit," says David Diniz, of Classic Jewellers International, a man of Chinese and Portuguese extraction, born in the north of China and raised in Shanghai, who worked as a motor car salesman in Vietnam during the war there before going into jewellery manufacturing in Hong Kong in 1972. "Sales are actually stimulated by the special thrill of acquiring something beautiful and being able to say that they got it 'like that'. When three or four Oriental women get together and discuss their jewellery, you can almost see the cloud of intrigue that envelops them."

The type of jewellery that is gifted at weddings and on occasions such as the birth of a child is generally of the kind known as *chum kam,* the traditional 24-carat gold jewellery of the East, designed more as a store of value than for display. Much of it is never worn,

Hong Kong socialite Brenda Chau (left), wife of Kai-Bong Chau, chief executive of the Association of Pacific Island Legislators, at home with her diamonds, some of them set in her evening gown.

Yvonne Ma (far left), wife of Hong Kong diamantaire Maximilian Ma, compares tote and bookmakers' prices on her portable television set at the horse races in Kowloon.

Tsuneo Takagi (right), managing director of Heiwado Jewellers in Tokyo, handles the 31-carat McLean diamond, which he bought for promotional purposes at the auction of the Duchess of Windsor's jewels.

At their home in São Paulo (left) Ida Kiung wears diamond jewellery given her by her husband Theodore and made entirely with diamonds from the mine near Diamantina that he once owned.

or intended to be worn, and is seen as a kind of dowry or investment, which, should the need arise, can be converted into cash. As weddings are usually on the first astrologically propitious date after the decision to marry is taken, betrothal and celebration may be only days apart. In the olden days the groom's parents presented jade jewellery to the parents of the bride, and in more recent times it has become usual also to give gold jewellery to their daughter-in-law. Young men too make presents of jewellery to their brides, and young women have come to expect a gold ring. Here De Beers has directed its marketing skills at changing allegiance from plain gold to gold with diamonds, and encouraging the idea that diamond jewellery should be worn and enjoyed.

"There is a move towards giving diamond jewellery at weddings," says Baldinger. "Not only the bride, but also her mother, sisters, mother-in-law and other women who have a role in the ceremony must receive jewellery. When the bride is getting a diamond, her mother-in-law may expect to receive a larger one for herself. It sometimes happens that for one wedding we make up five complete sets of jewellery."

Alongside the perception of diamonds as an investment against future adversity has grown up the perception that diamonds signify wealth and success, and that they are worn on special occasions not only for their brilliance, but as a symbol of social standing. "Open displays of sentiment and affection are less prevalent in Chinese culture," says Hong Kong jewellery manufacturer Anton Weder, who has lived in South-East Asia for over thirty years. "It is far more probable that a man who thinks it will enhance his status for his wife to be seen wearing diamond jewellery will tell her to go out and buy something appropriate."

Thomas Wong, a director of Chow Tai Fook Jewellery, in Hong Kong, does not exclude an element of sentiment, however. "The symbol of love to the practical Chinese mind is the value of love," he says, "and the value a man places on love, as expressed in the jewellery he buys his wife, is an indication of his status."

Chinese men seldom involve themselves in the actual purchasing process, however. It is generally the women who visit the jeweller, select or commission the piece, discuss the design and the price and, in many cases, sign the cheques themselves. "Men may come in to buy a birthday gift, but for the really serious stuff, items containing many gems, the lady comes herself," says Baldinger.

Largely as a result of De Beers' marketing programmes, Hong Kong women have acquired a relatively good knowledge of diamonds and, where the main considerations in the past were size and colour, they are prepared now to apply their knowledge and buy smaller stones in higher qualities. "In this part of the world all types of diamonds are saleable," says Wong. "But in the last few years sales of the better qualities in smaller sizes have grown appreciably."

"Customers in Hong Kong knew nothing about diamonds formerly," says Diniz. "Size was the main criterion. Colour was important, because in a white mounting the colour was visible, but if a stone looked clear to them it was pure, and a good cut was simply a matter of symmetry. They trusted implicitly the family jeweller, who used a local system of grading colour that had no precise standards. If he placed two stones side by side, they could see which had the better colour and accepted his grading. But today, De

Beers' television advertising has acquainted them with the Four Cs, they are aware of international standards, have learnt the GIA terminology and demand certificates. This is resisted by traditional jewellers, who are losing business to more sophisticated retailers. Having no traditional concepts about diamonds, the Japanese readily accepted international standards, whereas we are still in the process of transition."

Richard Liddicoat, founder of the Gemological Institute of America, talks to a group of his students (left) at the institute's headquarters in Santa Monica. The GIA's standards for certifying polished diamonds are universally recognized. The gift of love – (right) Mariko Nakagawa, a secretary in a Tokyo advertising agency, chooses her diamond engagement ring with her fiancé, business executive Yoshitaka Nomito, assisted by Yasuo Takeuchi, managing director of Shimbido Jewellers.

According to Diniz, the acquisition of knowledge has added spice to the excitement that Hong Kong women experience in buying diamond jewellery. "Husbands want their wives to wear the best jewels to indicate their own success in business, and the ladies enjoy competing with each other in displaying their newly acquired knowledge and showing that they have arrived socially."

"The buyers of important pieces are very sophisticated; they check prices and qualities, read up on diamonds, and there are probably more GIA graduates in Hong Kong than anywhere else outside the United States," says Baldinger. "Quite often when we show a customer some jewellery she takes out a magnifying glass and makes her own assessment of the stones. All that has to be discussed is the price. They have become experts."

"Although most Hong Kong jewellers create very expensive items for wealthy clients, the greatest volume of trade is in the smaller items sold to people with lower incomes, who attach more importance to the value of the materials than to the design," says Vincent Chow of Chow Sang Sang Jewellery, which has eleven retail jewellery stores in Kowloon and the New Territories. "In our market for medium range jewellery the soft, 24-carat gold that customers insist on limits design, but there is a move away from the traditional to a more cosmopolitan design in our gem-set pieces."

Because the jewellery purchased for investment in Hong Kong today is bought also for wearing, women are giving greater attention to design than they did previously. "Compared with the clean lines and larger surfaces that characterize European jewellery design today, typical Hong Kong design is a little elaborate, and not very precise, but it shows off a lot for comparatively little money," says Weder. "But because jewellers in Hong Kong have to cater also to the varied tastes of a large tourist market, other influences have been introduced."

"Ever since the 1920s, when Shanghai was the fashion capital of China and the wealthy women of the period were nurtured on Western jewellery, even basic Chinese gem-set jewellery has been heavily influenced by European and American design," says designer Benson Wong. "At the upper end of the market, particularly, Chinese ladies prefer the Western styles they have been exposed to in foreign magazines and through travel abroad."

"At one time a lot of the jewellery produced in South-East Asia was clearly identifiable as Chinese or Thai, but today we are seeing a movement towards cleaner-cut designs," says Liz Farrell, who supervises De Beers' marketing programmes in South-East Asia from the offices of the Ted Bates agency in Hong Kong. "The designs jewellers throughout the region have submitted over the past few years for our Diamonds of Distinction Collection are very stylish and would be equally at home in a showcase in Europe or Japan."

Asian markets differ from Western markets in being essentially self-purchase markets, says Liz Farrell. "Because the women who are going to wear the jewellery are the people

who go out and buy it, our programmes have been focused primarily on women of middle to upper status, who can afford to buy pieces costing more than $1000. We have only recently turned our attention to cultivating the romantic symbolism of the diamond in the younger, pre-marriage market. It would be nice to think that there would continue to be the attraction of a strong romantic connotation should the need for small, portable assets disappear."

"Although many of the older jewellers feel that a marketing programme based on the gift of love concept isn't feasible in this region, we regard it as our unique selling proposition," says Jonathan Harper, De Beers' market controller for South-East Asia, Korea and China. "There are many other good investments and there are many other status products; what distinguishes the diamond is that it is the symbol of love."

The economic growth of the newly-industrialized "tigers" of South-East Asia is reflected in the upsurge of diamond jewellery sales in the region. Today these countries consume nearly ten per cent by value, and a lot more by volume, of all the diamond jewellery produced in the world; indeed, they already account for almost half as much in value as the countries of Western Europe combined. In terms of the number of pieces purchased, the Philippines is the largest market, followed closely by Thailand, then South Korea, Indonesia, Hong Kong, Taiwan, Malaysia and Singapore. In terms of the value of the pieces sold, however, Taiwan, Thailand and South Korea are the principal "tigers". Understandably, manufacturing jewellers cast their eyes towards the distant prospect of mainland China as the ultimate consumer market. Already diamonds are mined and polished in the People's Republic, and Hong Kong jewellers manufacture some of their lines there – and when China awakes...?

During the diamond recession of the early eighties, although the international diamond market suffered, the world market for diamond jewellery actually grew steadily every year but one, and in the later eighties grew at an even faster pace, in the older markets as in the East.

"Women love diamonds for their beauty and are endlessly fascinated by these precious bits of carbon that come from the deepest parts of the earth and send their illumination skywards," says anthropologist Ellen Karp. "Their origins, physical attributes and tradition of feminine adornment have imbued diamonds with a rich symbolism. Alone of physical objects they can transcend time. Enriching the present with their evocative beauty, they refer also to the significance of the occasions in the past for which they were given and point like beacons to permanence in the future. Through their association with rites of passage and as heirlooms they chronicle a network of family relationships that are above time. For women they reflect a singular intimacy with one man, a broader love for kin and a universal love for all things of this earth."

"What is special about a diamond is that it has a love affair with light, and perhaps that is the secret of its hold over women," says author Evelyn Anthony. "Women are optimists by nature, and while they're prepared to laugh at superstition and risk a good weep when accepting that pearl choker, a woman prefers the cheerful sparkle, the ebullience of the diamond that seems to say to her, 'I'll give you some of my brightness and agelessness'."

"We owe a great deal to the nature of our product, which is uniquely and eternally desirable," says De Beers' chairman Julian Ogilvie Thompson, looking back with a touch of pride at his company's first century as the world leader of the diamond business, and looking forward with optimism to its second century. "We are very fortunate to have a product that is unaffected by fashion and that nothing can or will render obsolete; a product that combines beauty, brilliance, durability and singularity – and speaks of love."

Love's moment in all cultures – a traditional Shinto wedding at Chinzanso, a venue for marriages that is popular with Japanese couples. Today over seventy per cent of Japanese brides receive diamond engagement rings.

CONSULTING EDITOR FOR THE PROJECT
WAS BARRY MORTIMER.
DESIGN AND TYPOGRAPHY
ARE BY JOHAN HOEKSTRA.
PRODUCTION LIAISON BY MOLLY BUCHANAN.
ORIGINATION AND TYPESETTING
BY BEITH PROCESS & PHOTOTYPE CC.
PRINTED AND BOUND BY
DAI NIPPON PRINTING COMPANY LTD., TOKYO, JAPAN.
DIAMOND PEOPLE IS TYPESET
IN 11/12 CHELTENHAM ITC LIGHT.
PRINTED ON 157gsm SATIN KINFUJI.
PHOTOGRAPHS ON THE PAGES LISTED BELOW ARE BY:
PAGES 38 & 39: PETER JONES
PAGE 53 (TOP): TERRY SHEEN
PAGES 59 & 78: BARRY HAWTHORNE
PAGE 113 (DROP CAPITAL): MIKE CROWDER.
PAGE 124: ALAN HARPER
PAGE 125: ALAN BULLOCK
PAGE 134 (TOP LEFT): PETER CARMICHAEL
PAGE 134 (TOP RIGHT): ANDREW CUMINE
PAGE 166 (BOTTOM LEFT): MIKE CROWDER
PAGE 261 (DROP CAPITAL): MIKE CROWDER.
PAGE 261: JEFF KAUFMAN
OPPOSITE PAGE: HORST KLEMM

ENQUIRIES ABOUT THE BOOK SHOULD BE
ADDRESSED TO ANDREW LAMONT,
CORPORATE COMMUNICATIONS DEPARTMENT,
THE CENTRAL SELLING ORGANISATION,
17 CHARTERHOUSE STREET,
LONDON EC1N 6RA., ENGLAND.

1888 1988